# The Essential
# FergS

the
Horse

# The Essential
# Fergs the Horse

## The Life and Times of the World's Most Popular Cartoon Equine

Jean Abernethy

Foreword by Guy McLean

TRAFALGAR SQUARE
North Pomfret, Vermont

First published in 2015 by
Trafalgar Square Books
North Pomfret, Vermont 05053

Portions of this book have appeared online and in print.

**Disclaimer of Liability**

The author and publisher shall have neither liability nor responsibility to any person or entity with respect to any loss or damage caused or alleged to be caused directly or indirectly by the information contained in this book. While the book is as accurate as the author can make it, there may be errors, omissions, and inaccuracies.

Trafalgar Square Books encourages the use of approved safety helmets in all equestrian sports and activities.

**Library of Congress Cataloging-in-Publication Data**
Abernethy, Jean.
  The Essential Fergus the Horse : the life and times of the world's favorite cartoon equine / Jean Abernethy ; foreword by Guy McLean.
    pages cm

  Summary: "Artist and cartoonist Jean Abernethy takes us through the evolution of her massively popular cartoon character Fergus the Horse, and provides a collection of her best cartoons and comic strips"-- Provided by publisher.

  ISBN 978-1-57076-743-2 (paperback)

1.  Horses--Comic books, strips, etc. 2.  Caricatures and cartoons--United States--History--21st century. 3.  American wit and humor, Pictorial.  I. Title.

  PN6728.F444A26 2015
  741.5'973--dc23

                          2015022122

Book design by DOQ
Cover design by RM Didier
Typefaces:  Source Serif Pro and Tally Text

Printed in China

10 9 8 7 6 5 4 3 2 1

This book is dedicated to all the generous folk who've welcomed me into their stables and barns, and to all the dear friends I've ridden with over the years.

# Contents

Foreword by Guy McLean ............................................................... ix

Acknowledgments ......................................................................... xi

## Part One: Becoming Fergus      1

The Evolution of the Artist ........................................................ 3

The Evolution of the Horse ....................................................... 13

The Comic Strips .................................................................... 25

Fergus on Facebook ................................................................. 27

## Part Two: The Fergus Comics      35

The Ridden Word ..................................................................... 37

The Flies Have It ..................................................................... 51

Horse Wisdom ......................................................................... 59

Barn Smarts ........................................................................... 79

Sweet Companions .................................................................. 91

Wonderland ............................................................................ 115

# Foreword

I first came into contact with Fergus the Horse via Facebook in 2014 and was instantly hooked on him. He is an amazing character and reminds me of several very special individuals I have come in contact with in the past—from horses I met just once to a couple of my finest performance horses who "owned" the arena with the same kind of wit and true sense of self that Fergus exhibits in his every breath.

I had the extreme pleasure of meeting Fergus's dear friend Jean Abernethy a few months later, and I could see the same twinkle in her eye that shines out of any page that Fergus graces. I speak of Fergus here as a horse with his own identity, because to me, he is much more than just talented drawings and witty repartee—he is a fine representation of the incredible characters that can be found throughout the horse world. His undeniable voice brings valuable light to their existence.

I have always been one to see each individual horse as having his own true character and special attributes that make him "one of a kind," and Fergus fits this mold perfectly. I can't help but get caught up in his adventures, and I look forward to the next lesson (he teaches us humans) or the next adventure that he partakes in. For many years I have heard people say, "If only they could talk," when it comes to horses, and in these pages, Fergus is doing just that: sharing his everyday life and letting all of us know what's really going on in the intricate minds of our beloved equine friends. I believe that Fergus the Horse transcends the gap between childlike humor and adult-based wit and depth of story, and his growing legion of fans from all age groups is testament to this.

And who am I, to be given this wonderful honor of writing the foreword for Fergus's first book? Just a fan, mainly, but most of all a dreamer and devoted horse lover from the day I was born. I have chased these dreams to the other side of the world, and I'm proud to call Fergus my "Little Mate" and just like him, work to be the voice of horses worldwide, for their greater good.

Go get 'em Fergus, you little ripper, you.

Guy McLean
Australian Horseman, Bush Poet,
and International Entertainer
*www.guymcleanusatour.com*

# Acknowledgments

Thank you, Santa, for bringing the pony when I was little.

Accomplishments are always made easier by a loving, supportive family. To you, my family members, I am eternally grateful. To my brother Glen: The miles we rode when we were kids fueled fun and adventures that we still laugh about to this day, and in years since, I've had riding adventures that have kept the artistic muse well fed.

There are many people who've helped me throughout my career, and especially through the development of Fergus. To name a few, I might miss others. So I want to extend my gratitude to all those who have encouraged, advised, and offered me opportunity. You know who you are, and I thank you sincerely. I also want to thank all the publications that have featured Fergus over the years. You were/are instrumental in keeping it all going. Thank you, Fergus's Facebook fans. With your "likes" and your comments, you've been marvelously fun, and my gratitude to you is enormous.

Jean Abernethy

# Part One:

# Becoming Fergus

# The Evolution of the Artist

When you pick yourself up off the ground, and watch that pony run off—again—something clicks. You either quit, or you find it funny!

When I was little, I told my brother that I wanted to be a cowboy. He said I could not be a cowboy because I was a girl. But then, he knew more about the world than I did because he was eight. I was only five and the youngest of four children, all of us close in age. Humor was a part of learning to get along in the world—we had to learn to laugh at things.

I remember a hobbyhorse I got for my birthday when I was very small. It was a horse head on a stick. I'd wanted one that looked "real" and beautiful, with a pretty mane. This brown, plastic wonder had big round "buggey" eyes, a row of huge teeth set in a ridiculous grin, and a bottom jaw that swung like a trap door. It clapped shut when you pulled the plastic reins. Once revealed from its wrapping paper, I felt a little indignant, but mostly disappointed that this was not the black stallion who danced in my dreams. But it was a gift. Even at that tender age, I knew it was a gift from parents of modest means. I had to just buck up, smile, and be grateful. I named him "Charlie Horse" because I'd heard those words somewhere. The name made my parents and grandparents laugh. I rode that character all through the house. He turned out to be a lot of fun!

Santa delivered a real pony to our small family farm when I was seven. Her name was Dusty. She was three, and very green. My brother Glen, with grit, determination, and encouragement from Dad, got Dusty going nicely. She was not an easy pony. Slight, skittish, and fast, she'd had a few frightening escapades before Santa delivered her to us. As a growing child, I was very small, consistently the size of kids about two years my junior. Riding Dusty was simply not a safe option for me for the first few months. I did an awful lot of brushing and hoof-picking until summer came and Glen and Dusty reached an understanding. She was always high-strung and spooky, but she was also affectionate, and had learned that carrying a rider could be rather fun.

Mother said I could have some boots if I could get on the pony. There was no saddle. But Dusty was patient and eventually I learned to swing myself on. Dusty gave me a whole set of challenges, too, when I started to ride her. Charlie Horse didn't see much of me after that. Glen had bought a larger pony, and we rode through a lot of adventures together, following back roads and snowmobile trails. I wonder if Santa knew when he delivered that first pony that he had initiated careers for my brother and me. Glen is now a skilled horseman in his own right.

As a kid, I could never find enough horse books in the school library to satisfy me. I signed out every one, read it, and copied the illustrations diligently, often frustrated that my efforts at drawing did not produce the quality that I strove for. I guess I could call this my self-imposed education, for the "art instruction" at school, for the most part, was about gluing pasta to construction paper. I could make anything look like a horse!

I also read the how-to books. I remember taking a book of knots and a piece of rope to the barn, and practiced tying the knots on the pony. I crawled into bed with a booklet from the Department of Agriculture called "Judging Livestock." The book would fall open at the photograph of the Clydesdale with names and arrows all around it, and there, I studiously memorized the points of equine conformation. These critically important subjects were not being taught at school.

I was 15 when I made this graphite drawing. By then I had been trying for several years to emulate the beautiful drawings by C.W. Anderson.

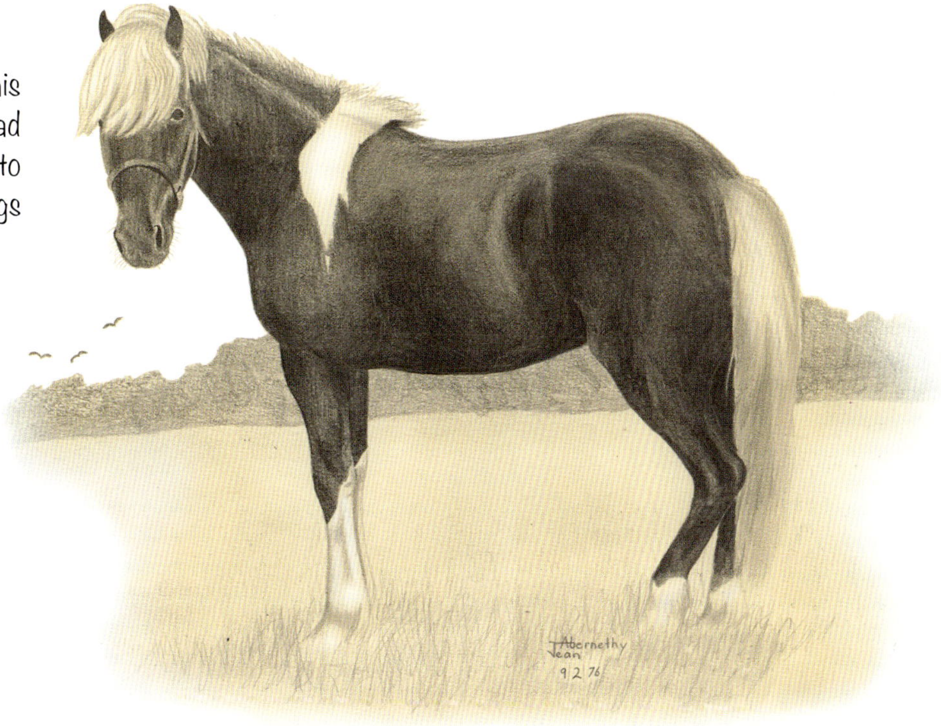
Abernethy
Jean
9 2 76

By the time I'd made the drawing of Dusty on page 5 I'd outgrown her and bought a young horse. At six months, he'd been weaned from his mother, cold turkey, and needed a friend. A flashy young lad, with a lot of white on his face, he was my world. I taught him to lead, then to pull, wearing a harness, and later to ride. Well, I *thought* I was teaching him, and I suppose I was, but in retrospect, considering my youthful, teenage mistakes, he was actually teaching *me.* Forty years later, he still is.

By the time I finished the eighth grade, I'd outgrown the pony who was all of 10 hands high. For $75 of my savings I bought a weanling colt who grew into a fine young man. He was my world. I would have been about 17 when I made this drawing of him.

6

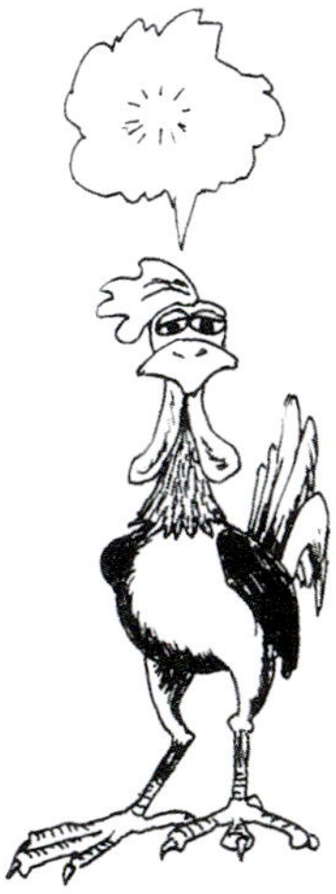

Indeed, what does a chicken think about...really?

During my high school years, my armful of books was always topped with a sketchbook. Drawing had become a means of studying the things I truly loved, and my talent for it was becoming evident. My peers on the school bus would ask, "Can I see your sketchbook?" almost on a daily basis. I'd hand it off and get it back in 15 minutes or so. They were eager to see the drawings, and seemed amazed by them, although to me, it didn't seem like such a big deal. It was just something I enjoyed doing. For me, those blank white pages were for practicing, exploring, experimenting. I drew in it constantly. When classes at school were completely uninteresting, I kept my passion with me in the pages of my sketchbook.

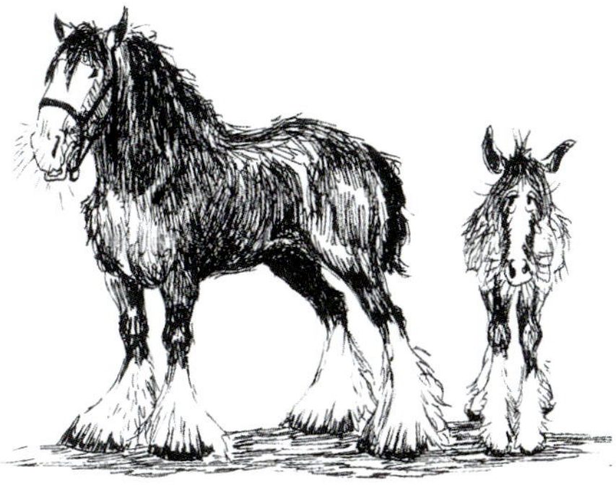

An early exploration of Clydesdales: the furrier, the better.

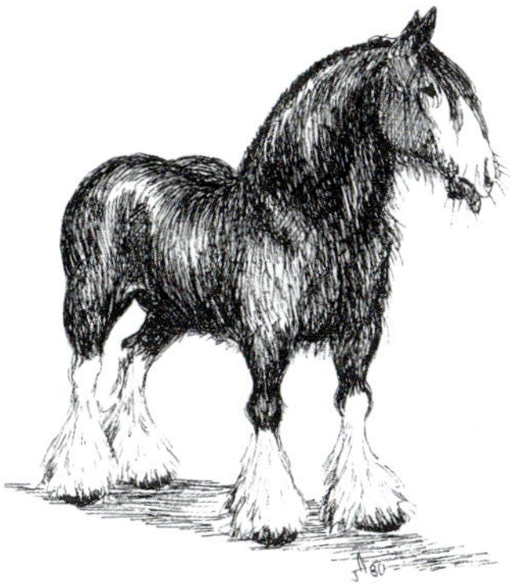

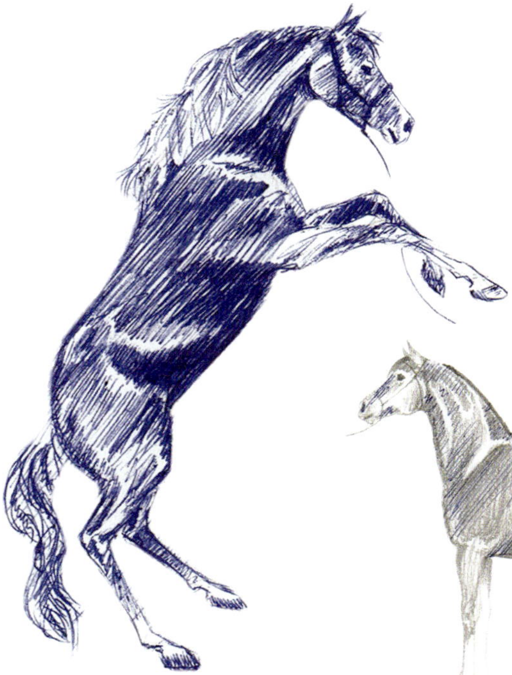

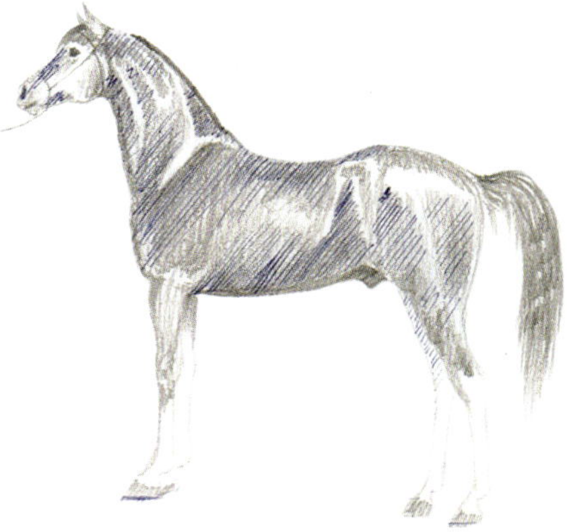

Artistic experimentation: the Clydesdale is drawn with radiograph pen, the rearing horse, ball-point pen, and the Arabian with graphite and pen.

I strove in parallel to both depict beautiful anatomically correct horses and develop a style of comical drawing.

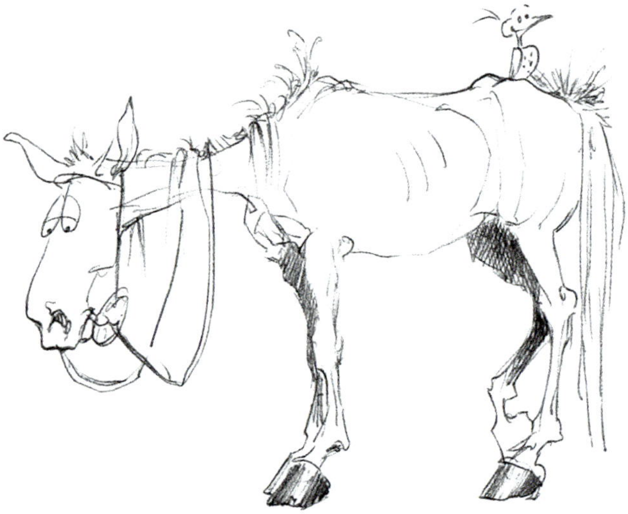

I often toyed with humor in my sketches.

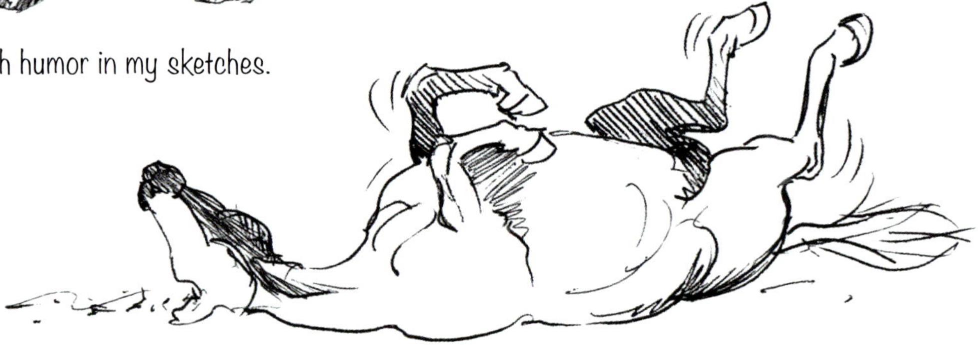

Gesture drawing to practice proportion, movement, foreshortening. I drew constantly to explore horses and farm animals in various ways. I was never bored if I had a pen.

After high school I enrolled in an Equine Studies program at Humber College in West Toronto, Ontario, Canada. My studies there opened doors that exposed this farm kid to a world of professional equestrians of every stripe.

I loved it and hungrily soaked up new knowledge. But even then, the artist in me would not be stilled. I doodled in my notebooks to an extent that gained the attention of instructors who commissioned me to make drawings for

career projects they were working on. Eventually, I made the shift to pursue an art degree at Ontario College of Art. (Now, OCAD University.) There, I learned the real value of life drawing, and was introduced to a myriad of professional artist's materials and mediums to explore.

Throughout my four years at OCA, I sold equine-related comics and illustrations on a freelance basis, having previously established connections through the Humber College equestrian program.

Ontario is a province endowed with all kinds of horses and equestrian sports, and when I was in college, there were thriving harness-racing and Thoroughbred-racing industries. I created cartoons for many equine sports, breeds, and disciplines. The booming Standardbred industry com-

These drawings were further exploration in humor. The overweight, sandwich-eating jockey is a joke in itself. I learned that matching facial expressions on various characters would cause people to smile.

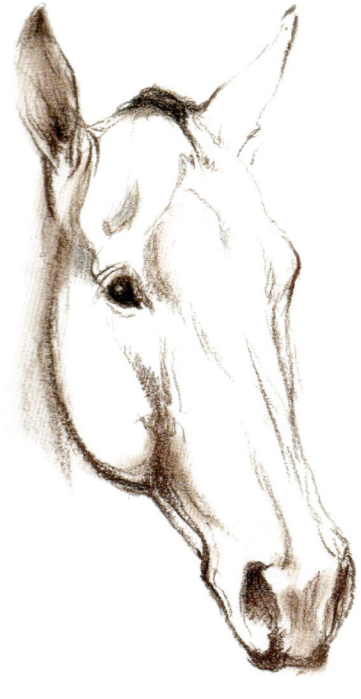

A charcoal drawing of a polo pony. Life drawings involving horses are challenging in that you must be close enough to see your subject, yet somehow far enough away so your sketchbook is out of nibbling range.

missioned a lot of comical illustration through the eighties. But generic horse comics could be more widely distributed, so as much as possible, I made an effort to keep my drawings from being pigeon-holed in any particular segment of the horse industry. Most of my cartoon horses were generic.

©ABERNETHY

"Now grip his sides with your legs."

7 6 5 4 3 2 1
©J. ABERNETHY

"We better get some jumper cables. The horses are on the far turn."

©J. ABERNETHY

So far this year you've earned $450,000.00. Repairs to harness, carts and hub rails add up to $449,637.89.

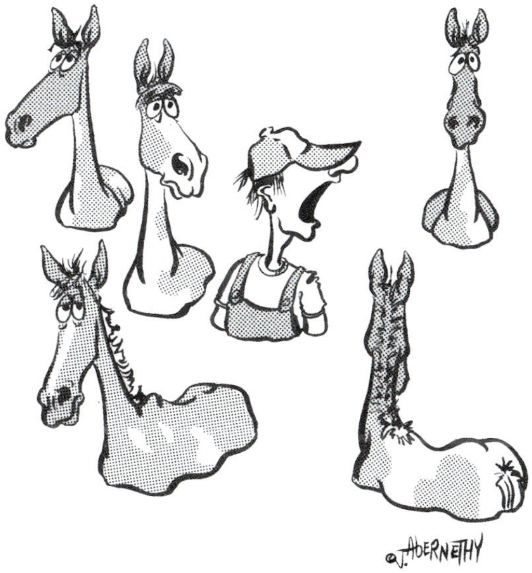
©J. ABERNETHY

"Dad, the waterbowl's still leakin'!"

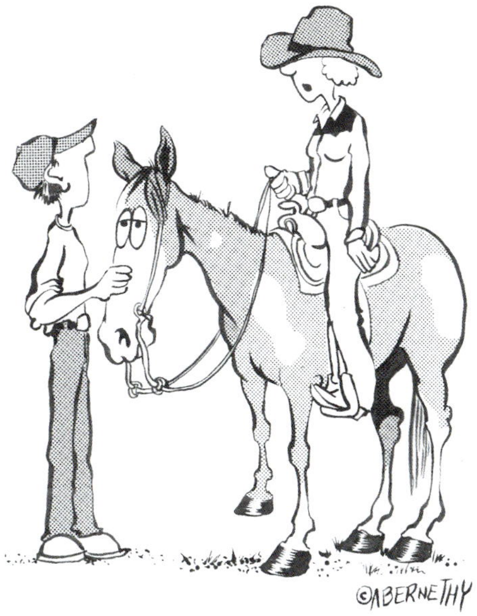
©ABERNETHY

"I give up. Why are you selling her?"

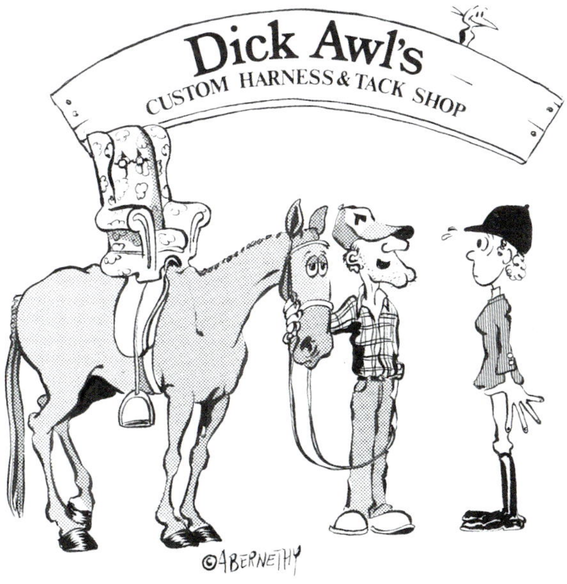
Dick Awl's
CUSTOM HARNESS & TACK SHOP
©ABERNETHY

"I've had the seat rebuilt on your old saddle!"

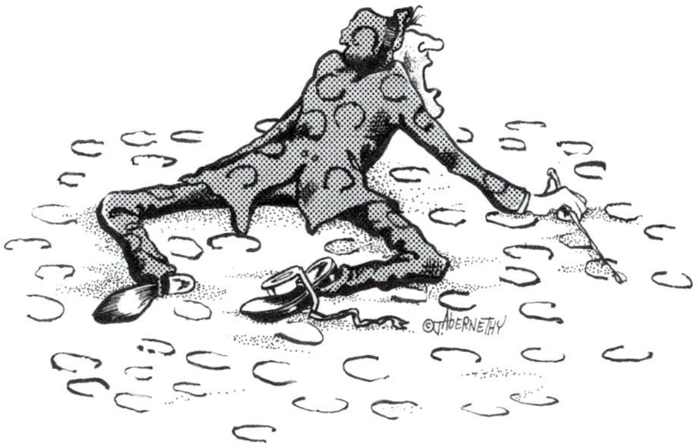
©J. ABERNETHY

"And what are her other four gaits?"

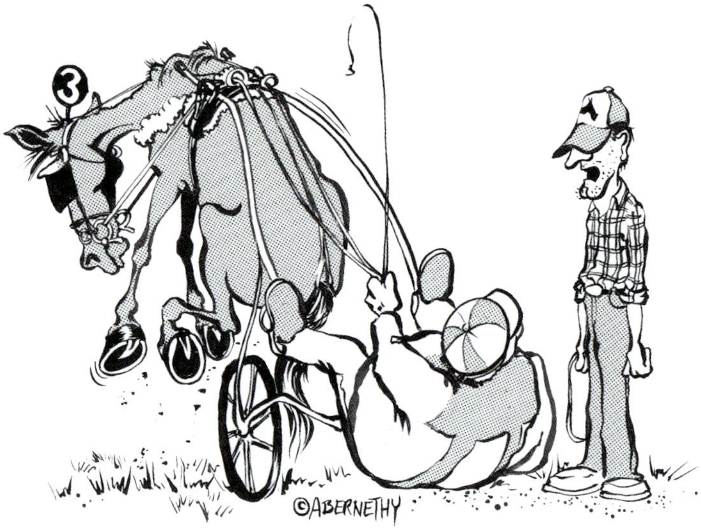

©ABERNETHY


"Maybe if you give me your dentures
and wallet, he'll touch down."

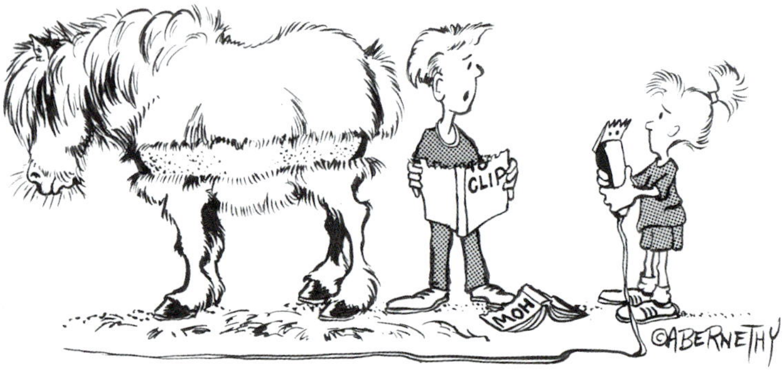

CLIP
MOM
©ABERNETHY


"We're in trouble now!"

# The Evolution of the Horse

©ABERNETHY 2008

Throughout those years of cartooning, a recurring question came up: "What is your horse's name?" Perhaps it was the consistency of those non-horse-like eyes on my equine characters that suggested to readers I was always drawing the same horse. I can't be sure. But the question came up more and more often, and hinted that perhaps readers wanted an individual horse character.

By the late nineties, my comics had appeared in a good many horse publications across the United States and Canada, and the time seemed ripe to try something new. So, I drew a little horse with those same ridiculous eyes and named him "Fergus," thinking that the letter "u" could perfectly be replaced by a horseshoe.

I drew him, stuffed him into a fax machine, and sent him off to a dear friend in England. He emerged there in a comic storyline, announcing that he would rather travel by satellite than by horse trailer!

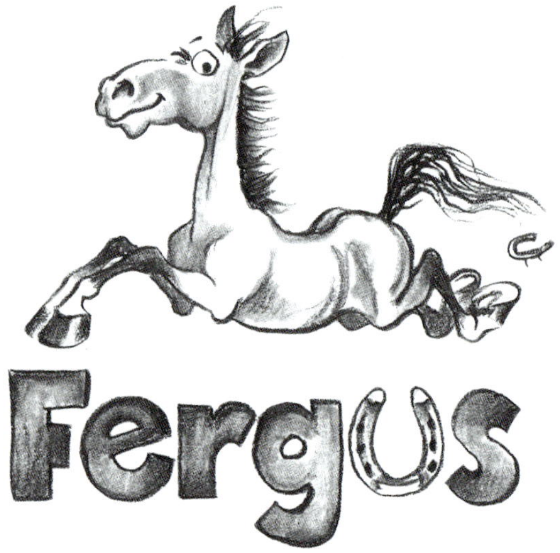
Fergus

What's in a name, anyway?

Fergus was born. I actually drew him many times before settling on his color and markings. The handsome young gelding who was my companion through my high school years was a direct influence on my choice for Fergus's markings.

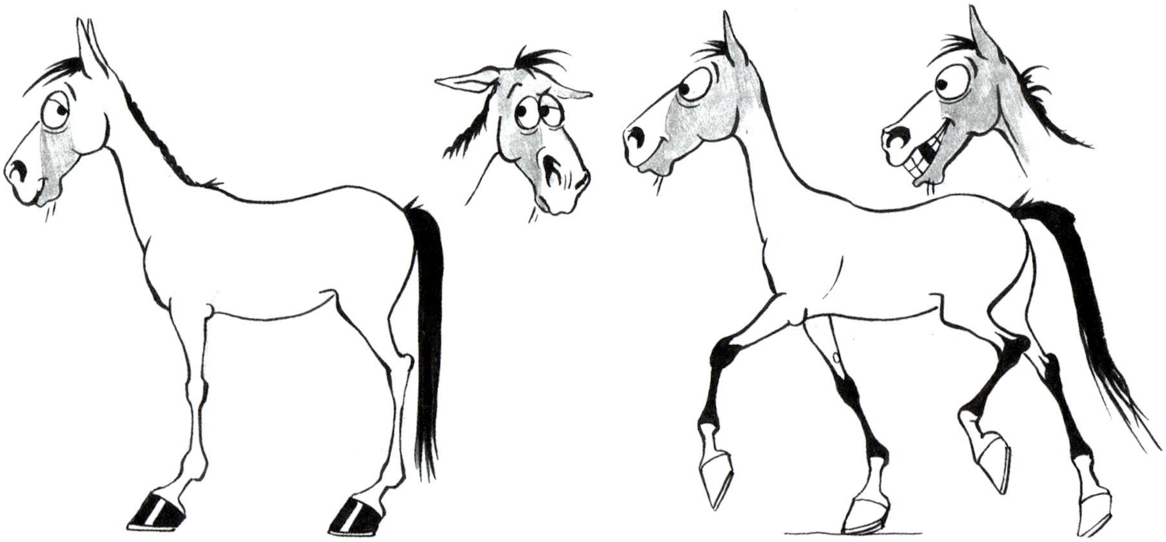

I sought to capture Fergus's thoughts in his forever changing expressions.

At this point in my life, I had met and worked with enough horses to know the similarities they share, and also how different they can be. I decided that Fergus should embody the quintessential "average" horse: he eats, he spooks, and he really does not understand human logic at all.

This befuddlement personified the rift between equine and *Homo sapiens* logic, and made him a perfect candidate to communicate training methods in Monty Roberts' quarterly magazine, *Join-Up Journal*. Fergus also promoted equine feeds for Seminole, a Florida-based company, and he added a touch of humor to many editorial articles.

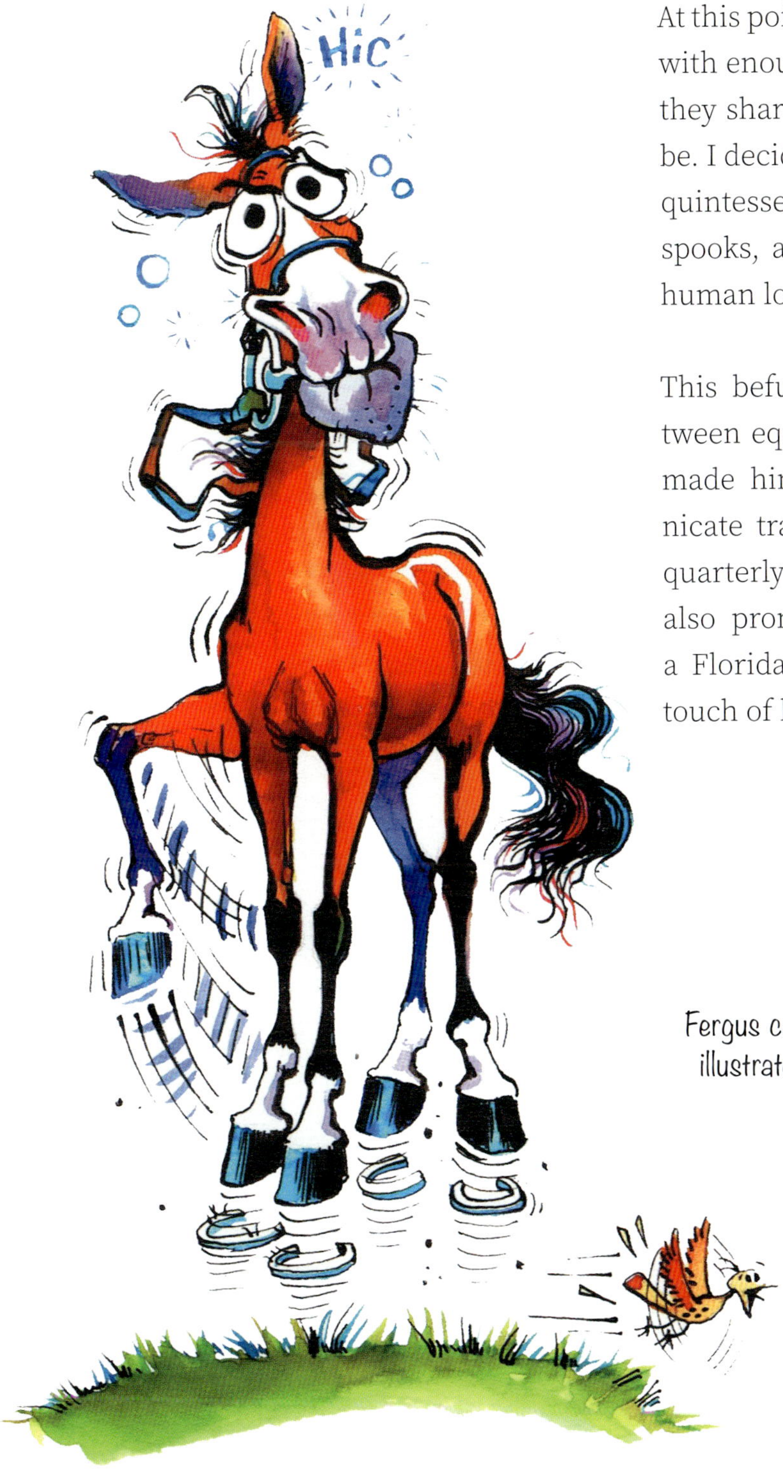
Hic

Fergus came down (or went up) with hiccups to illustrate an article about how horses can get hiccups in *Equus Caballus*.

©ABERNETHY 05

ABERNETHY

These early drawings of Fergus graced an article about clipping in *Equus Caballus* magazine. I did them with brush and India ink, watercolor, and Dr. Martin's colored inks.

©ABERNETHY '04

What I love about horse people is their lack of inhibition about the grittier subjects of horsekeeping. Here's an editorial illustration that appeared in an article on manure management...

YOU'RE GOING TO PUSH IT WHERE?!
©JEAN ABERNETHY 2003

...and yet another in which Fergus graced an article on taking a horse's temperature.

# NOT MY HEAD!

BY JEAN ABERNETHY

**DON'T HURT MY HEAD!**

**THERE NOW, FERGUS BUDDY.**

**EASY BOY**

**WHOA FERGUS**

MANY THINGS CAN MAKE A HORSE HEAD-SHY. HITTING A HORSE'S HEAD IS THE WORST KIND OF HORSEMANSHIP...

**MAYBE I SHOULD HIT HIS HEAD! THAT'S WHERE THE PROBLEM IS!**

... OR LETTING A YOUNGSTER OUTGROW ITS HALTER IS A DREADFULLY PAINFUL MISTAKE!

**OW! MY HEAD!**

**ELBY DARND LOOK HOW THAT COLT HAS GROWN!**

©JEAN ABERNETHY 2005

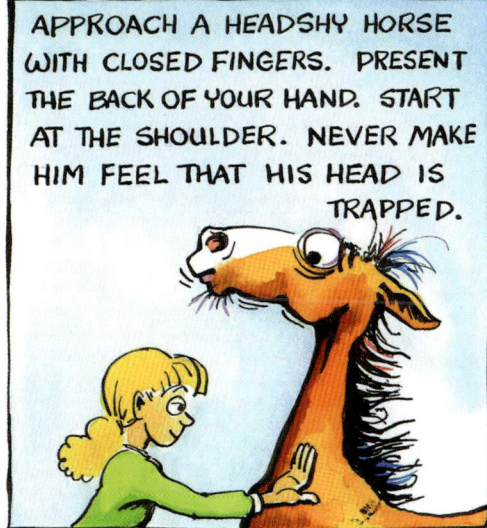

APPROACH A HEADSHY HORSE WITH CLOSED FINGERS. PRESENT THE BACK OF YOUR HAND. START AT THE SHOULDER. NEVER MAKE HIM FEEL THAT HIS HEAD IS TRAPPED.

A HAIR DRYER WORKS TOO. THE HORSE FEELS AIR TOUCH HIS HEAD, BUT IT DOESN'T HURT.

WITH PATIENCE & PERSISTANCE YOU WILL TEACH HIM THAT YOU WILL CAUSE HIM NO PAIN.

**SIGH!**

While developing Fergus for printed media, I was also attempting to get a line of T-shirts and sweatshirts going—a request from Fergus fans—and also to generate some income. Jerre Kelsh invented this quote, and I was so taken with it that I asked her permission to use it in a T-shirt design. Jerre consented.

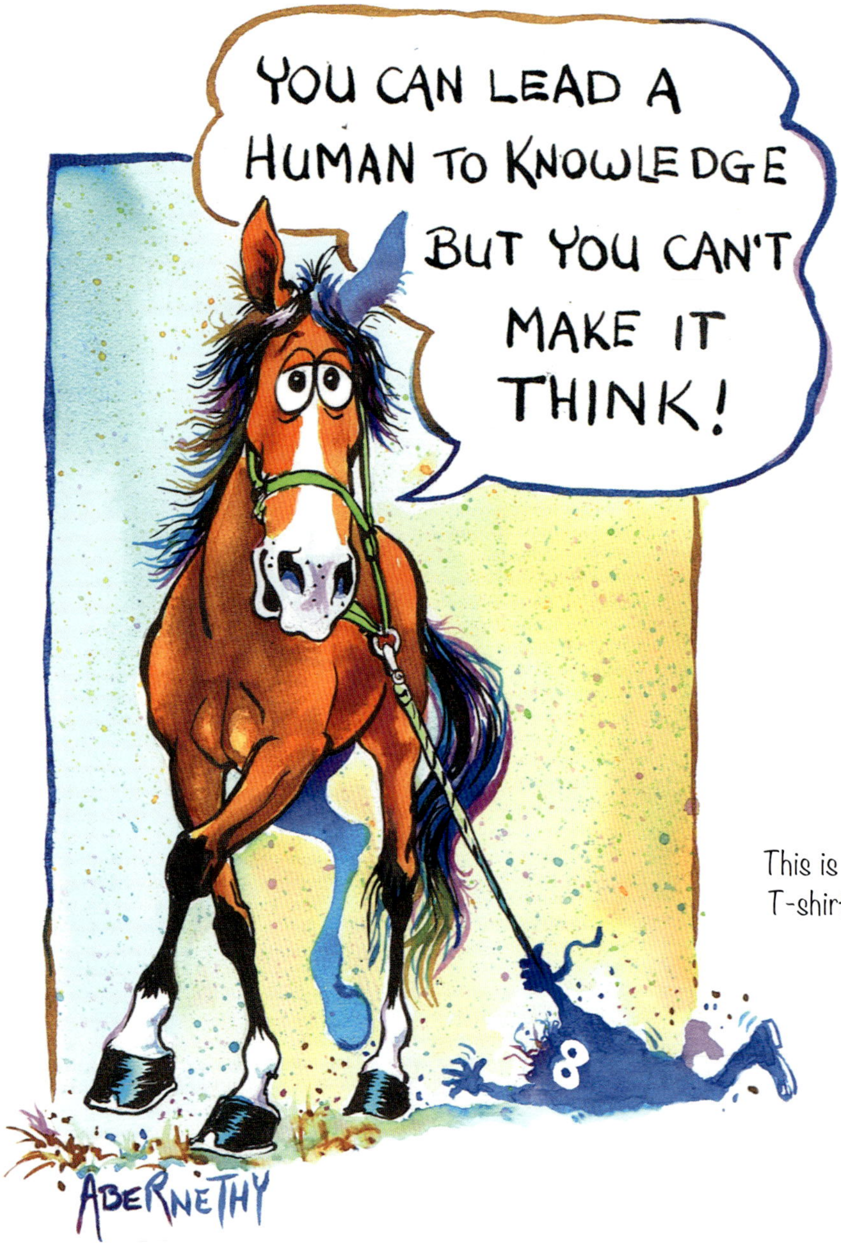
YOU CAN LEAD A HUMAN TO KNOWLEDGE BUT YOU CAN'T MAKE IT THINK!
ABERNETHY

This is the original version of the T-shirt artwork, featuring Jerre Kelsh's quote.

Fergus needed a pedigree. Let me see—we have the GSB (General Stud Book); we also have the AQHA, the APHA, the AApA, AHA, AHHS, AHS, ASH, ASHA, AMHA, ASPC. We have the CHBA, FSA, SPSS, C.T.H.S., BWP/NAD, KTOB, KNN, KWPN, LAA, LANA, IHSGB, FEIF, FPS, HSGB, POA, RHBBA, NSH, NSSHA, NAAAHA, TWHBEA...Some countries are more given to acronyms than others, but it seemed reasonable that Fergus should become the foundation gelding of the FLHWBGE (Funny Little Horse With Big Googley Eyes) society.

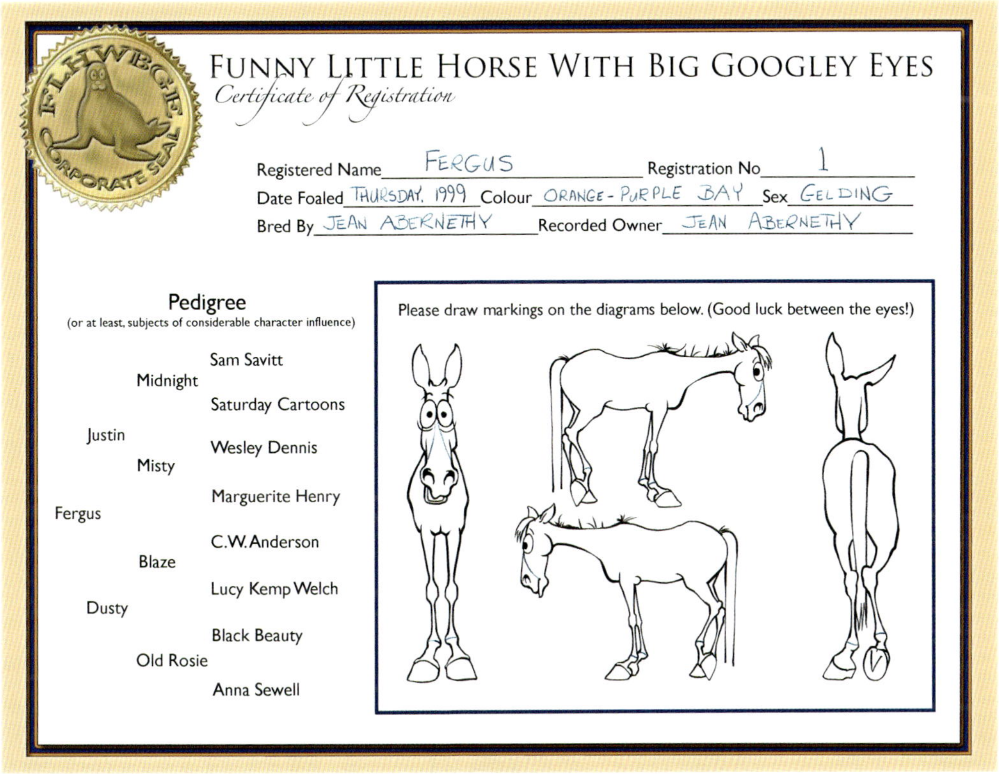
FLHWBGE
CORPORATE SEAL
FUNNY LITTLE HORSE WITH BIG GOOGLEY EYES
Certificate of Registration
Registered Name FERGUS Registration No 1
Date Foaled THURSDAY, 1999 Colour ORANGE-PURPLE BAY Sex GELDING
Bred By JEAN ABERNETHY Recorded Owner JEAN ABERNETHY
Pedigree
(or at least, subjects of considerable character influence)
Fergus
Justin
Midnight
Sam Savitt
Saturday Cartoons
Misty
Wesley Dennis
Marguerite Henry
Dusty
Blaze
C.W. Anderson
Lucy Kemp Welch
Old Rosie
Black Beauty
Anna Sewell
Please draw markings on the diagrams below. (Good luck between the eyes!)

Fergus's original Certificate of Registration.

With just one star character, my whole slant on delivering humor had to change. I needed support characters that could hold conversations with my starring actor. So I kept drawing and a variety of beasts developed that could carry out storylines with Fergus. Grace the pony was inspired by a neighbor's pony of my childhood years called "Trigger." Trigger knew way too much and gave me the highest adrenaline ride of my life. It happened because on that summer day, with our assorted horses, ponies and kids, I was the only one still small enough to ride him.

The "gentle giants" were represented by Claymore the Clydesdale, whose name I later changed to Hugh. Kase the Friesian appeared, and Dottie, the Appaloosa, with her daughter, Ditto. There was Art the Paint Horse, a mule named Clevis—the list is infinite, actually. I still invent them as I need them.

My sketch page developing characters, drawn with brush and India ink. Clockwise, starting at the top left: Grace the pony, Hugh the Clydesdale, Ditto the foal, Dottie the Appaloosa mare, Kase the Friesian, Art the Paint Horse. And of course Himself (with all four shoes!)

Note to trivia-seekers: The comic on p. 78 explains explains why Ditto's spots are on her head instead of her rump.

I worked on human characters too, but the humor seemed to come more readily when slanted toward the personalities of the horses.

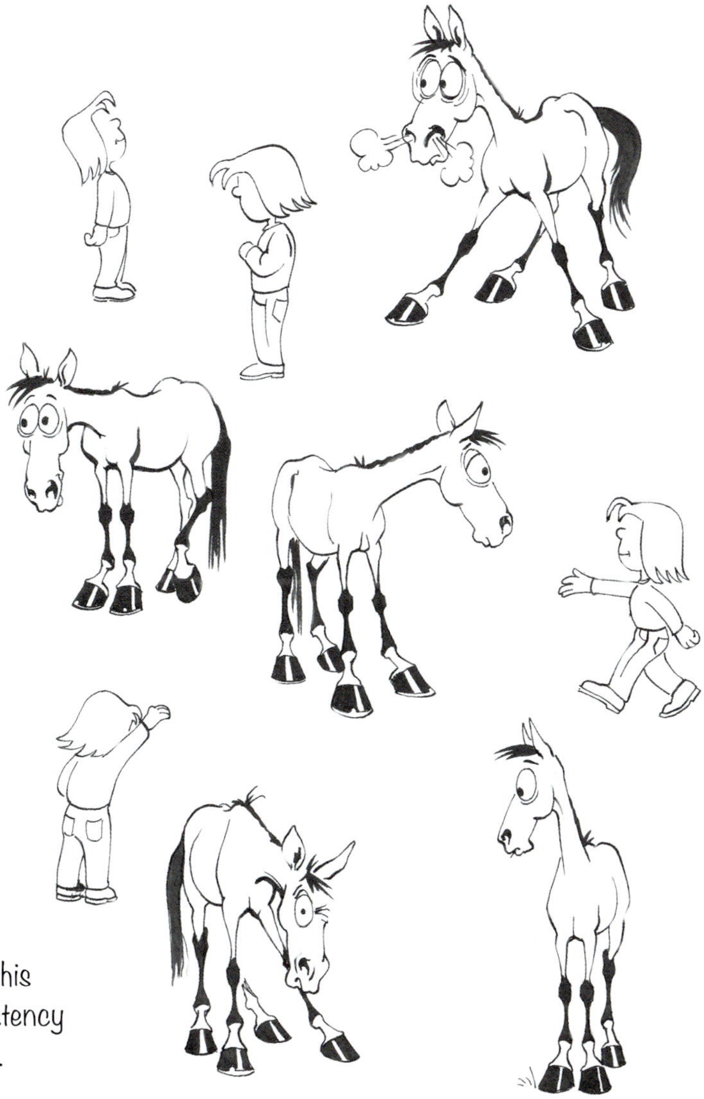

Practicing pages like this helped me develop consistency with the characters.

My interest in history was taken up by *Blaze Magazine,* a quarterly horse periodical for kids, and, for a few years, Fergus presented history trivia in illustrated story pages.

Through those years the look of my illustrations was changing noticeably, because my knowledge of computer graphics was expanding. In my *Blaze* features, I was learning to combine handmade artwork with computer-generated techniques. Note for trivia-seekers: "Horse Latitudes" on page 24 was actually never published by *Blaze,* though it was written to follow "Fergus Goes to Sea."

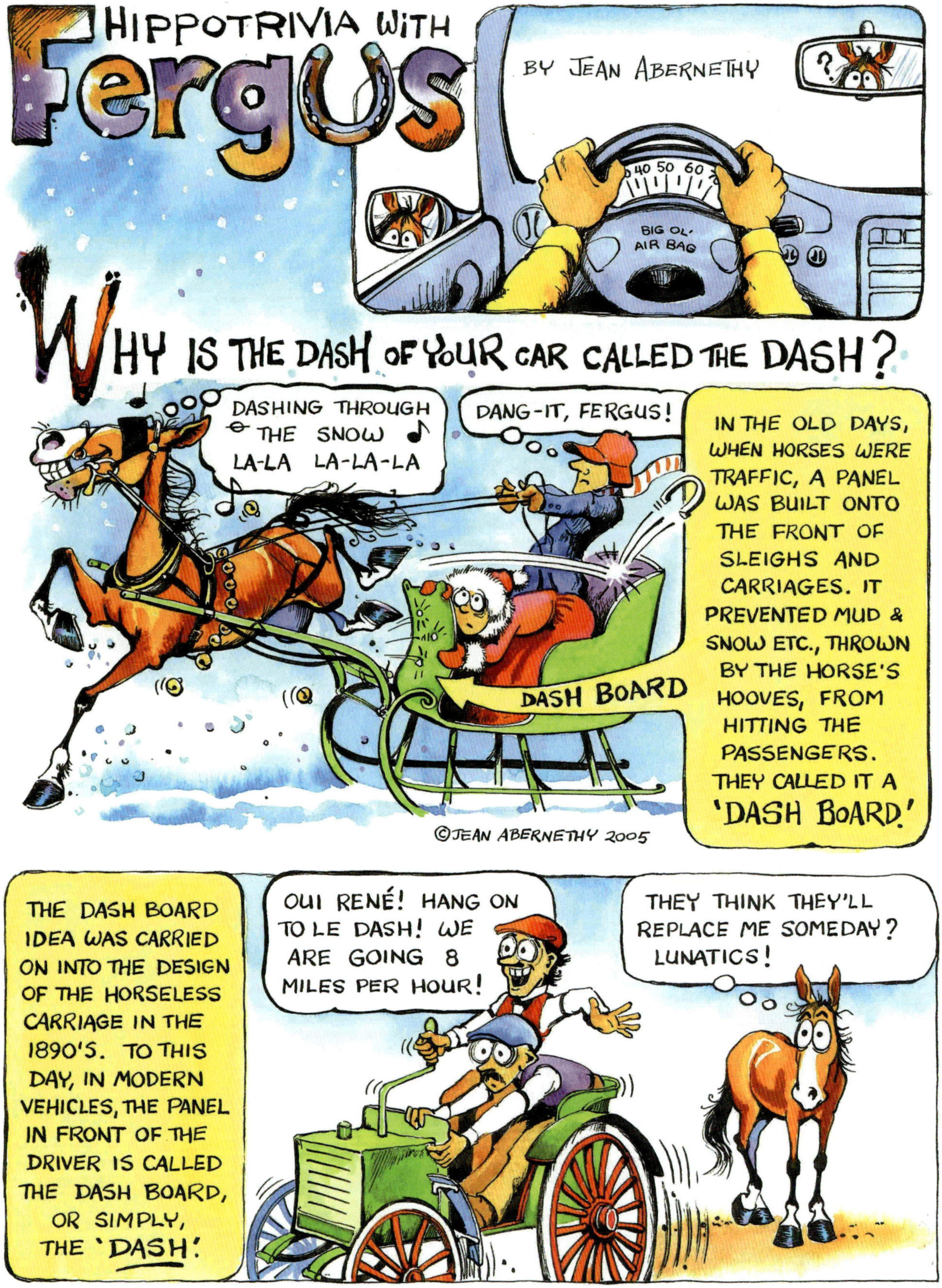

HIPPOTRIVIA WITH
Fergus
BY JEAN ABERNETHY
40 50 60
BIG OL' AIR BAG
WHY IS THE DASH OF YOUR CAR CALLED THE DASH?
DASHING THROUGH THE SNOW LA-LA LA-LA-LA
DANG-IT, FERGUS!
IN THE OLD DAYS, WHEN HORSES WERE TRAFFIC, A PANEL WAS BUILT ONTO THE FRONT OF SLEIGHS AND CARRIAGES. IT PREVENTED MUD & SNOW ETC., THROWN BY THE HORSE'S HOOVES, FROM HITTING THE PASSENGERS. THEY CALLED IT A 'DASH BOARD.'
DASH BOARD
©JEAN ABERNETHY 2005
THE DASH BOARD IDEA WAS CARRIED ON INTO THE DESIGN OF THE HORSELESS CARRIAGE IN THE 1890'S. TO THIS DAY, IN MODERN VEHICLES, THE PANEL IN FRONT OF THE DRIVER IS CALLED THE DASH BOARD, OR SIMPLY, THE 'DASH'.
OUI RENÉ! HANG ON TO LE DASH! WE ARE GOING 8 MILES PER HOUR!
THEY THINK THEY'LL REPLACE ME SOMEDAY? LUNATICS!

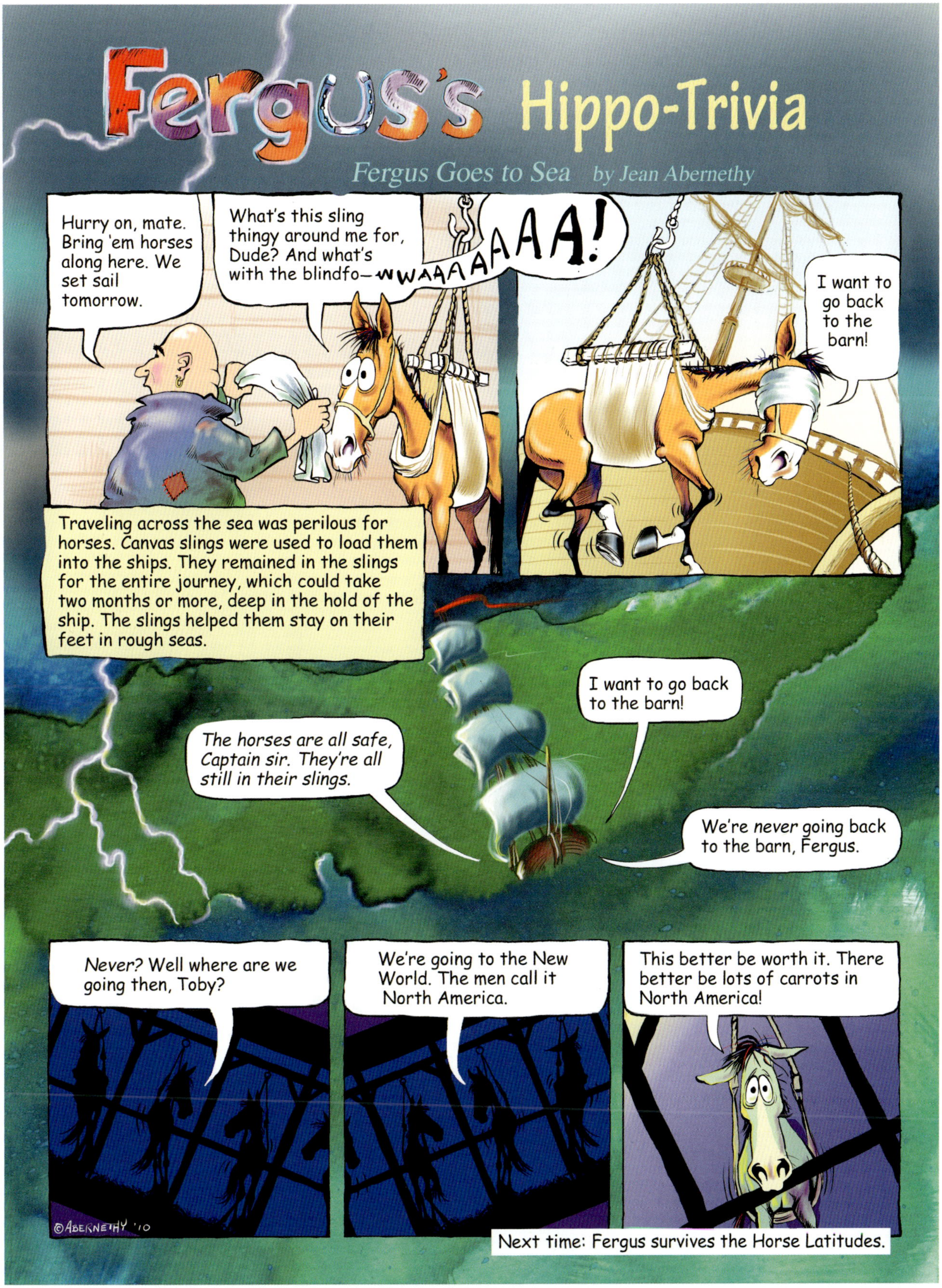
Fergus's Hippo-Trivia
Fergus Goes to Sea by Jean Abernethy
Hurry on, mate. Bring 'em horses along here. We set sail tomorrow.
What's this sling thingy around me for, Dude? And what's with the blindfo—WWAAAAAAAA!
I want to go back to the barn!
Traveling across the sea was perilous for horses. Canvas slings were used to load them into the ships. They remained in the slings for the entire journey, which could take two months or more, deep in the hold of the ship. The slings helped them stay on their feet in rough seas.
I want to go back to the barn!
The horses are all safe, Captain sir. They're all still in their slings.
We're never going back to the barn, Fergus.
Never? Well where are we going then, Toby?
We're going to the New World. The men call it North America.
This better be worth it. There better be lots of carrots in North America!
©ABERNETHY '10
Next time: Fergus survives the Horse Latitudes.

# Hippo-Trivia with Fergus

## Fergus Survives the Horse Latitudes
*by Jean Abernethy*

A sailing ship bound for the New World carries tools and horses for the colonists. Fergus has been in the dark hold of the ship all summer long. But now there is another challenge to survive.

Aye, lads, we've reached the Horse Latitudes.

Captain, we're running short of fresh water!

There's no wind, sir. We're not going anywhere.

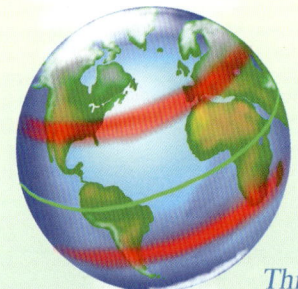

At 30 to 35 degrees latitude both North and South of the Equator there are bands of hot, dry air, with little or no wind. Ships could be stranded there for days or weeks. The horses below decks required water to stay alive. But so did the ship's sailors and there was only a limited amount aboard.

A grim choice, but the men must live. Some of the horses have to go. Keep the healthiest ones, boys.

*This difficult decision became so common that these areas of the sea became known as the Horse Latitudes.*

Wind! We're moving! Toby, we're moving!

Toby?

In Autumn the ship finally arrives.

LAND HO!

I smell grass!!

Look, Mama, a new horse! He's thin. Can I give him a carrot?

Wow! A barn, a kid and a carrot! I think I like this New World!

© ABERNETHY '10

# The Comic Strips

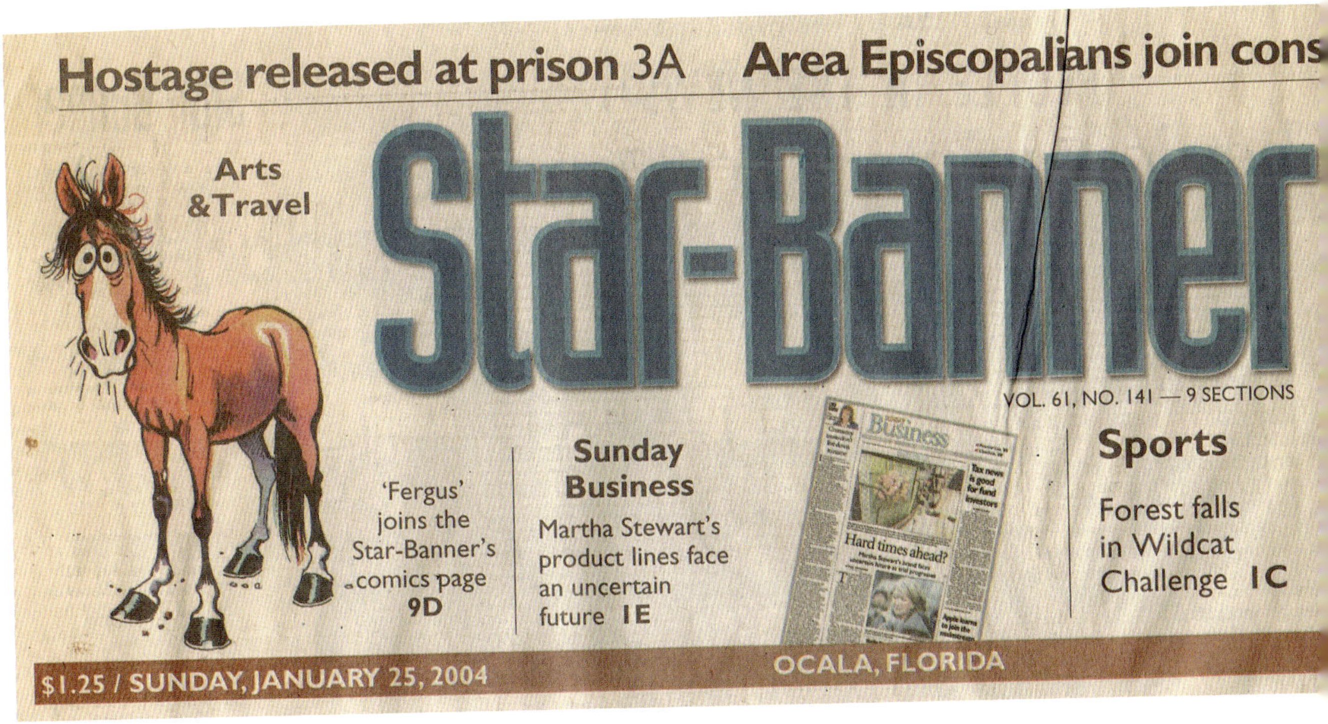
Hostage released at prison 3A
Area Episcopalians join cons
Star-Banner
Arts &Travel
'Fergus' joins the Star-Banner's comics page 9D
Sunday Business
Martha Stewart's product lines face an uncertain future 1E
Business
Hard times ahead?
VOL. 61, NO. 141 — 9 SECTIONS
Sports
Forest falls in Wildcat Challenge 1C
$1.25 / SUNDAY, JANUARY 25, 2004
OCALA, FLORIDA

In 2004, another challenge presented itself. I was asked if I could create a weekly comic strip for a newspaper. The answer, of course, was "Yes!" Then I had to figure out how to do it.

Appearing every Sunday on the "Comics Page" of the *Ocala Star-Banner,* Fergus entered the world of newspaper comics. In forging humor for this audience, I had to create punchlines that could be understood by everyone, not simply the equestrian readers. This was when I started having fun with a beaver, crows, and an armadillo.

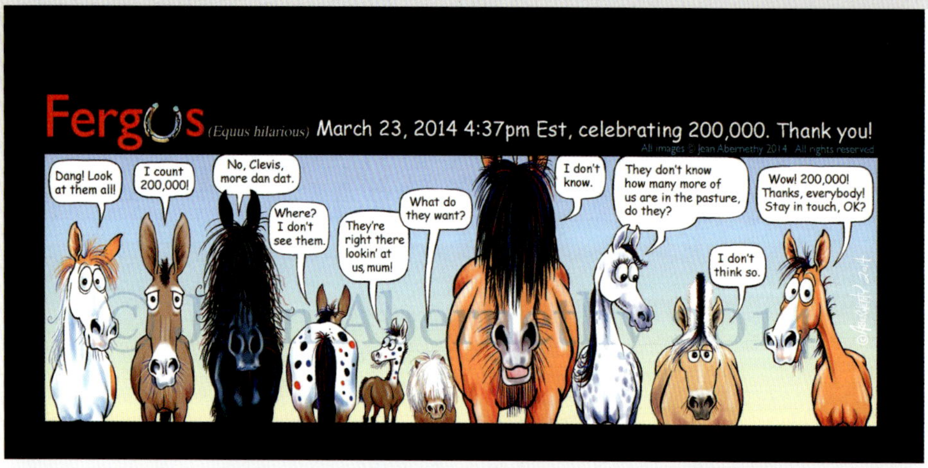
Fergus (Equus hilarious) March 23, 2014 4:37pm Est, celebrating 200,000. Thank you!
All images © Jean Abernethy 2014 All rights reserved
Dang! Look at them all!
I count 200,000!
No, Clevis, more dan dat.
Where? I don't see them.
They're right there lookin' at us, mum!
What do they want?
I don't know.
They don't know how many more of us are in the pasture, do they?
I don't think so.
Wow! 200,000! Thanks, everybody! Stay in touch, OK?

Fergus the Horse
March 23, 2014 · Edited ·

Thank you

Like · Comment · Share
11,190 people like this.
1,287 shares
View previous comments 6 of 213

Ha ha, I can definitely see the resemblance. 🙂
March 26, 2014 at 6:13am · Like

❤
March 27, 2014 at 2:25pm · Like

am I the only one that was reading with different voices??
April 8, 2014 at 7:31pm · Like · 10

You betcha
May 24, 2014 at 12:52am · Like

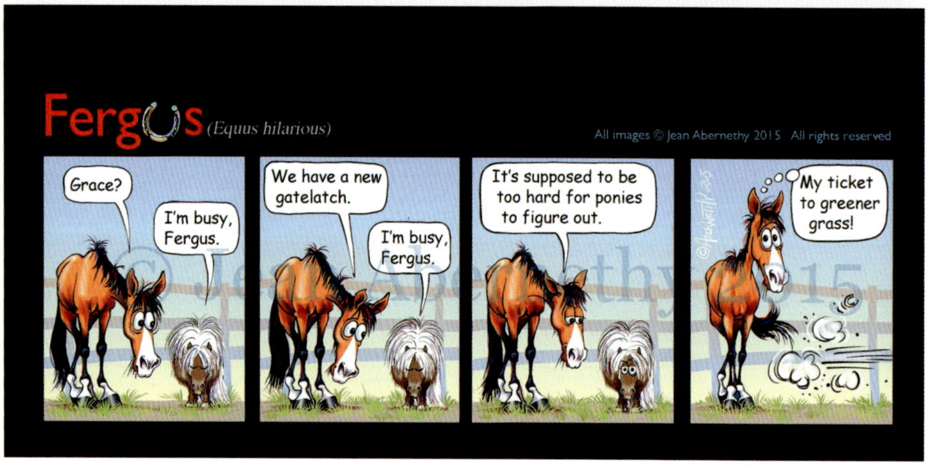
Fergus (Equus hilarious)
All images © Jean Abernethy 2015 All rights reserved
Grace?
I'm busy, Fergus.
We have a new gatelatch.
I'm busy, Fergus.
It's supposed to be too hard for ponies to figure out.
My ticket to greener grass!

Fergus the Horse
January 15 ·

Like · Comment · Share
10,007 people like this.
3,804 shares
View previous comments 6 of 177

Derfor safira alltid står igjen og Orlando er på jakt etter grønt gress med pontus?! 😔 Hallvar
See Translation
Like · Reply · January 24 at 4:03pm

Jepp, hun lurer Ollis på samme måte etterpå 😊
See Translation
Like · Reply · 1 · January 24 at 4:04pm

Men Ollis og pontus opnet kun nok til at dem kommer gjennom så Safira måtte stå att og se dem kose seg 😎
See Translation
Like · Reply · January 24 at 4:05pm

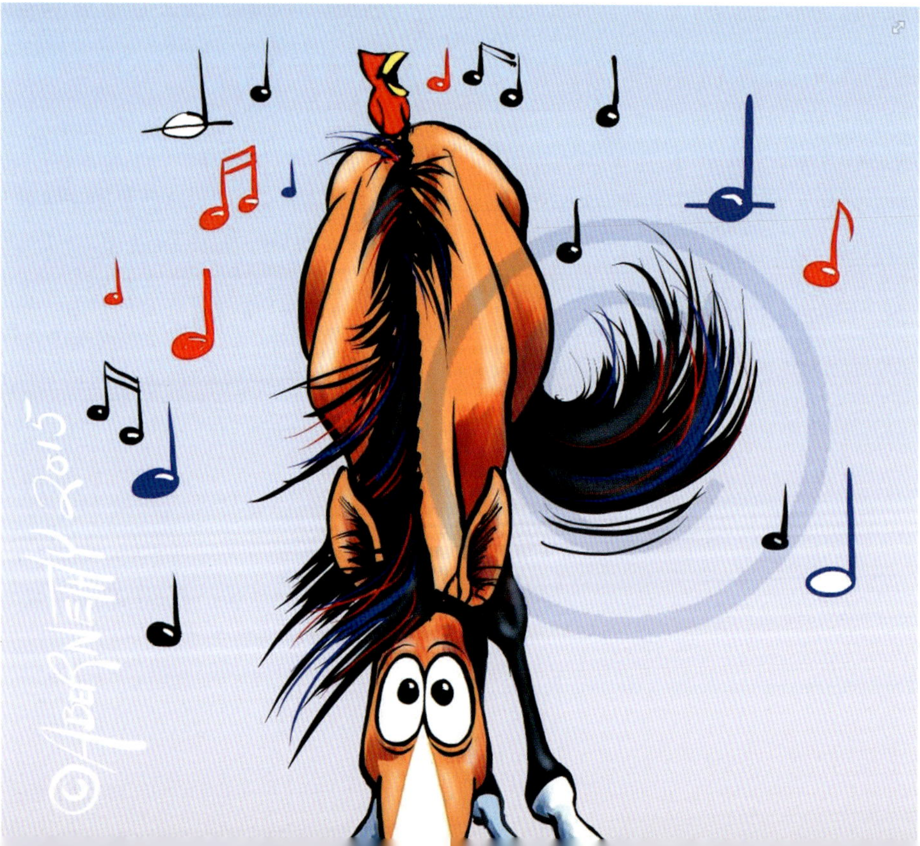

Fergus the Horse
April 26 ·

Like · Comment · Share
6,503 people like this.
848 shares
View previous comments 6 of 50

Love this.
Like · Reply · April 27 at 11:42am

Love It !!!
Like · Reply · April 27 at 4:53pm

the cardinal is singing My OLe Kentucky Home!!!
Like · Reply · April 27 at 6:33pm

Love you Fergy....lol
Like · Reply · April 27 at 7:14pm

Te amo bonito.....
See Translation
Like · Reply · April 27 at 11:50pm

it's Boycie 😔😔
Like · Reply · May 15 at 9:05am

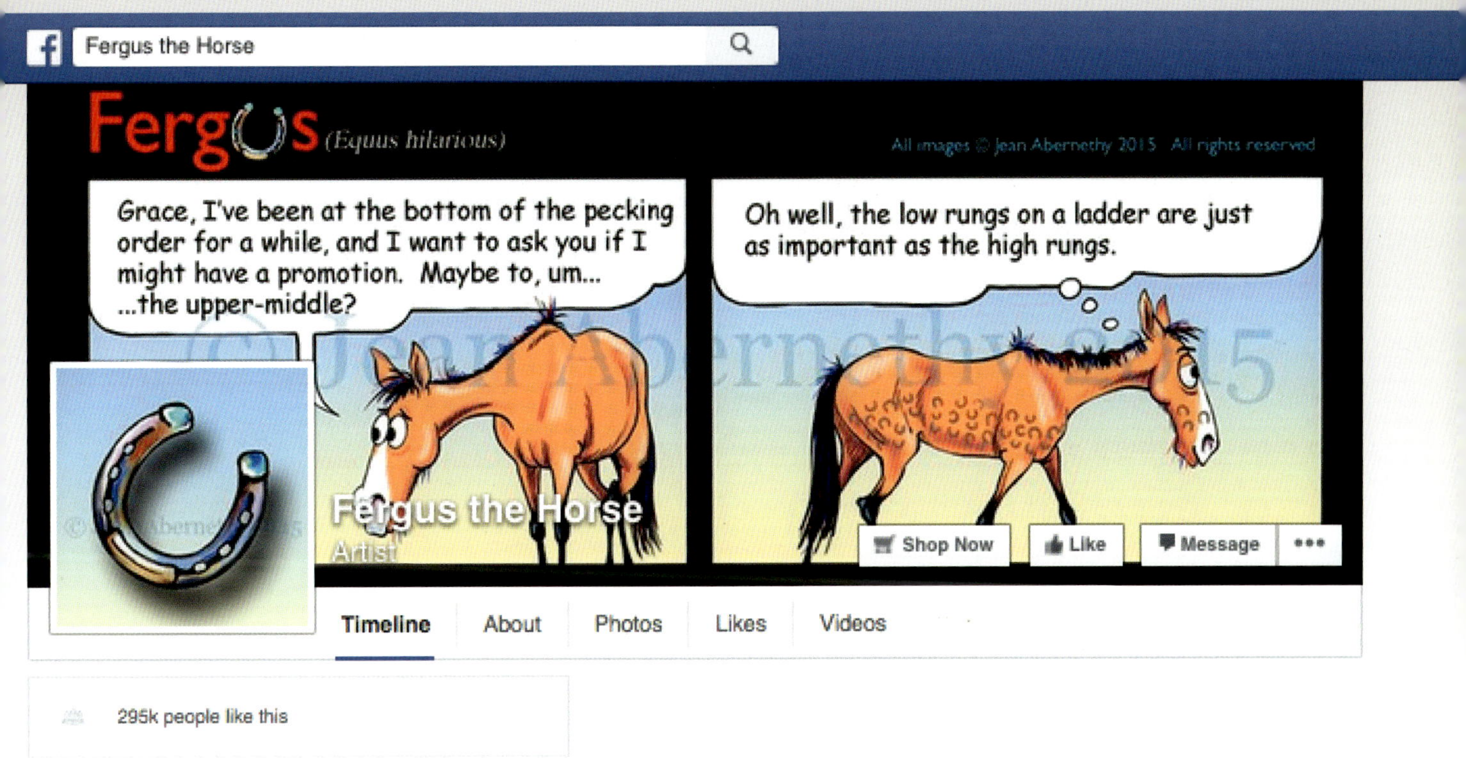
Fergus the Horse
Fergus (Equus hilarious)
All images © Jean Abernethy 2015 All rights reserved
Grace, I've been at the bottom of the pecking order for a while, and I want to ask you if I might have a promotion. Maybe to, um... ...the upper-middle?
Oh well, the low rungs on a ladder are just as important as the high rungs.
Fergus the Horse
Artist
Shop Now
Like
Message
Timeline
About
Photos
Likes
Videos
295k people like this

# Fergus on Facebook

As the publishing industry was turned on its head by the birth of the internet, illustration changed, too. More and more of my illustrations were created for the screen, and fewer for print. I found myself changing computers and changing programs, while drawing mediums also continued to shift. I began working on an electronic tablet. I wore out a small one, then purchased a bigger one.

Then social media arrived. Fergus found his way to Facebook in 2012 and suddenly the little horse I'd come to believe in was exposed to the whole world. I now watch with amazement as more and more people join the fun. When fans say "Fergus reminds me of my horse!" I could not be paid a higher compliment.

**Regarding Hunters & Jumpers.**   Dear horses everywhere,

People often talk about **Hunters & Jumpers**. They have definitions for those, but I don't know what they are. It might have something to do with having one's mane braided into little knots, but I am not certain. However, we horses have fundamentally clear definitions for **Hunters** and **Jumpers**:

"**Hunters**" (fig. 1) are those sinister beings which lurk in one's path. They *do not move*, but are obviously poised to pounce. Give them a wide berth!

"**Jumpers**" (fig. 2) are those beings which *actually do move* in to attack. They might even *touch* you!!! The only reasonable response when one encounters a **Jumper** is to pack yourself and your little rider off to the barn without a moment's hesitation, and take the rest of the day off.

With your safety in mind, **Fergus**

Fig 1   Hunters

Fig 2   Jumpers

## Equine Anatomy

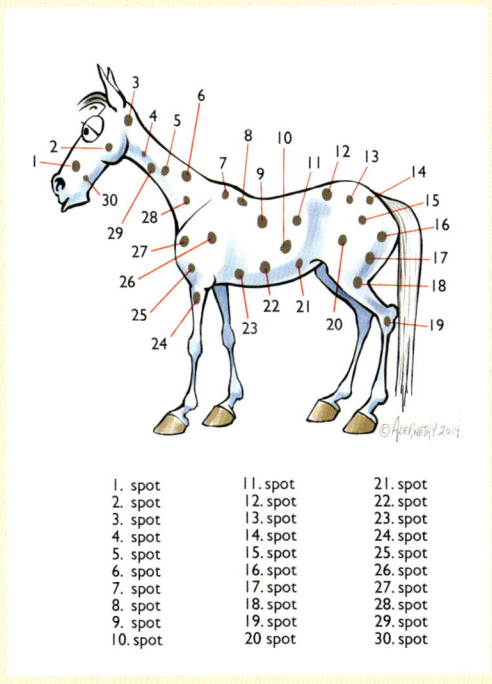

| 1. spot | 11. spot | 21. spot |
|---|---|---|
| 2. spot | 12. spot | 22. spot |
| 3. spot | 13. spot | 23. spot |
| 4. spot | 14. spot | 24. spot |
| 5. spot | 15. spot | 25. spot |
| 6. spot | 16. spot | 26. spot |
| 7. spot | 17. spot | 27. spot |
| 8. spot | 18. spot | 28. spot |
| 9. spot | 19. spot | 29. spot |
| 10. spot | 20 spot | 30. spot |

Fergus © Jean Abernethy 2014

The Facebook platform offered a place for experimentation in ways to present Fergus to his audience other than in comic-strip form.

Dear horses everywhere,

You may often hear equestrians speak of the "double oxer" yet they only ride us over fences. I never quite understood this until the day we encountered these characters. The moment I spotted them, I knew *this* was what we'd been training for! I set out to prove myself, but as I collected my stride for the jump, communication with my rider deteriorated quickly. Consequently our landing was not ideal, but we cleared them! *No faults!*

Never let your rider undermine your self-confidence.

--- **Fergus**

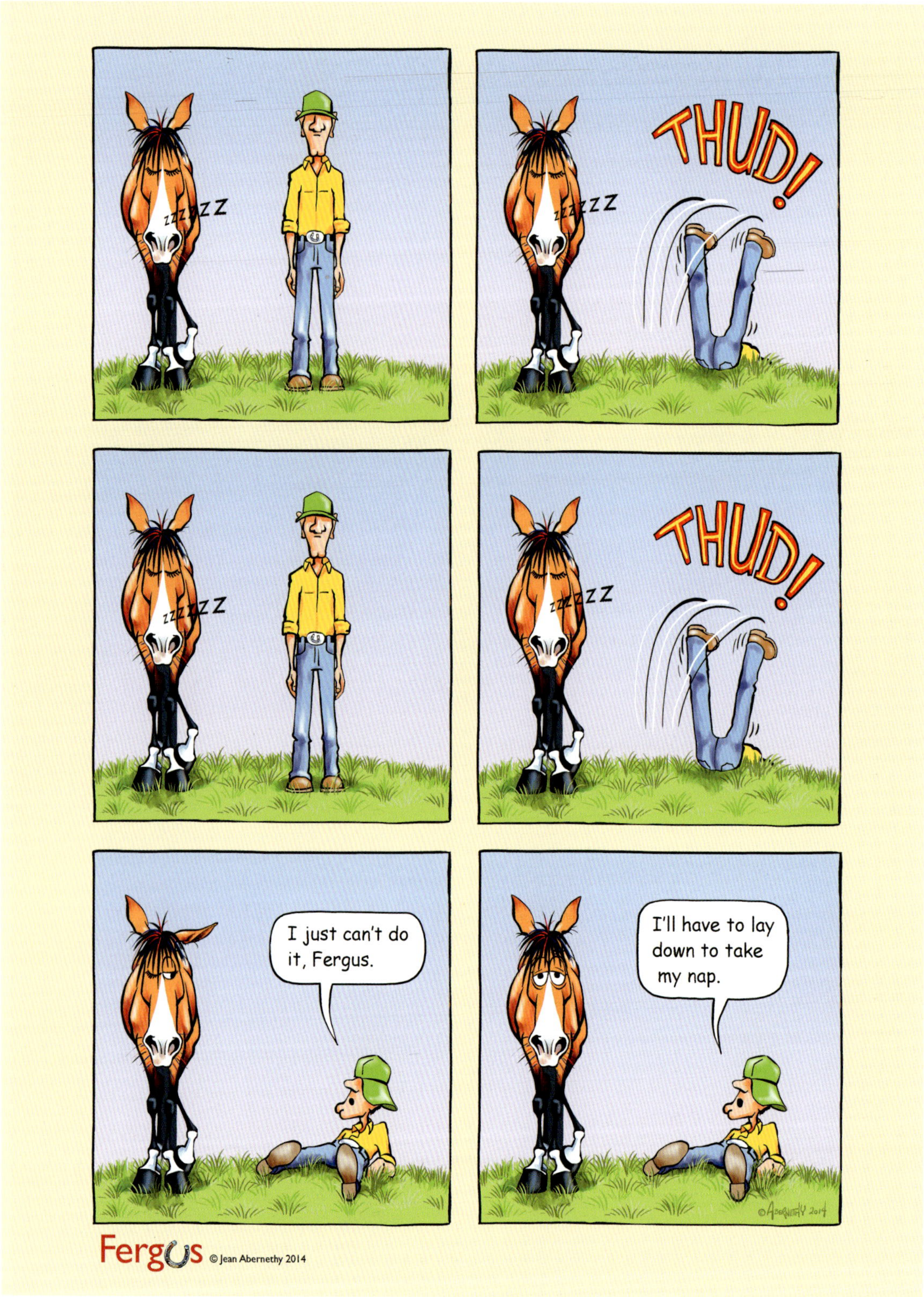
zzzzZZ
zzzzZZ
THUD!
zzzzZZ
zzzzZZ
THUD!
I just can't do it, Fergus.
I'll have to lay down to take my nap.
©ABERNETHY 2014
Fergus © Jean Abernethy 2014

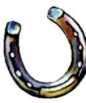

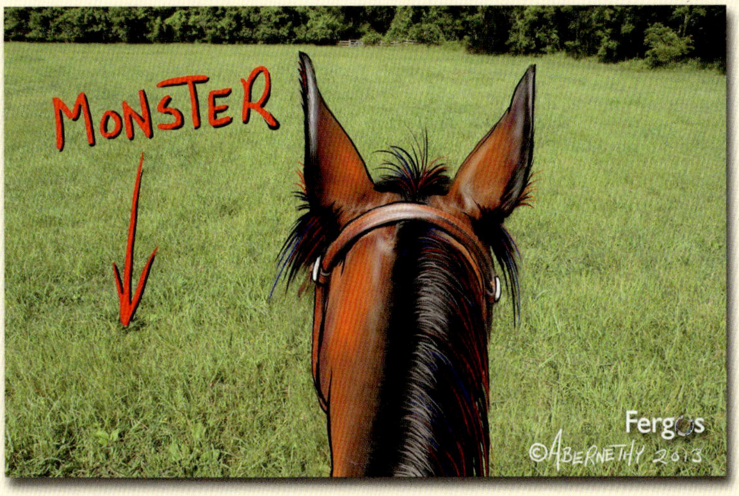
MONSTER
Fergus
©ABERNETHY 2013

Dear Horses everywhere,

Humans are clever, and training them is no small task. Just when you're getting onto their pattern of requests, they switch it up and ask for something different, leaving us looking like the fool. They say they don't want us anticipating, but instead, want us always attentive.

That's fair enough, I suppose.

But the "relationship" is mutual, is it not? Humans have busy little minds, and it is sometimes an effort to keep them on task. They must be schooled to be attentive leaders. Here is an exercise which, through practice, they learn by default to be attentive.

See the arrow indicating the hidden monster in this photo? Well, there is actually nothing there. But if you bolt sideways about 5 meters at this point, you will assuredly bring your rider out of daydream. He or she cannot possibly anticipate this, and will not easily forget the lesson.

*Adrenaline is an astute teacher.* You will have the courtesy of your rider's focused attention for a long while.

Best of luck with it, Fergus

I've been grateful to the horses who've been a part of my life over the years. It is they who've guided me in bringing Fergus and his friends to life. My friend "Vinnie" inspired this essay on training through anticipation.

There are many trails untraveled for Fergus, and I wonder sometimes if this book is simply a beginning. There is one thing Fergus and the real horses in my life continue to assure me...

# Courage
## keeps us
## going,

© Jean Abernethy 2013

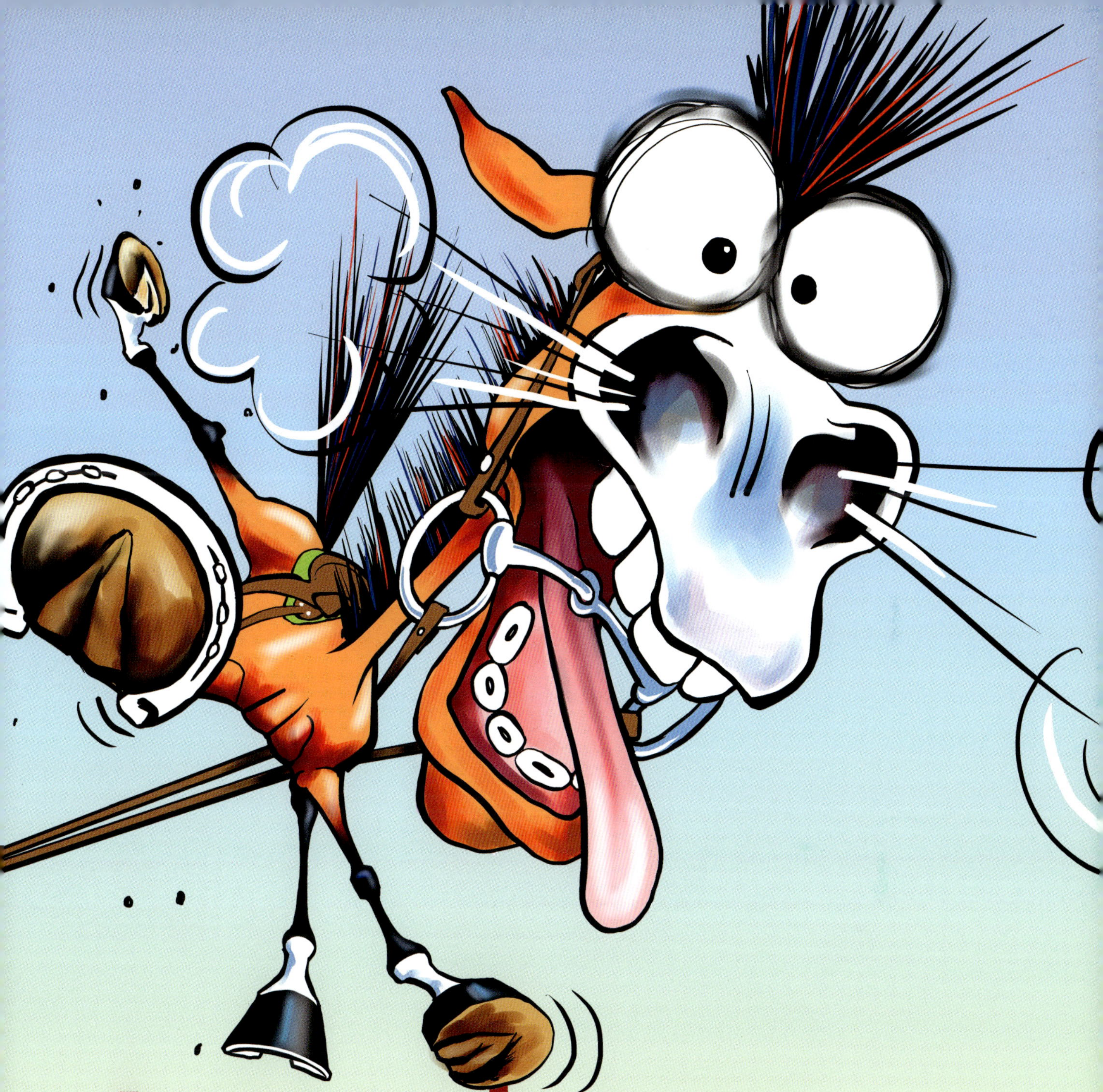

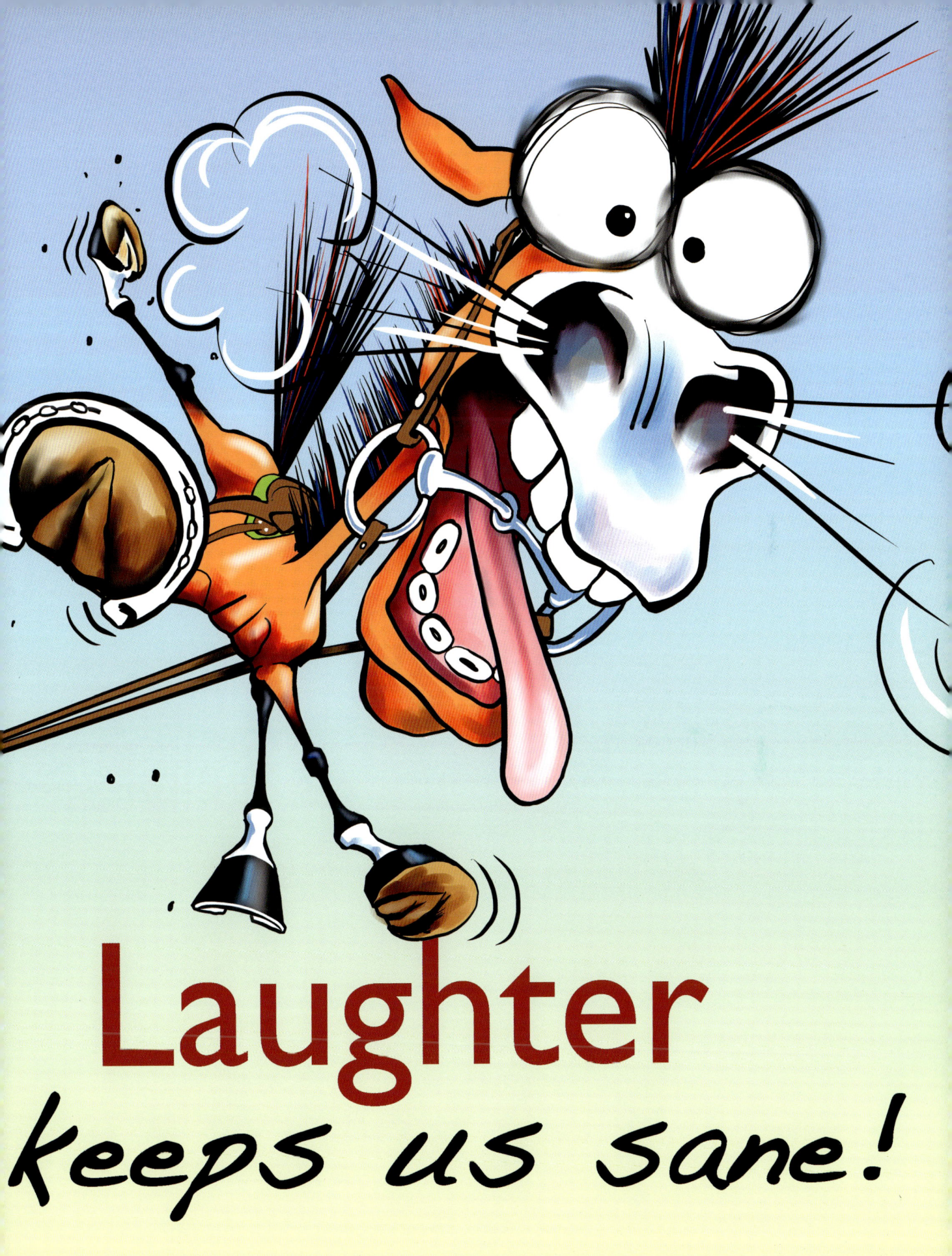

# Laughter

*keeps us sane!*

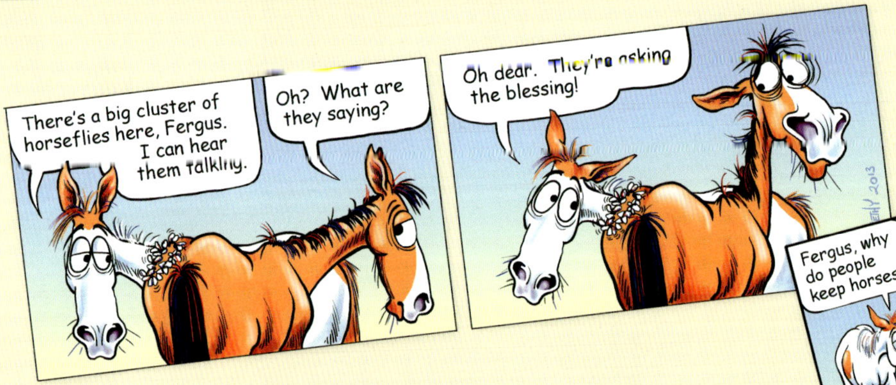
There's a big cluster of horseflies here, Fergus. I can hear them talking.
Oh? What are they saying?
Oh dear. They're asking the blessing!
THY 2013

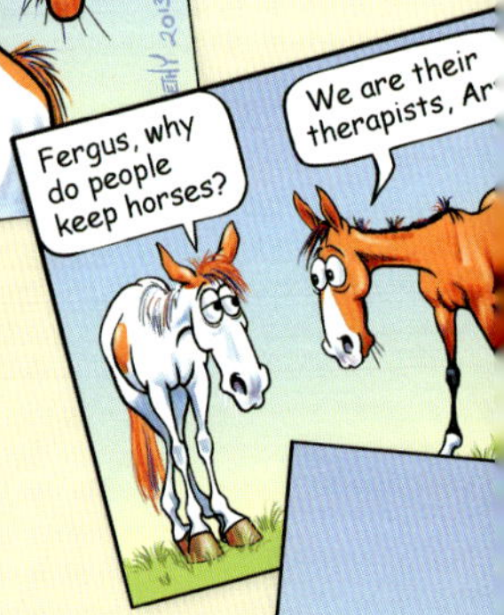
Fergus, why do people keep horses?
We are their therapists,

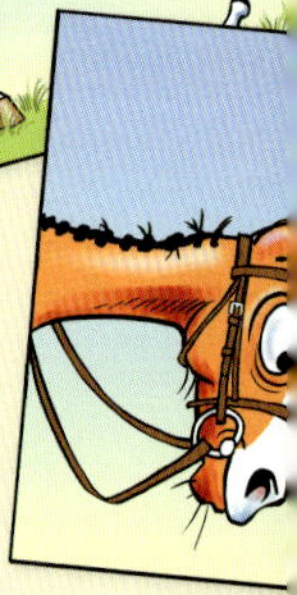

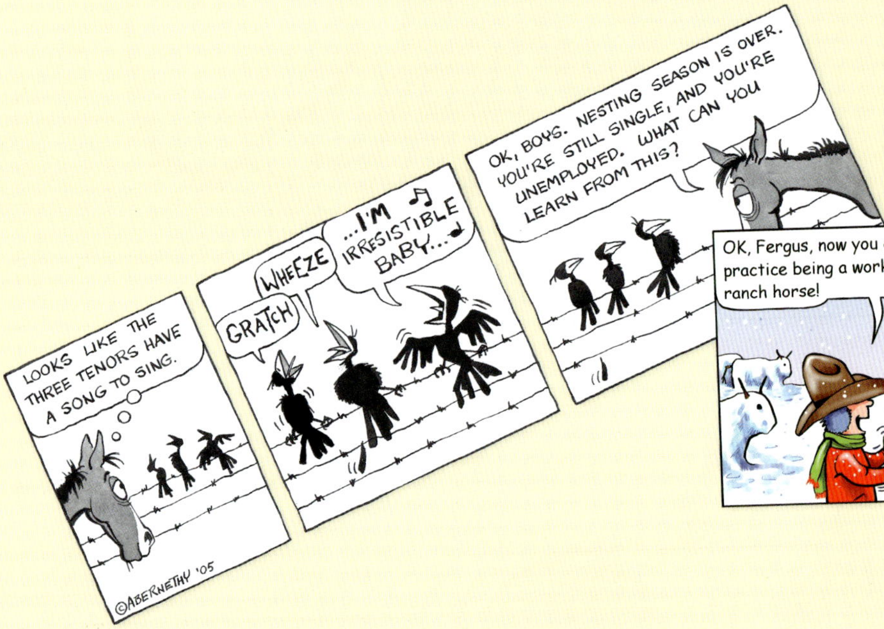
LOOKS LIKE THE THREE TENORS HAVE A SONG TO SING.
©ABERNETHY '05
GRATCH
WHEEZE
...I'M IRRESISTIBLE BABY...
OK, BOYS. NESTING SEASON IS OVER. YOU'RE STILL SINGLE, AND YOU'RE UNEMPLOYED. WHAT CAN YOU LEARN FROM THIS?

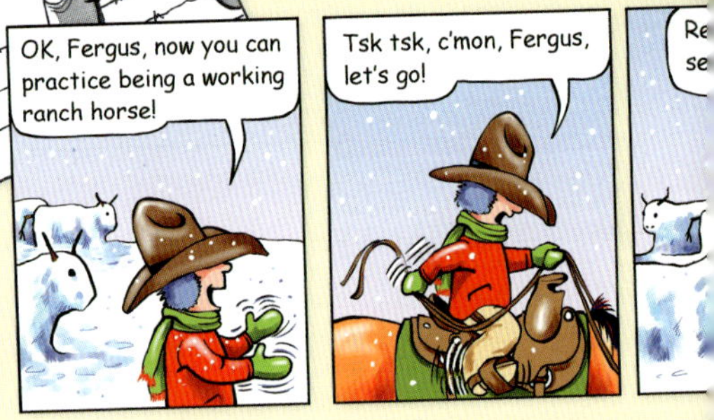
OK, Fergus, now you can practice being a working ranch horse!
Tsk tsk, c'mon, Fergus, let's go!

# Part Two:

# The Fergus Comics

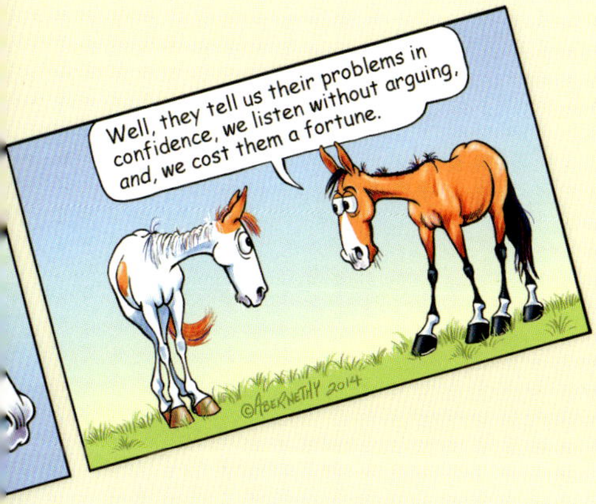
Well, they tell us their problems in confidence, we listen without arguing, and, we cost them a fortune.
©ABERNETHY 2014

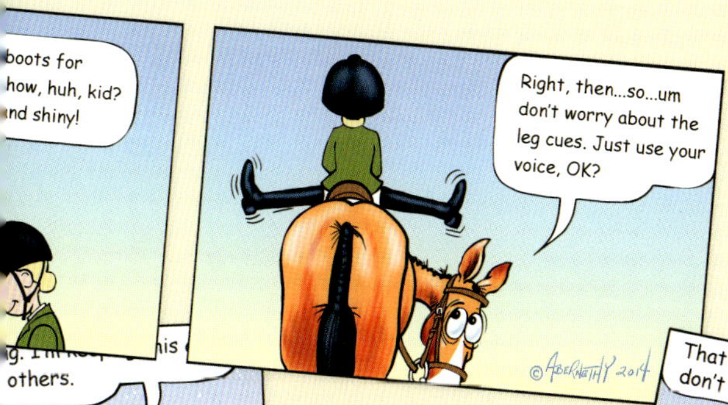
Right, then...so...um don't worry about the leg cues. Just use your voice, OK?
©ABERNETHY 2014

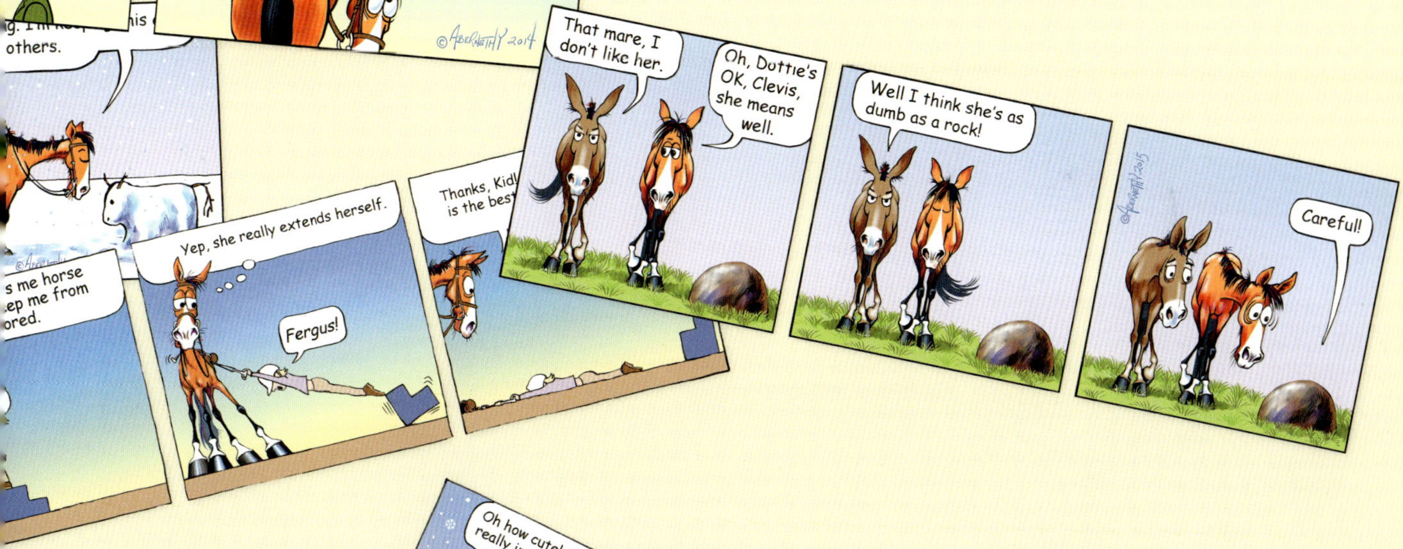
Yep, she really extends herself.
Fergus!
That mare, I don't like her.
Oh, Dottie's OK, Clevis, she means well.
Well I think she's as dumb as a rock!
©ABERNETHY 2015
Careful!

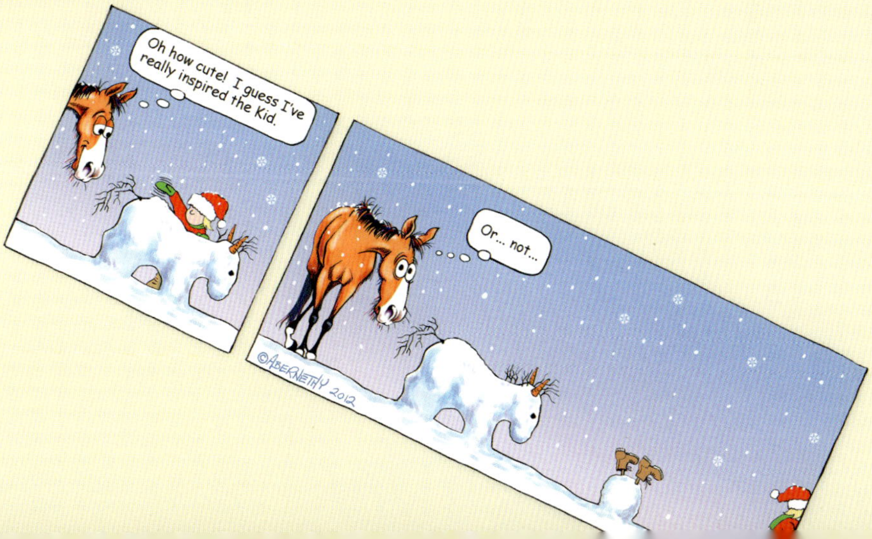
Oh how cute! I guess I've really inspired the Kid.
Or... not...
©ABERNETHY 2012

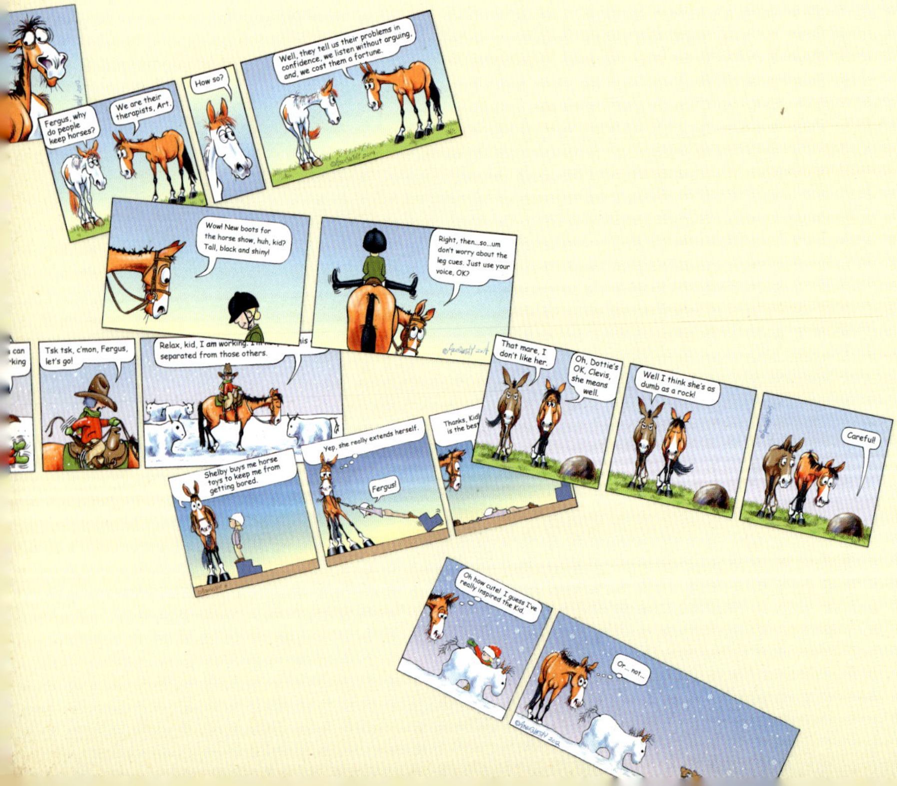

Fergus, why do people keep horses?
We are their therapists, Art.
How so?
Well, they tell us their problems in confidence, we listen without arguing, and, we cost them a fortune.
Wow! New boots for the horse show, huh, kid? Tall, black and shiny!
Right, then...so...um don't worry about the leg cues. Just use your voice, OK?
Tsk tsk, c'mon, Fergus, let's go!
Relax, kid, I am working.
separated from those others.
That mare, I don't like her.
Oh, Dottie's OK, Clevis, she means well.
Well I think she's as dumb as a rock!
Careful!
Shelby buys me horse toys to keep me from getting bored.
Yep, she really extends herself.
Fergus!
Oh how cute! I guess I've really inspired the Kid.
Or... not...

# The Ridden Word

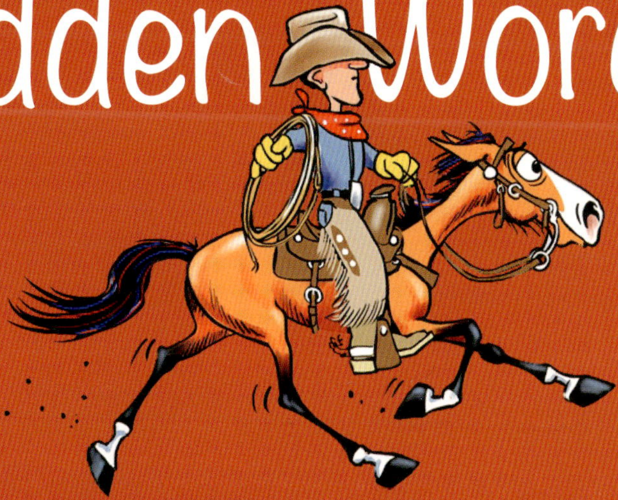

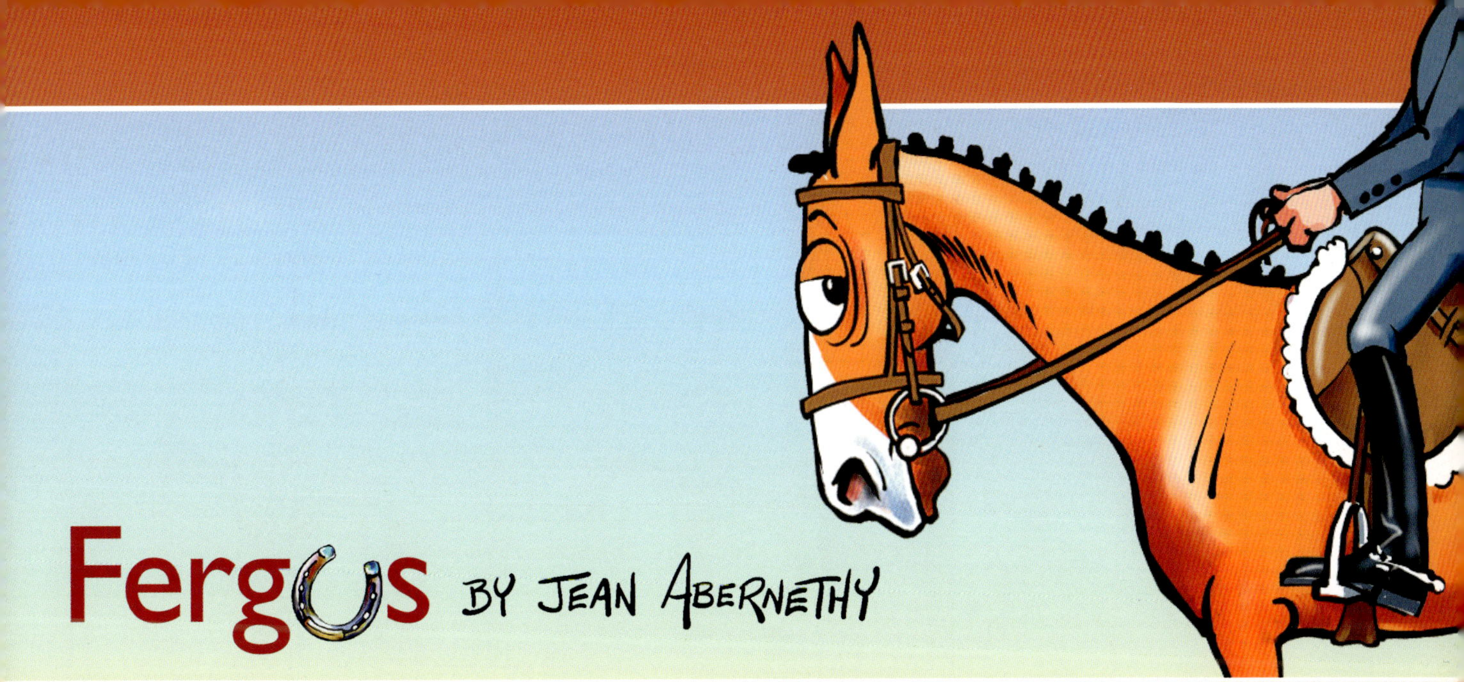
Fergus BY JEAN ABERNETHY

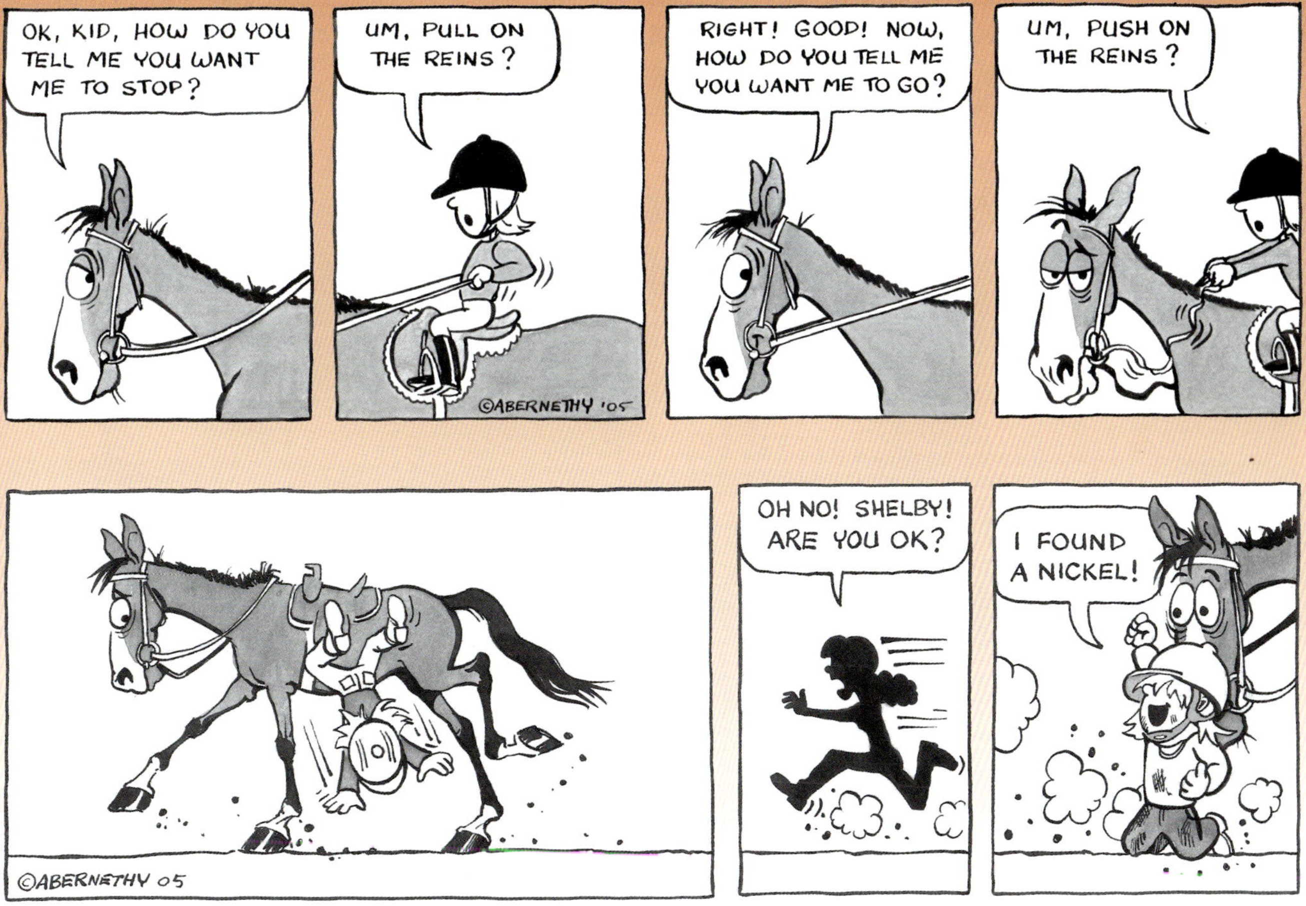
OK, KID, HOW DO YOU TELL ME YOU WANT ME TO STOP?
UM, PULL ON THE REINS?
©ABERNETHY '05
RIGHT! GOOD! NOW, HOW DO YOU TELL ME YOU WANT ME TO GO?
UM, PUSH ON THE REINS?
©ABERNETHY 05
OH NO! SHELBY! ARE YOU OK?
I FOUND A NICKEL!

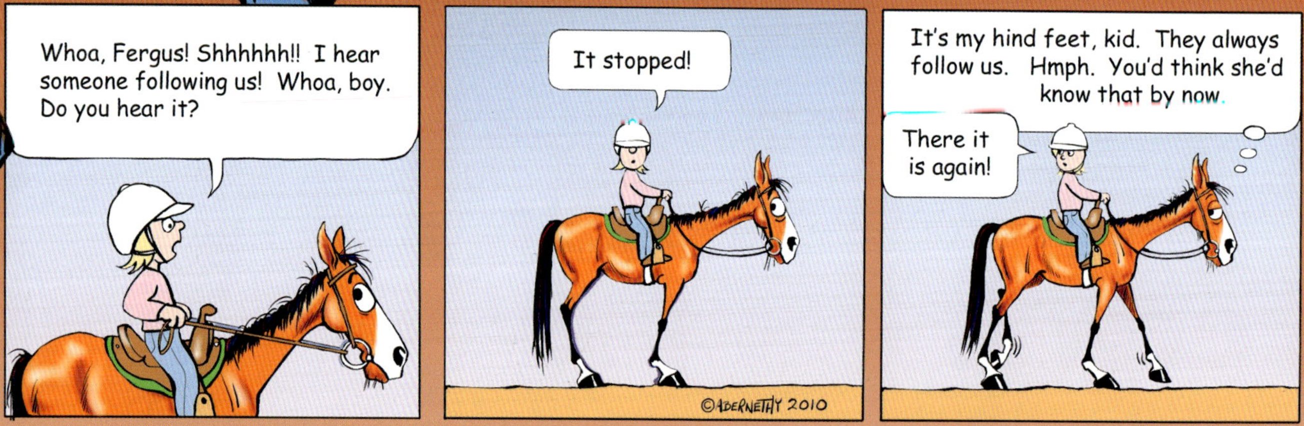
Whoa, Fergus! Shhhhhh!! I hear someone following us! Whoa, boy. Do you hear it?
It stopped!
©ABERNETHY 2010
It's my hind feet, kid. They always follow us. Hmph. You'd think she'd know that by now.
There it is again!

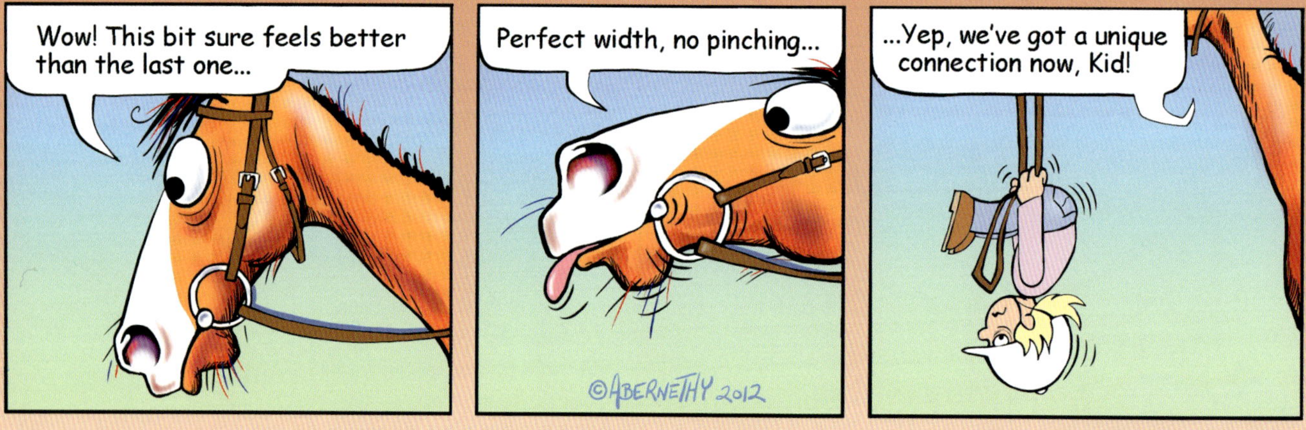
Wow! This bit sure feels better than the last one...
Perfect width, no pinching...
©ABERNETHY 2012
...Yep, we've got a unique connection now, Kid!

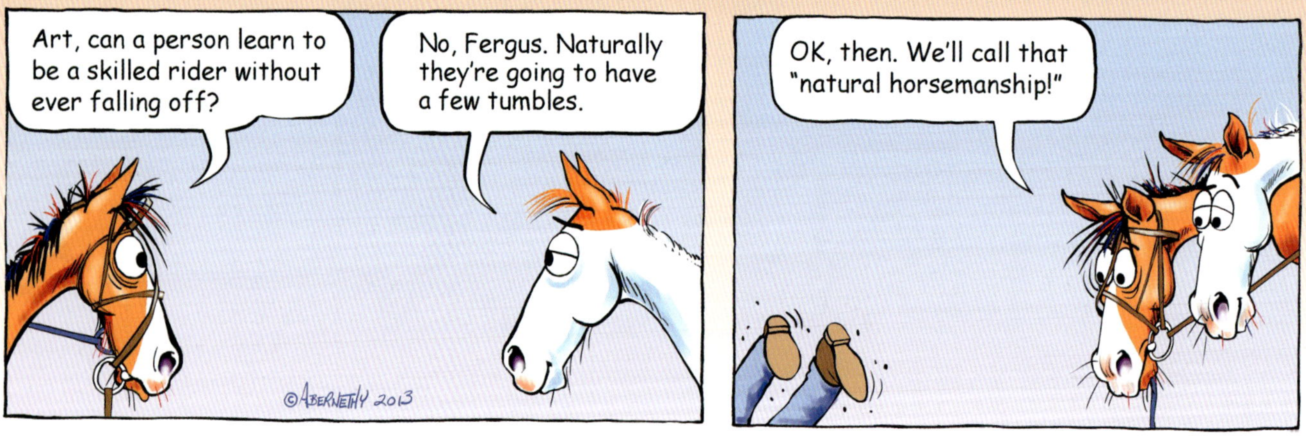
Art, can a person learn to be a skilled rider without ever falling off?
No, Fergus. Naturally they're going to have a few tumbles.
©ABERNETHY 2013
OK, then. We'll call that "natural horsemanship!"

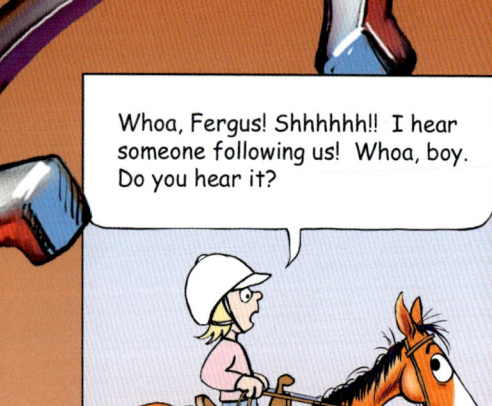

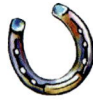

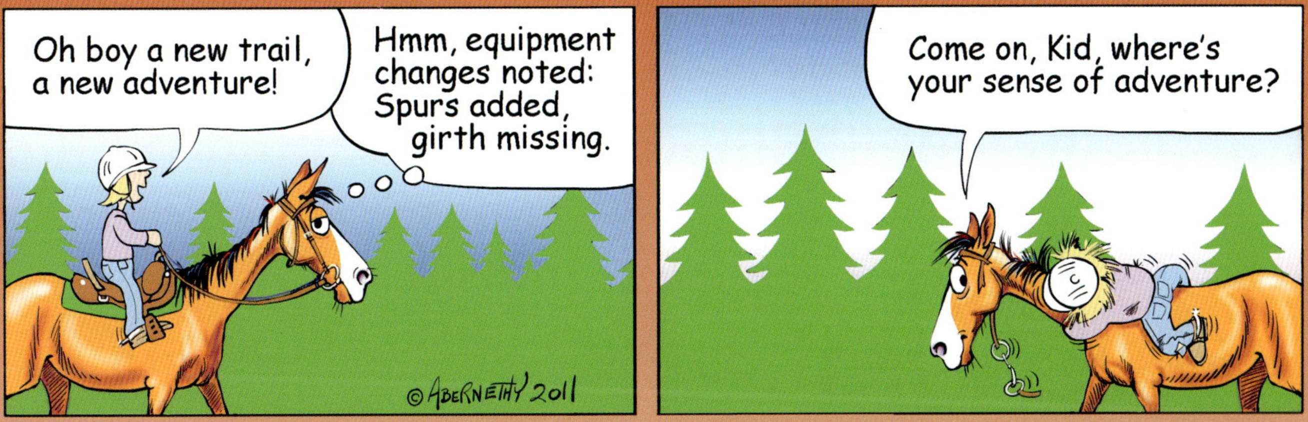
Oh boy a new trail, a new adventure!
Hmm, equipment changes noted: Spurs added, girth missing.
©ABERNETHY 2011
Come on, Kid, where's your sense of adventure?

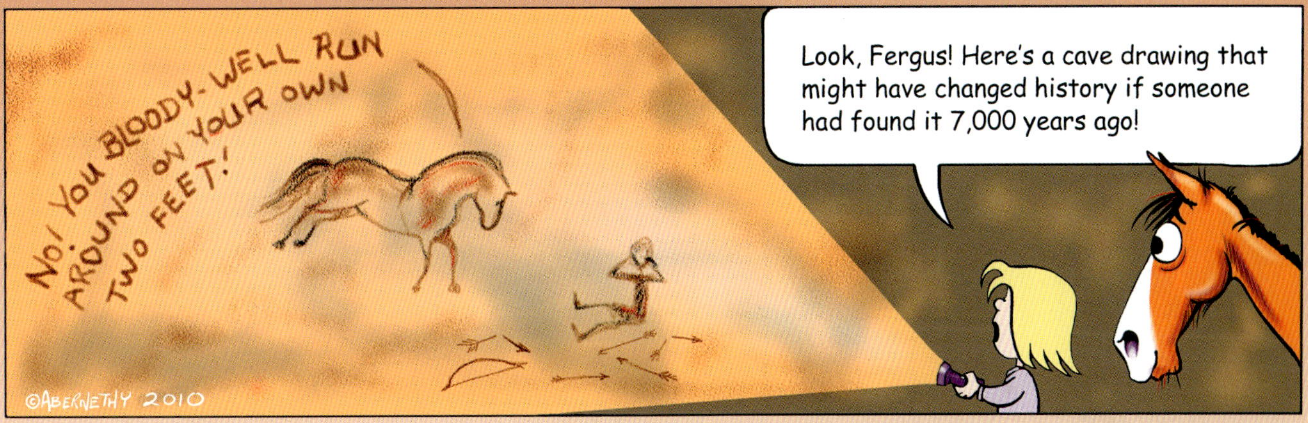
NO! YOU BLOODY-WELL RUN AROUND ON YOUR OWN TWO FEET!
©ABERNETHY 2010
Look, Fergus! Here's a cave drawing that might have changed history if someone had found it 7,000 years ago!

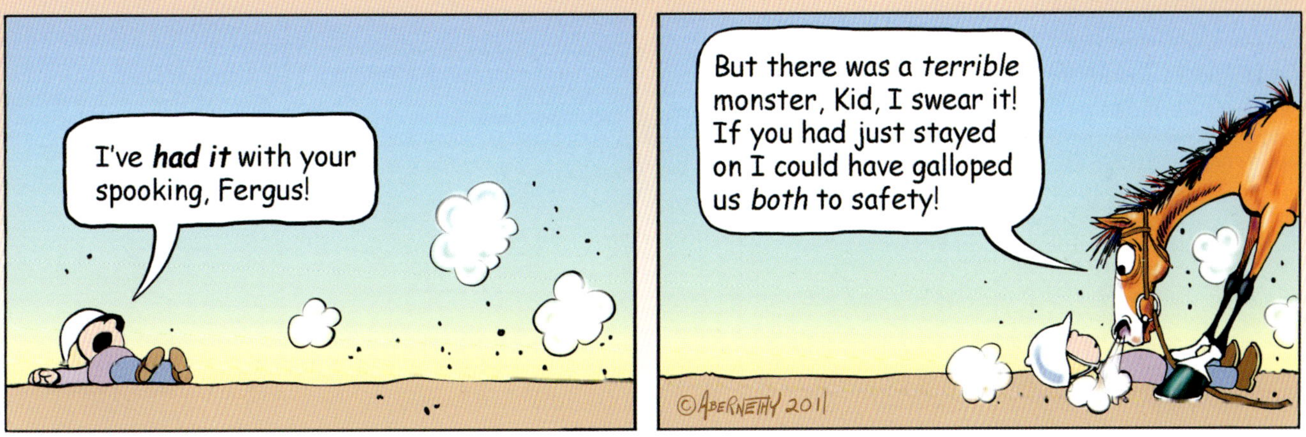
I've *had it* with your spooking, Fergus!
But there was a *terrible* monster, Kid, I swear it! If you had just stayed on I could have galloped us *both* to safety!
©ABERNETHY 2011

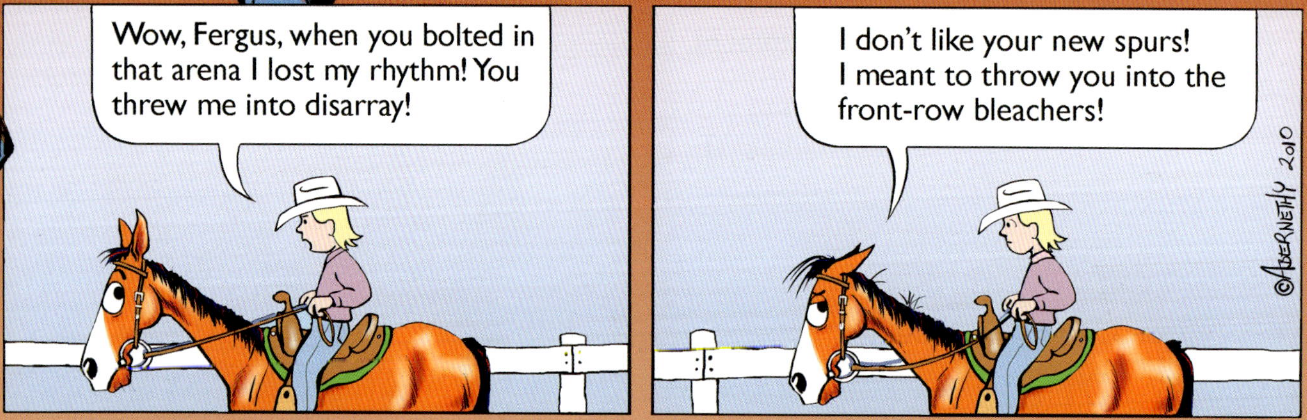
Wow, Fergus, when you bolted in that arena I lost my rhythm! You threw me into disarray!
I don't like your new spurs! I meant to throw you into the front-row bleachers!
©ABERNETHY 2010

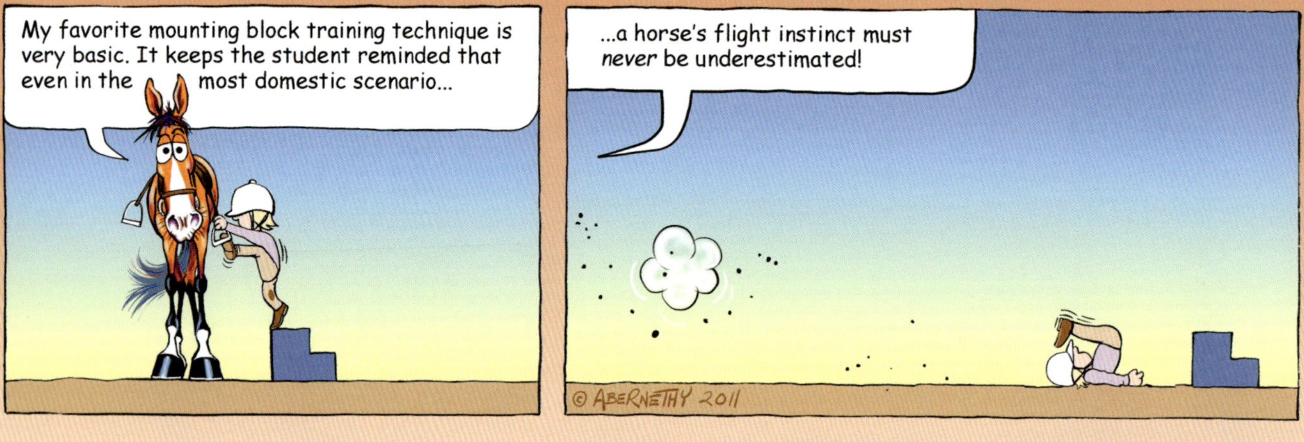
My favorite mounting block training technique is very basic. It keeps the student reminded that even in the most domestic scenario...
...a horse's flight instinct must *never* be underestimated!
© ABERNETHY 2011

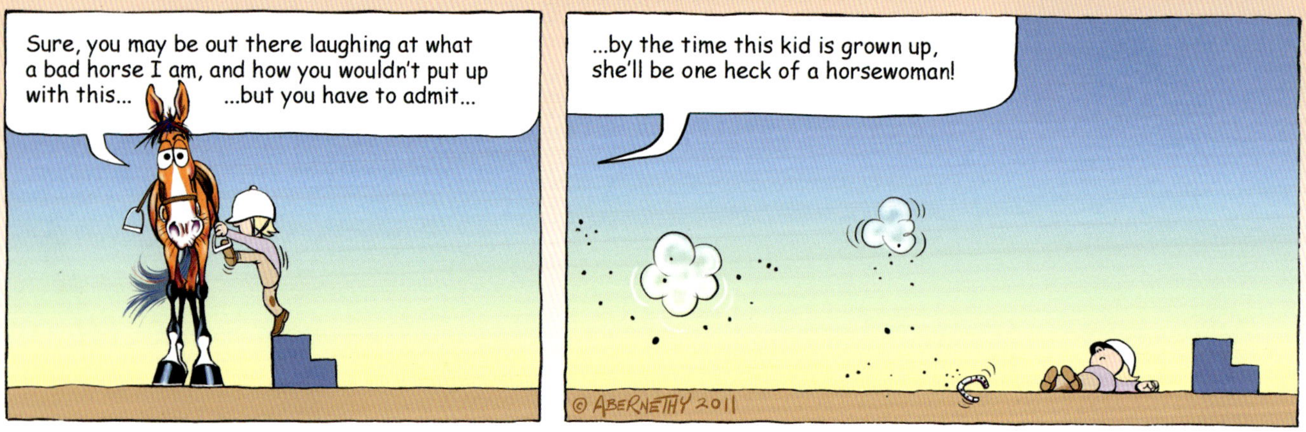
Sure, you may be out there laughing at what a bad horse I am, and how you wouldn't put up with this... ...but you have to admit...
...by the time this kid is grown up, she'll be one heck of a horsewoman!
© ABERNETHY 2011

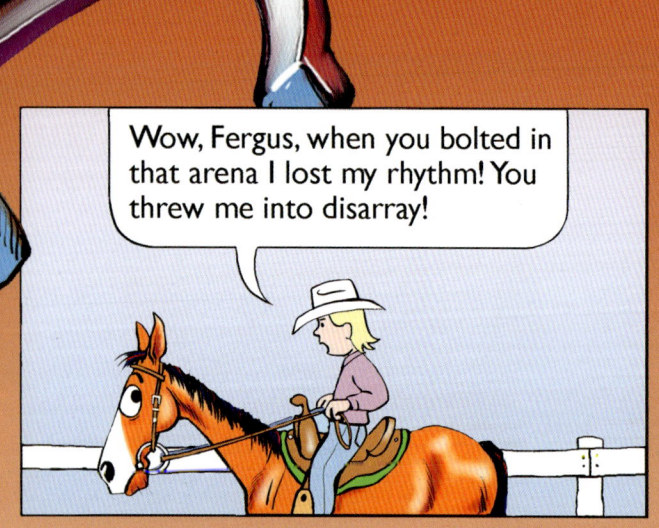

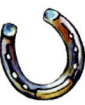

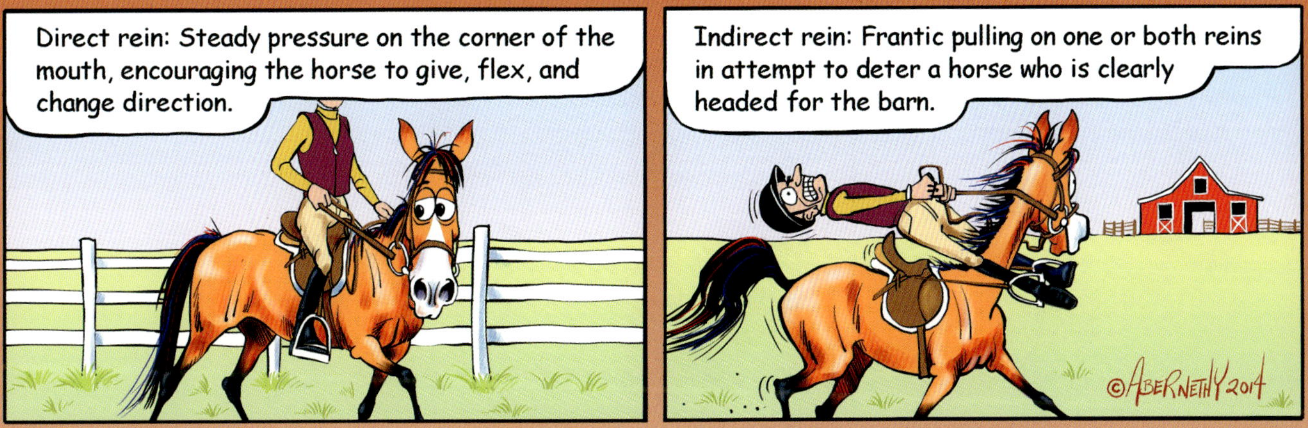
Direct rein: Steady pressure on the corner of the mouth, encouraging the horse to give, flex, and change direction.
Indirect rein: Frantic pulling on one or both reins in attempt to deter a horse who is clearly headed for the barn.
©ABERNETHY 2014

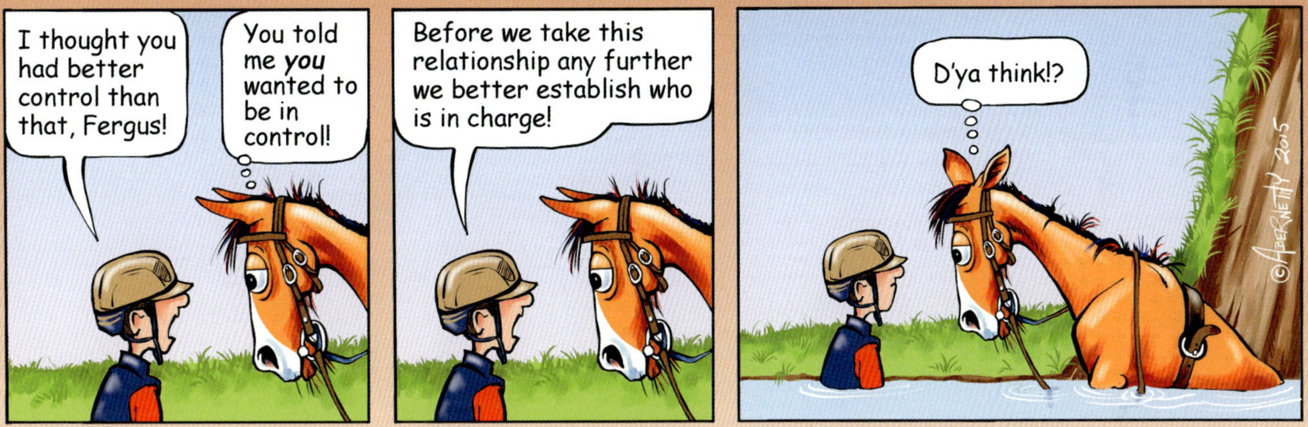
I thought you had better control than that, Fergus!
You told me *you* wanted to be in control!
Before we take this relationship any further we better establish who is in charge!
D'ya think!?
©ABERNETHY 2015

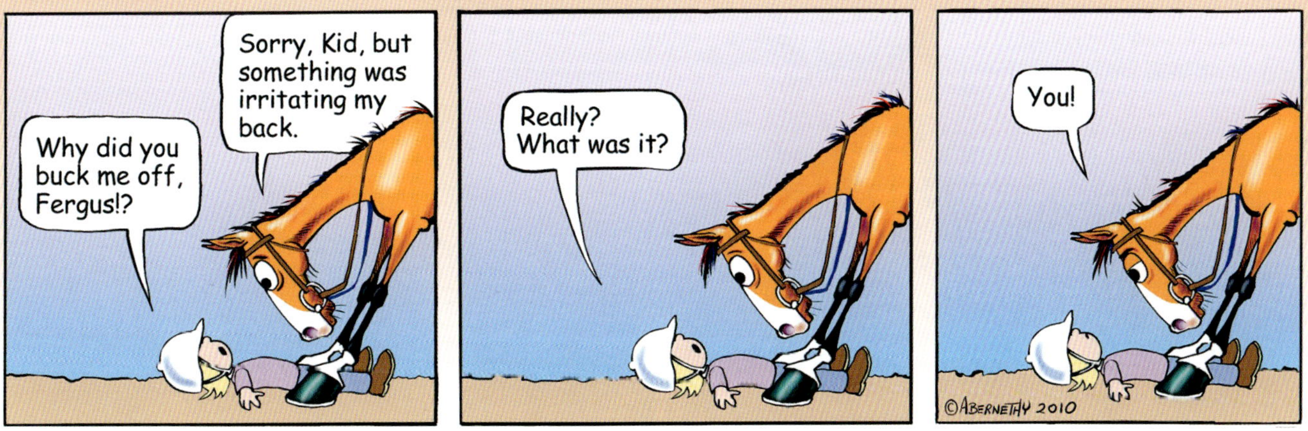
Why did you buck me off, Fergus!?
Sorry, Kid, but something was irritating my back.
Really? What was it?
You!
©ABERNETHY 2010

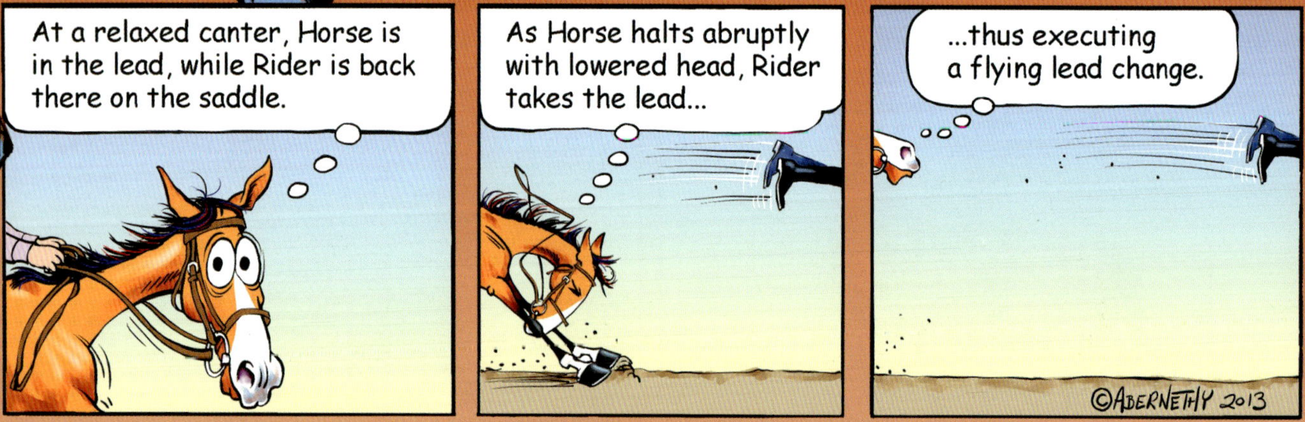
At a relaxed canter, Horse is in the lead, while Rider is back there on the saddle.
As Horse halts abruptly with lowered head, Rider takes the lead...
...thus executing a flying lead change.
©ABERNETHY 2013

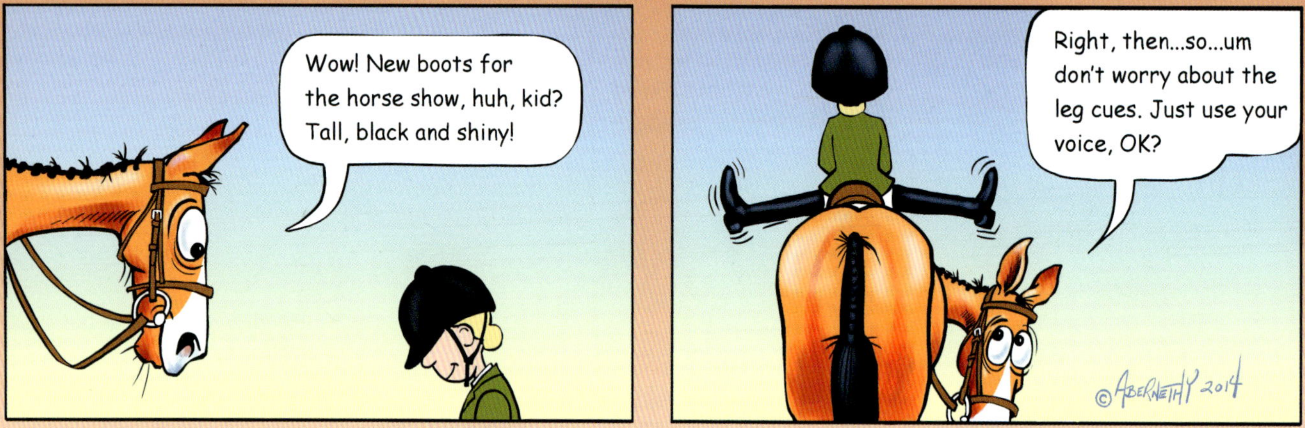
Wow! New boots for the horse show, huh, kid? Tall, black and shiny!
Right, then...so...um don't worry about the leg cues. Just use your voice, OK?
©ABERNETHY 2014

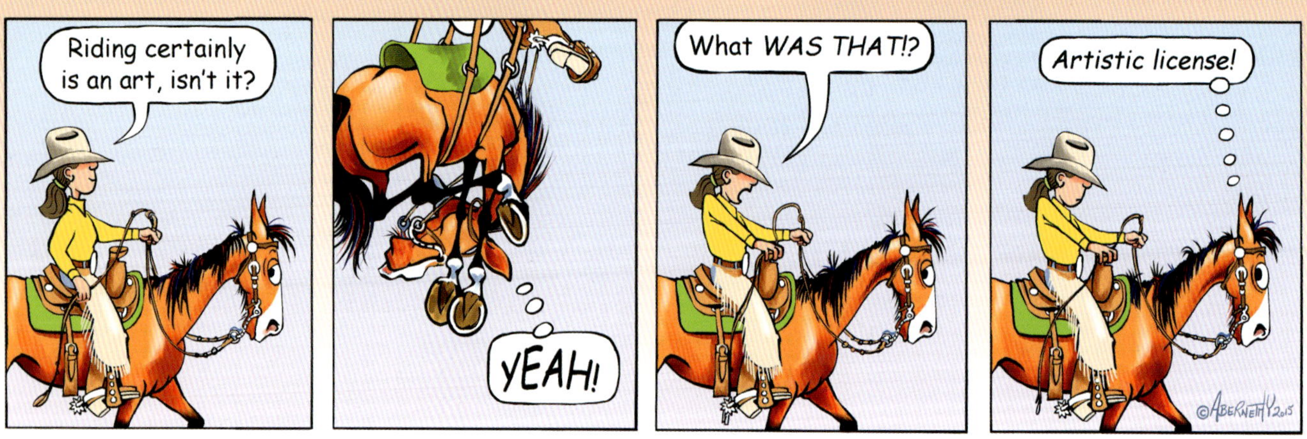
Riding certainly is an art, isn't it?
YEAH!
What *WAS THAT*!?
*Artistic license!*

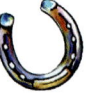

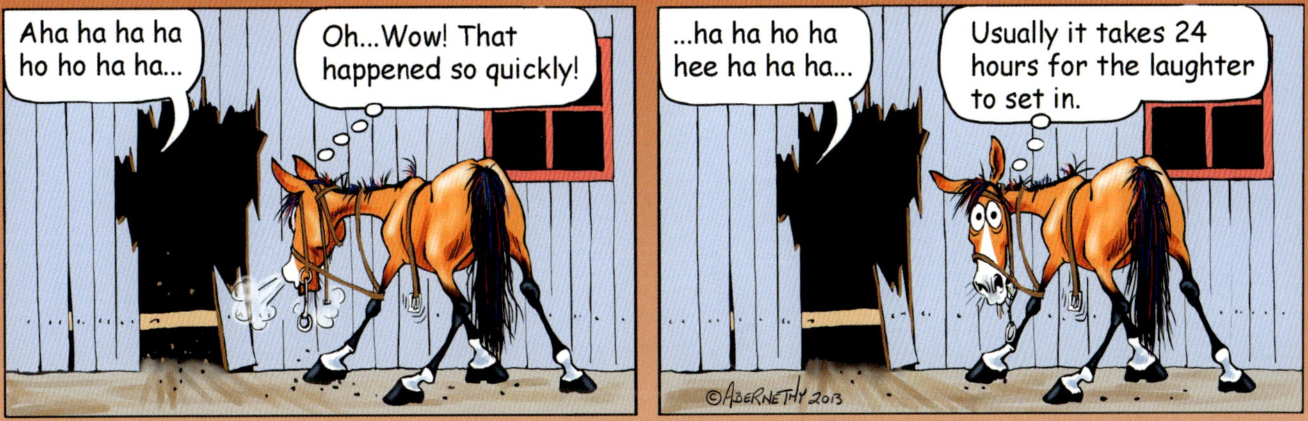
Aha ha ha ha
ho ho ha ha...
Oh...Wow! That happened so quickly!
...ha ha ho ha
hee ha ha ha...
Usually it takes 24 hours for the laughter to set in.
©ABERNETHY 2013

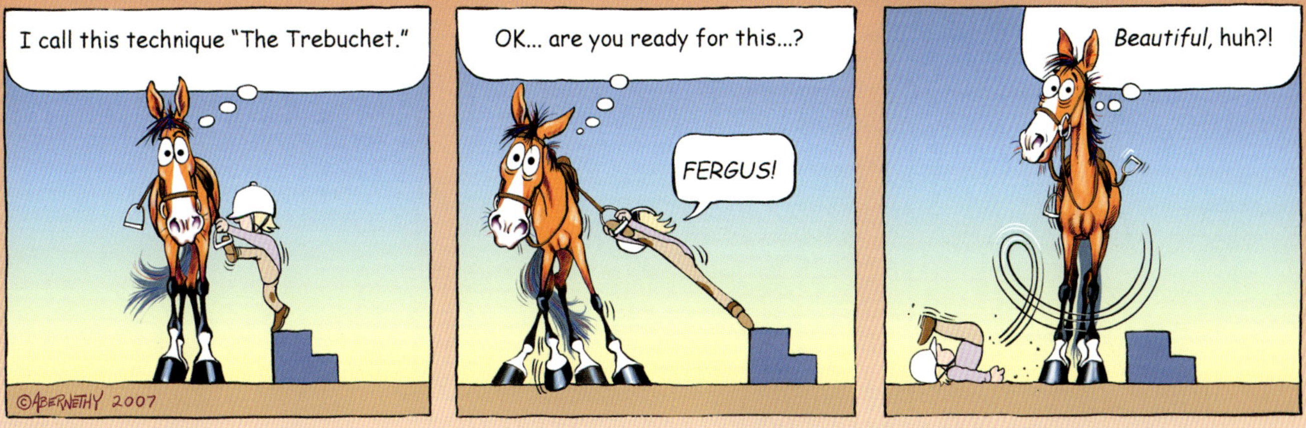
I call this technique "The Trebuchet."
©ABERNETHY 2007
OK... are you ready for this...?
FERGUS!
*Beautiful*, huh?!

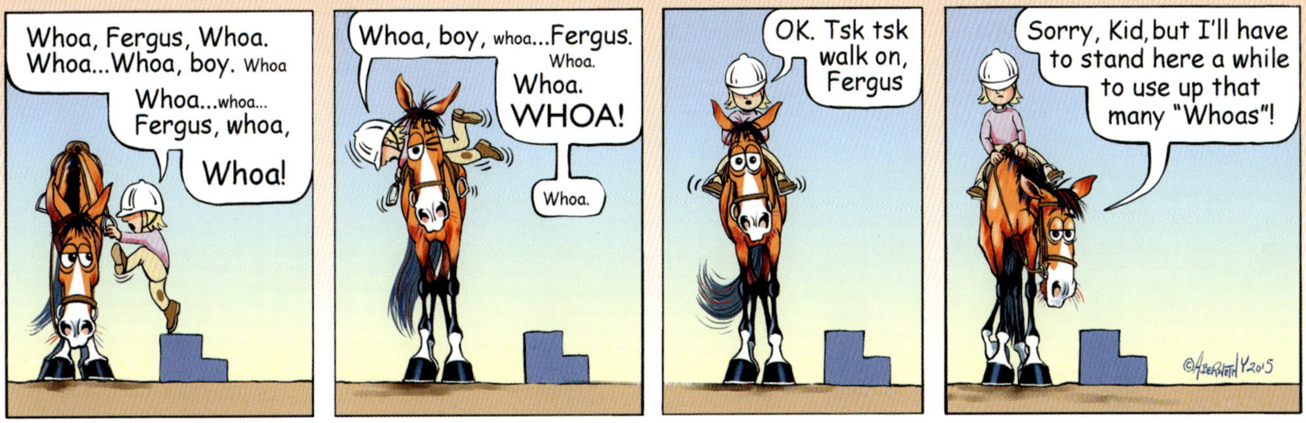
Whoa, Fergus, Whoa.
Whoa...Whoa, boy. Whoa
Whoa...whoa...
Fergus, whoa,
Whoa!
Whoa, boy, whoa...Fergus.
Whoa.
Whoa.
WHOA!
Whoa.
OK. Tsk tsk walk on, Fergus
Sorry, Kid, but I'll have to stand here a while to use up that many "Whoas"!
©ABERNETHY 2015

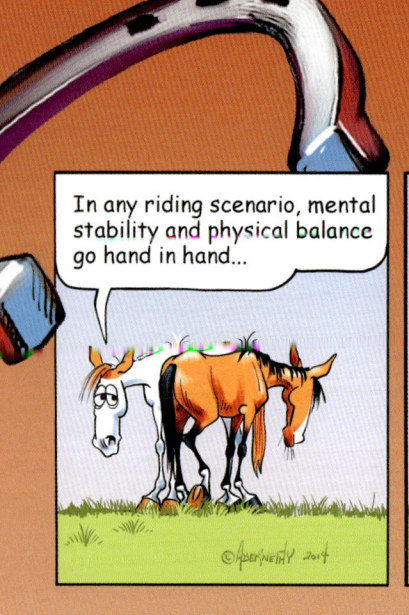

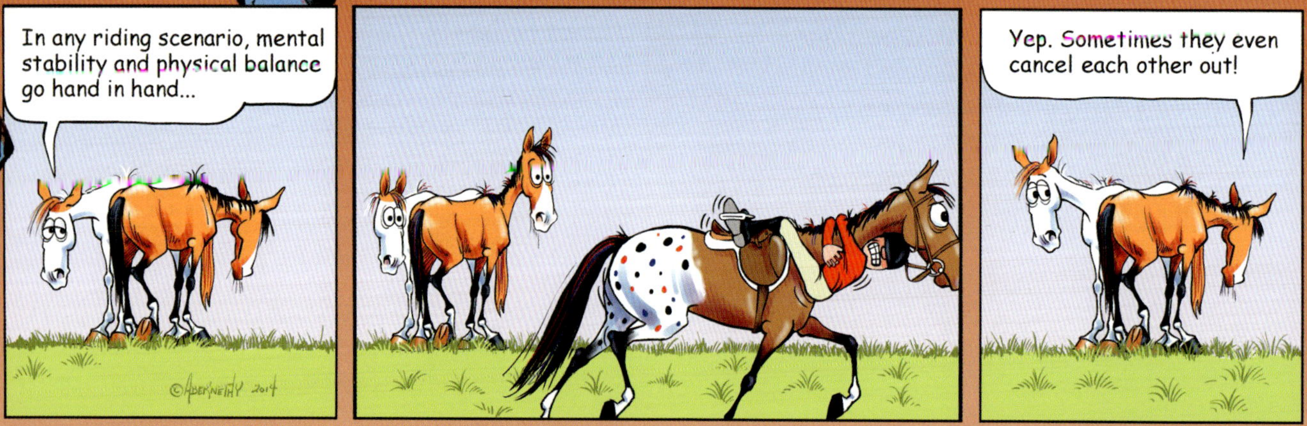
In any riding scenario, mental stability and physical balance go hand in hand...
Yep. Sometimes they even cancel each other out!

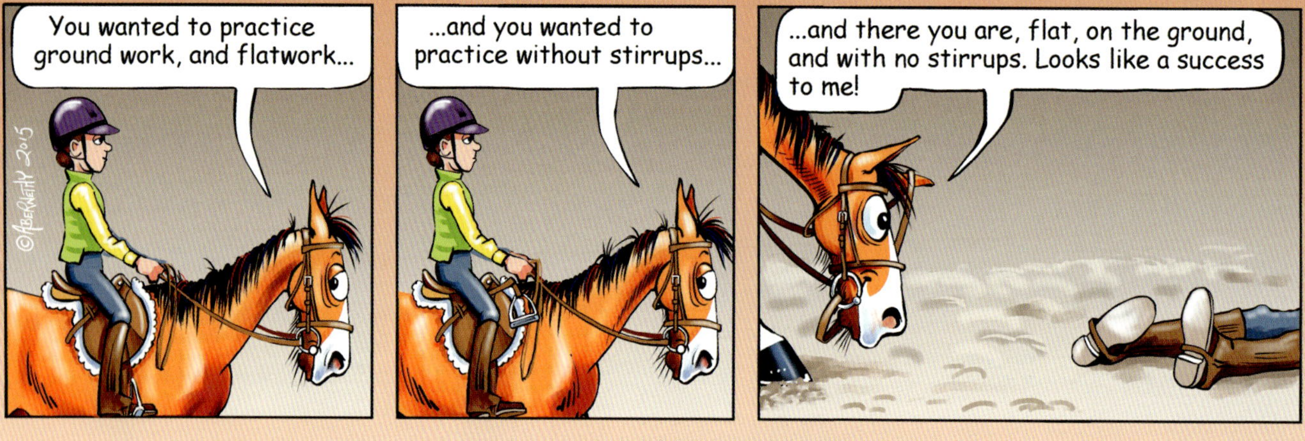
You wanted to practice ground work, and flatwork...
...and you wanted to practice without stirrups...
...and there you are, flat, on the ground, and with no stirrups. Looks like a success to me!

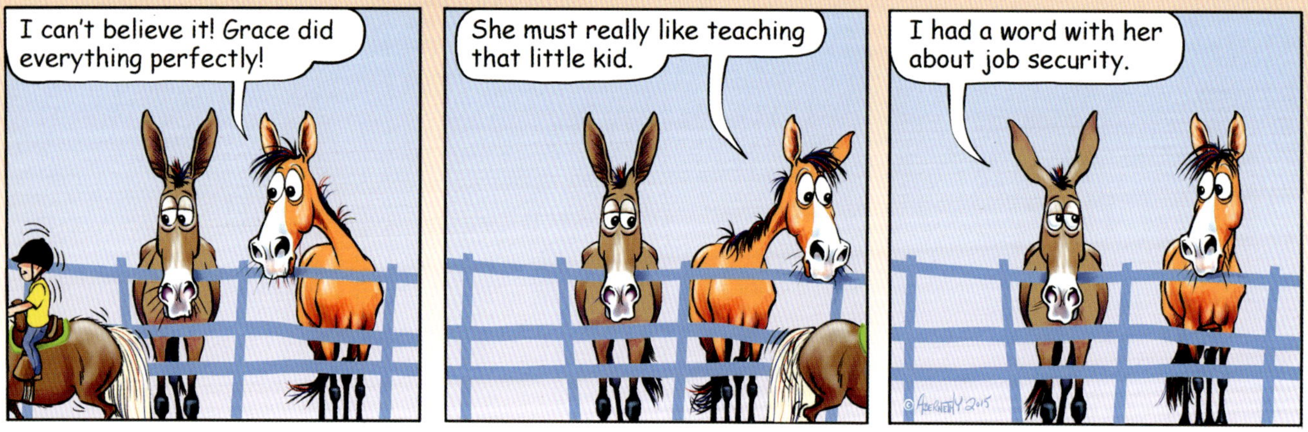
I can't believe it! Grace did everything perfectly!
She must really like teaching that little kid.
I had a word with her about job security.

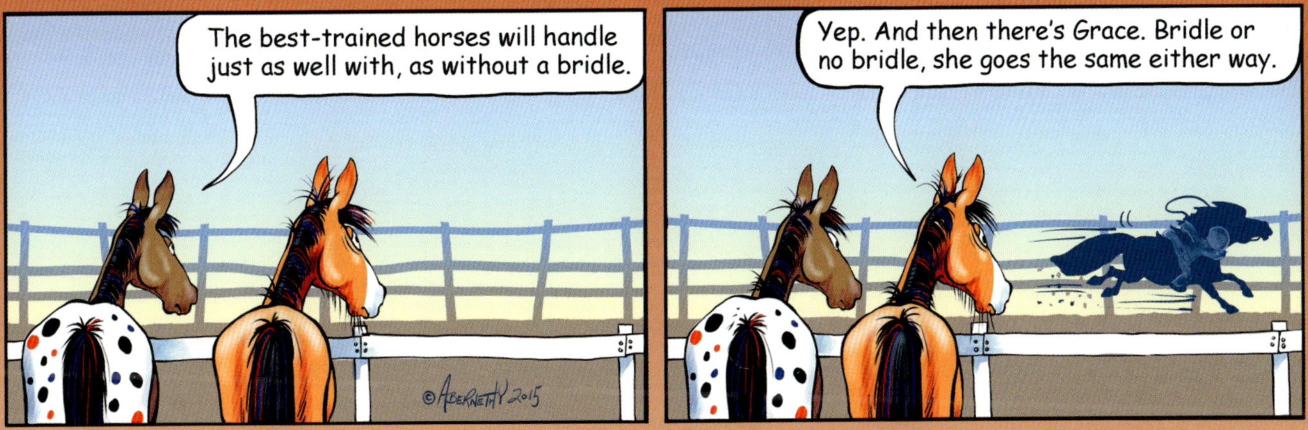
The best-trained horses will handle just as well with, as without a bridle.
Yep. And then there's Grace. Bridle or no bridle, she goes the same either way.
©ABERNETHY 2015

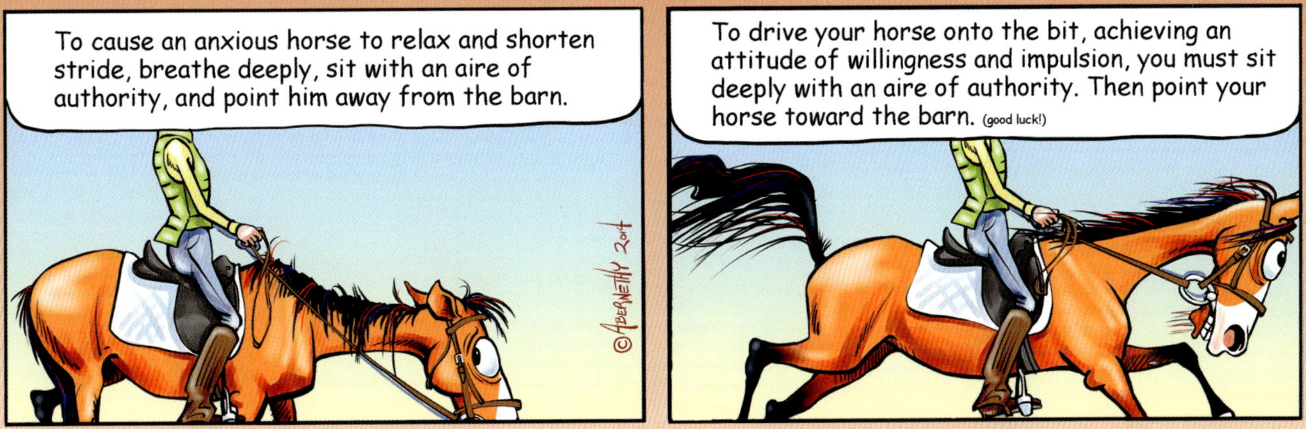
To cause an anxious horse to relax and shorten stride, breathe deeply, sit with an aire of authority, and point him away from the barn.
©ABERNETHY 2014
To drive your horse onto the bit, achieving an attitude of willingness and impulsion, you must sit deeply with an aire of authority. Then point your horse toward the barn. (good luck!)

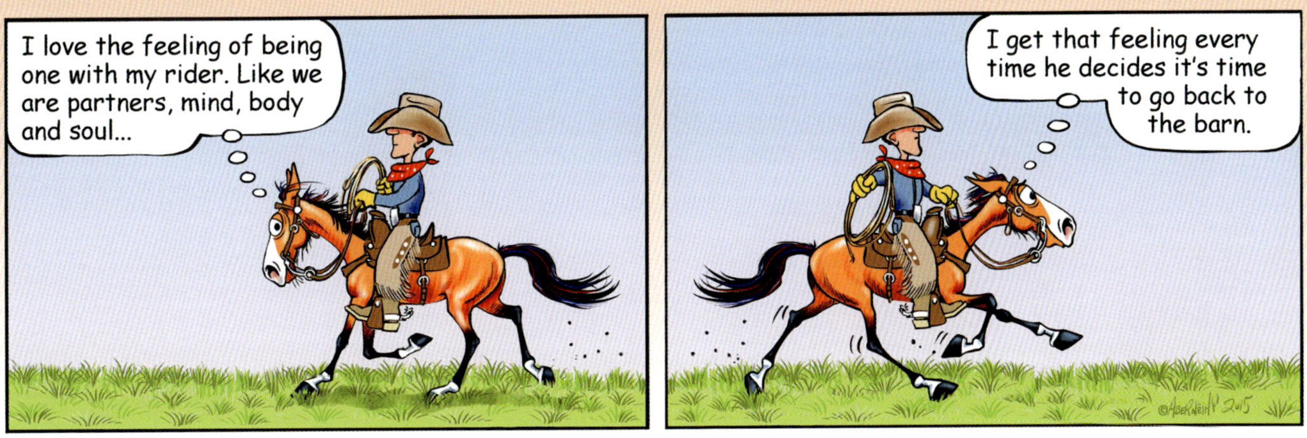
I love the feeling of being one with my rider. Like we are partners, mind, body and soul...
I get that feeling every time he decides it's time to go back to the barn.

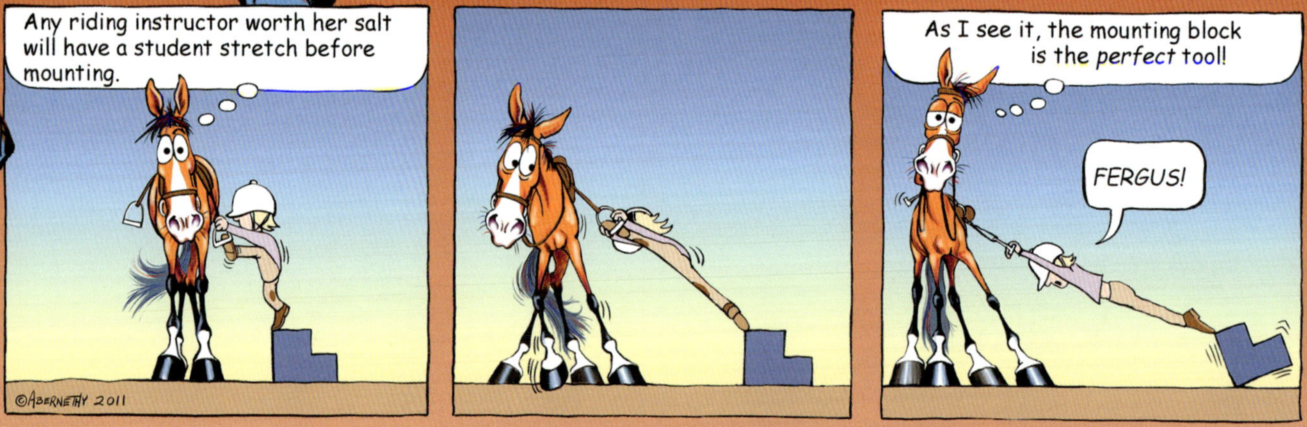
Any riding instructor worth her salt will have a student stretch before mounting.
©Abernethy 2011
As I see it, the mounting block is the *perfect* tool!
FERGUS!

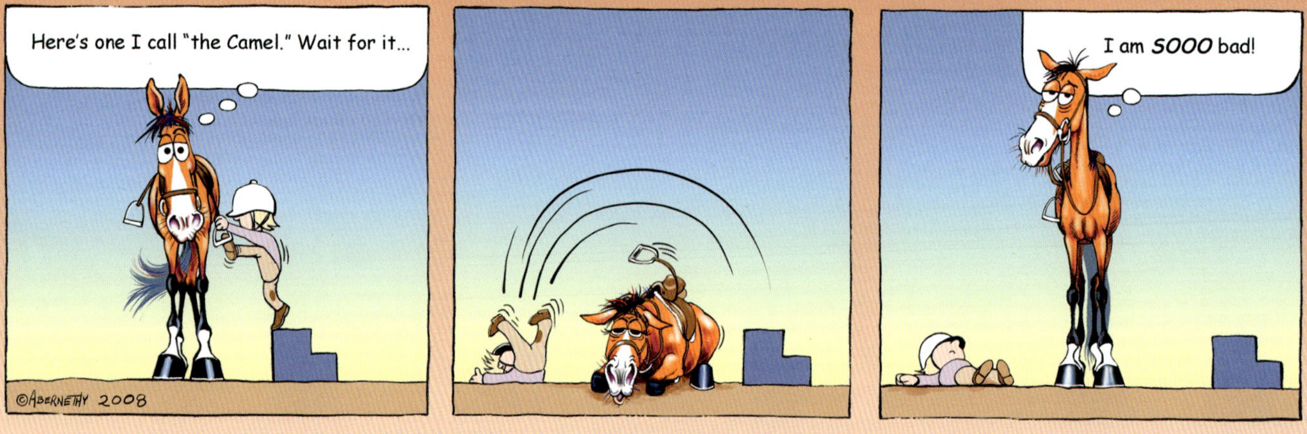
Here's one I call "the Camel." Wait for it...
©Abernethy 2008
I am SOOO bad!

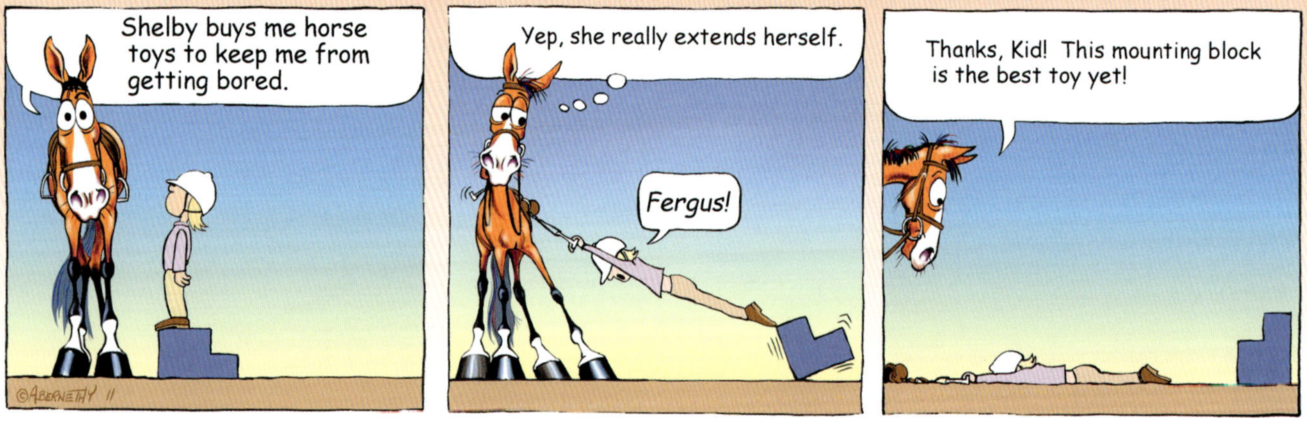
Shelby buys me horse toys to keep me from getting bored.
©Abernethy 11
Yep, she really extends herself.
Fergus!
Thanks, Kid! This mounting block is the best toy yet!

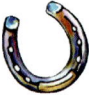

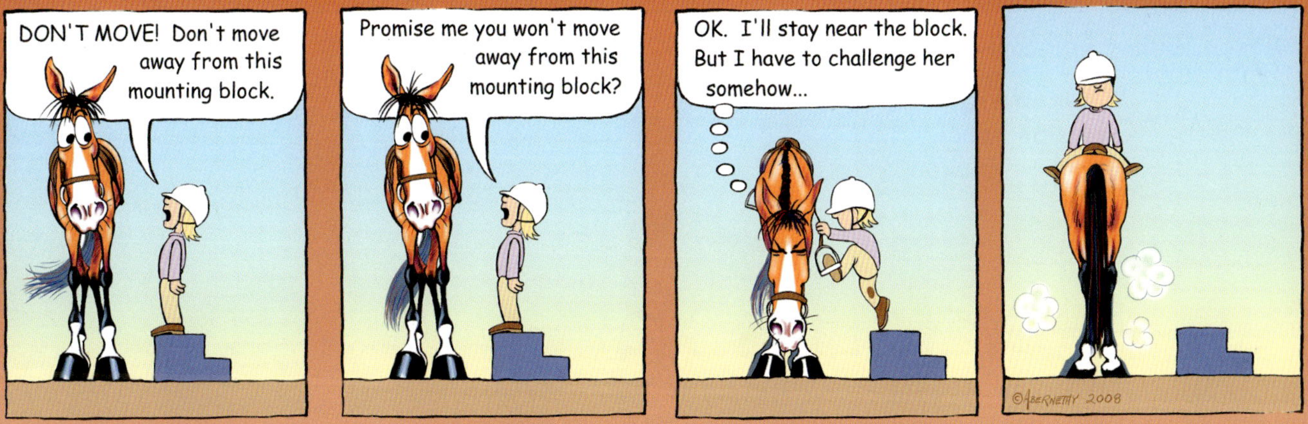
DON'T MOVE! Don't move away from this mounting block.
Promise me you won't move away from this mounting block?
OK. I'll stay near the block. But I have to challenge her somehow...
©ABERNETHY 2008

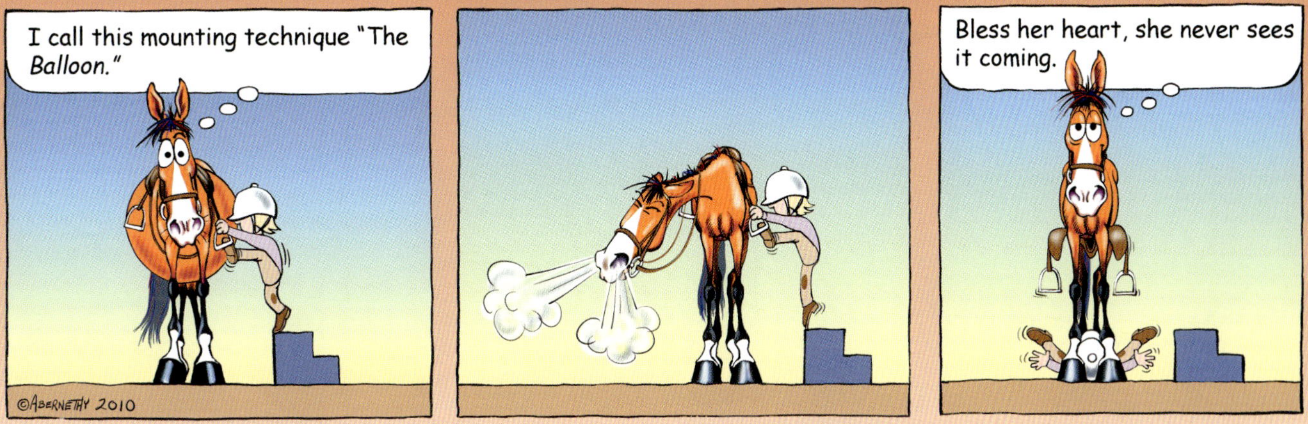
I call this mounting technique "The Balloon."
Bless her heart, she never sees it coming.
©ABERNETHY 2010

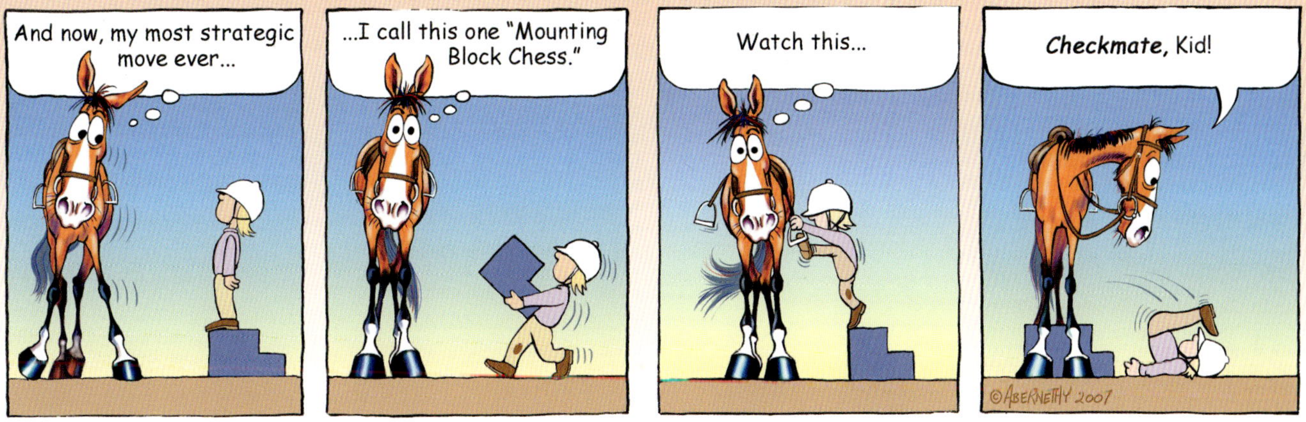
And now, my most strategic move ever...
...I call this one "Mounting Block Chess."
Watch this...
**Checkmate,** Kid!
©ABERNETHY 2007

No! I don't want to go that way!

Chsk, chsk, walk on Fergus.

Wait a minute...Hey! I don't want to go that way, either!

Dang! Now she's got me all mixed up and I don't know which direction to balk in!

Wow, Shelby sure likes a good slapstick, crash-and-burn type comedy!

Although sometimes it takes a few minutes for the humor to set in.

Fergus! ...you...!!

# The Flies
# Have It

# Fergus BY JEAN ABERNETHY

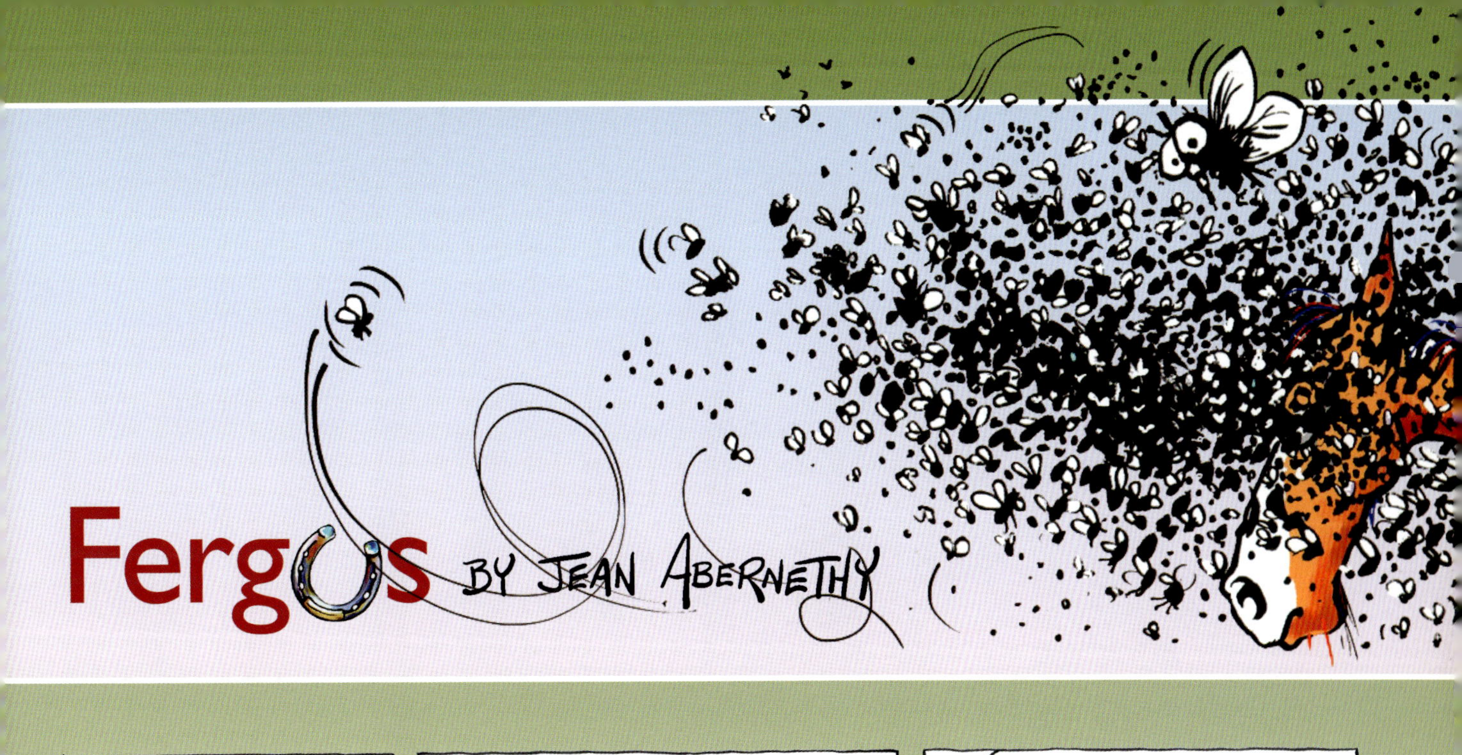

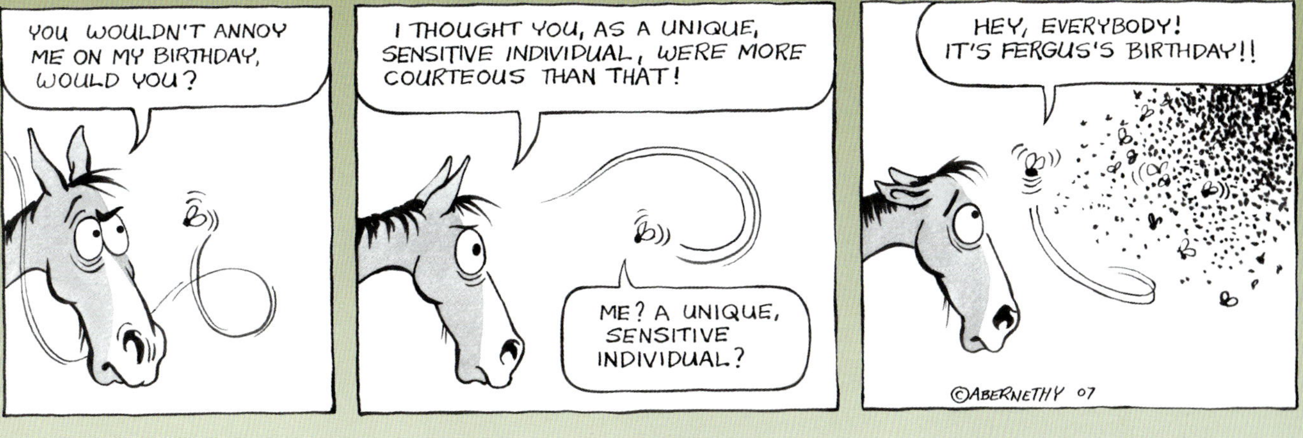

YOU WOULDN'T ANNOY ME ON MY BIRTHDAY, WOULD YOU?
I THOUGHT YOU, AS A UNIQUE, SENSITIVE INDIVIDUAL, WERE MORE COURTEOUS THAN THAT!
ME? A UNIQUE, SENSITIVE INDIVIDUAL?
HEY, EVERYBODY! IT'S FERGUS'S BIRTHDAY!!
©ABERNETHY 07


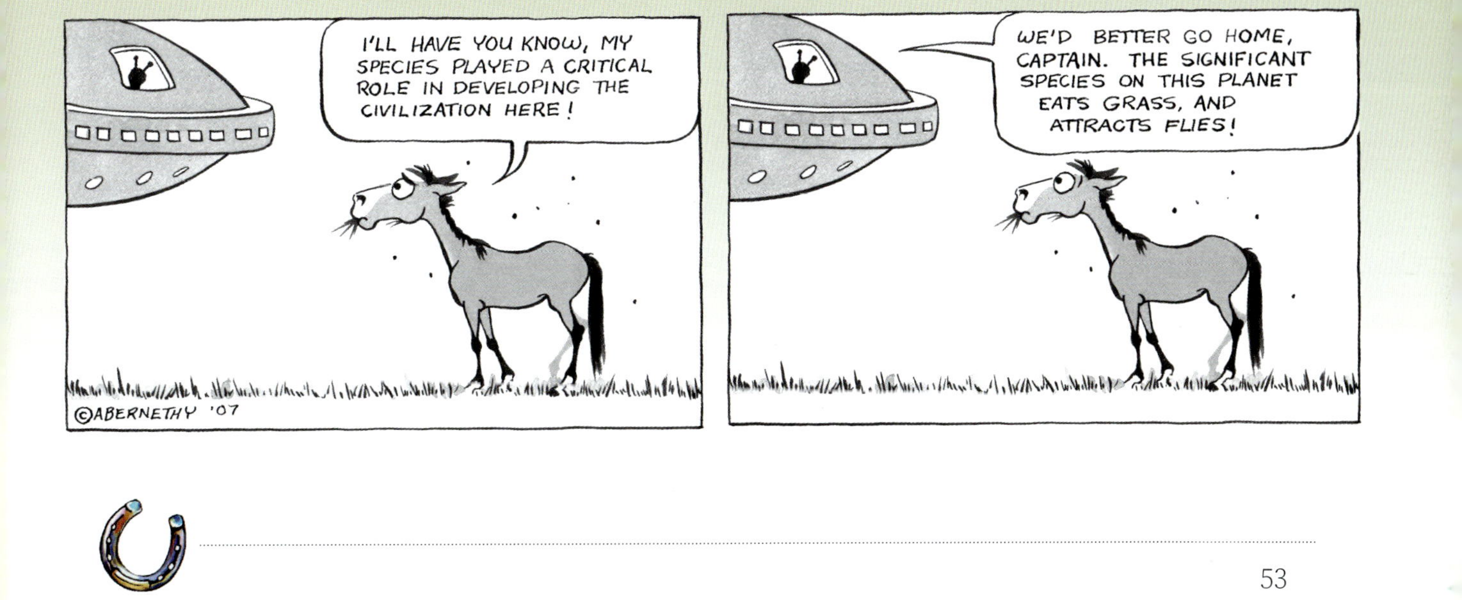

I'LL HAVE YOU KNOW, MY SPECIES PLAYED A CRITICAL ROLE IN DEVELOPING THE CIVILIZATION HERE!
©ABERNETHY '07
WE'D BETTER GO HOME, CAPTAIN. THE SIGNIFICANT SPECIES ON THIS PLANET EATS GRASS, AND ATTRACTS FLIES!

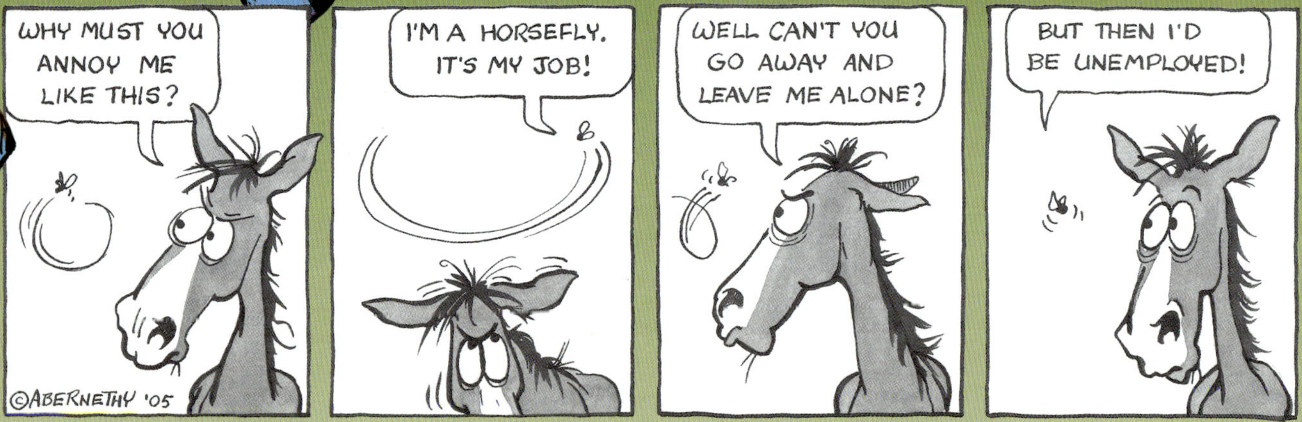
WHY MUST YOU ANNOY ME LIKE THIS?
I'M A HORSEFLY. IT'S MY JOB!
WELL CAN'T YOU GO AWAY AND LEAVE ME ALONE?
BUT THEN I'D BE UNEMPLOYED!
©ABERNETHY '05

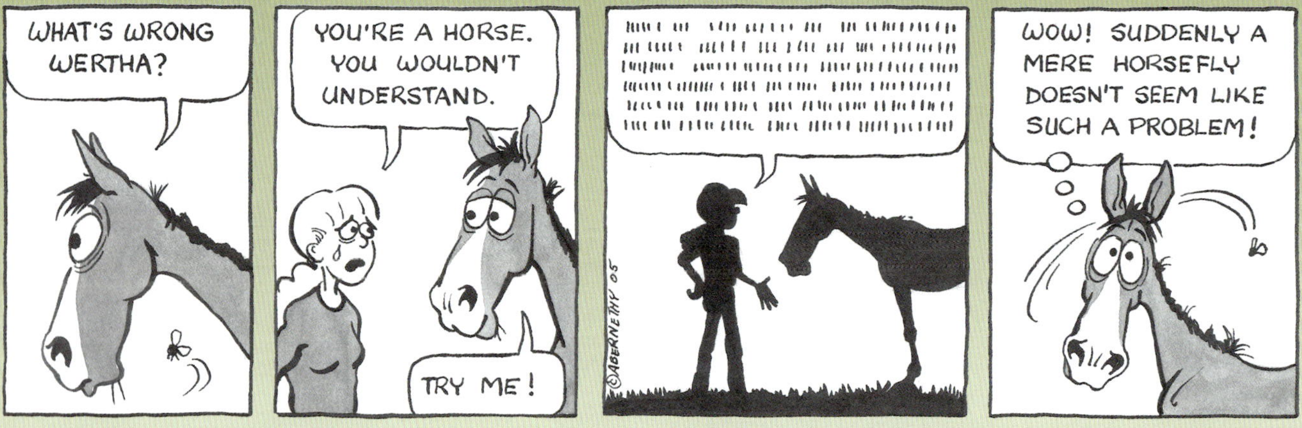
WHAT'S WRONG WERTHA?
YOU'RE A HORSE. YOU WOULDN'T UNDERSTAND.
TRY ME!
WOW! SUDDENLY A MERE HORSEFLY DOESN'T SEEM LIKE SUCH A PROBLEM!
©ABERNETHY 05

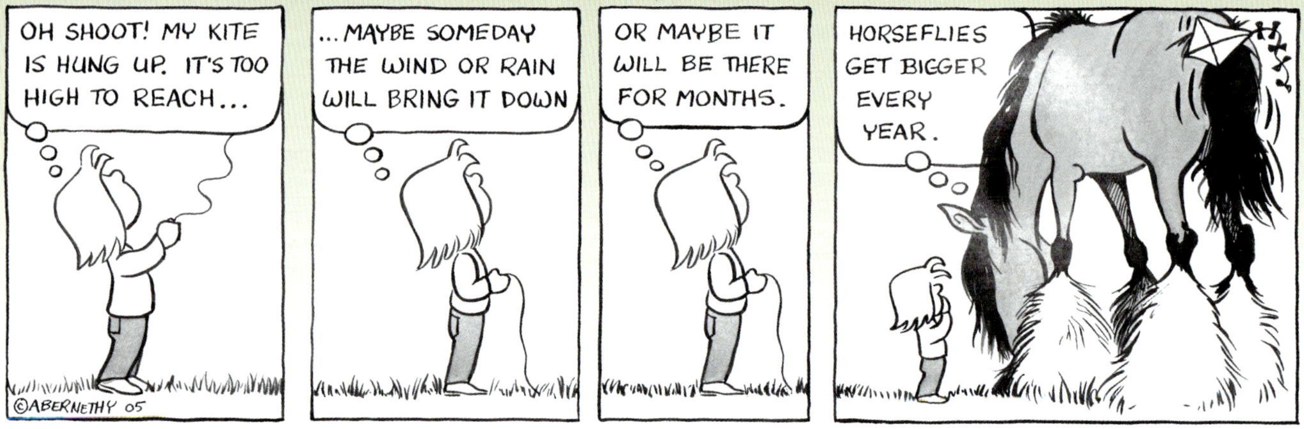
OH SHOOT! MY KITE IS HUNG UP. IT'S TOO HIGH TO REACH...
...MAYBE SOMEDAY THE WIND OR RAIN WILL BRING IT DOWN
OR MAYBE IT WILL BE THERE FOR MONTHS.
HORSEFLIES GET BIGGER EVERY YEAR.
©ABERNETHY 05

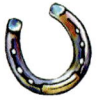

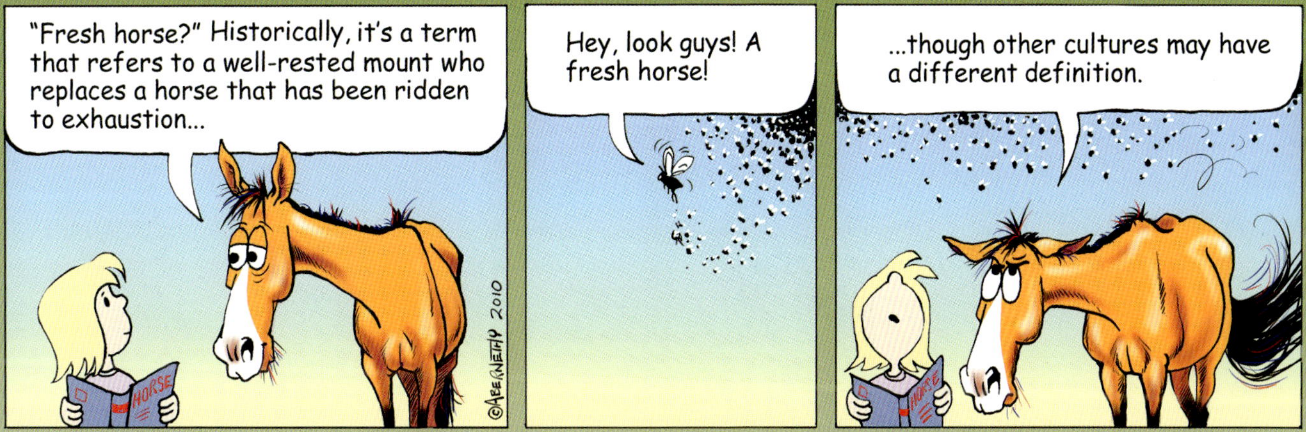
"Fresh horse?" Historically, it's a term that refers to a well-rested mount who replaces a horse that has been ridden to exhaustion...
©ABERNETHY 2010
Hey, look guys! A fresh horse!
...though other cultures may have a different definition.

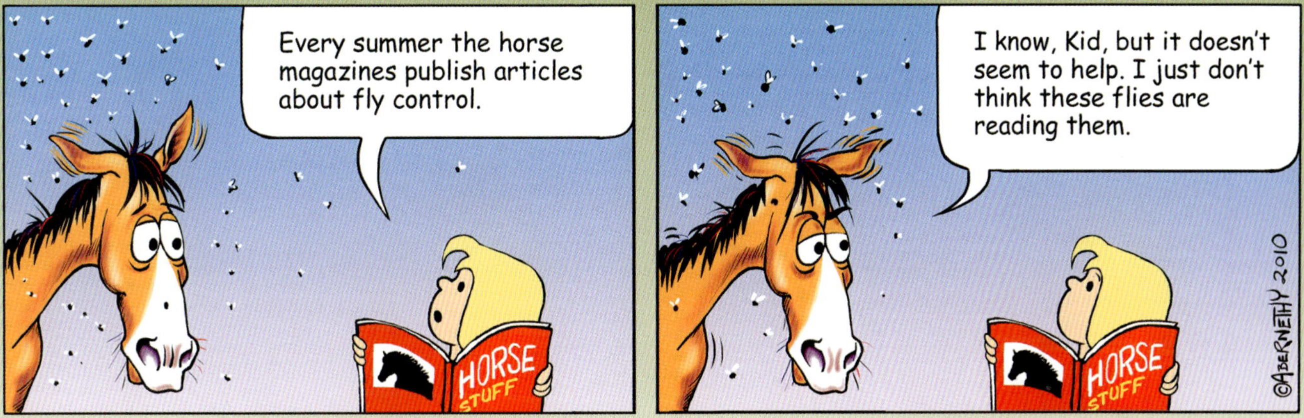
Every summer the horse magazines publish articles about fly control.
HORSE STUFF
I know, Kid, but it doesn't seem to help. I just don't think these flies are reading them.
HORSE STUFF
©ABERNETHY 2010

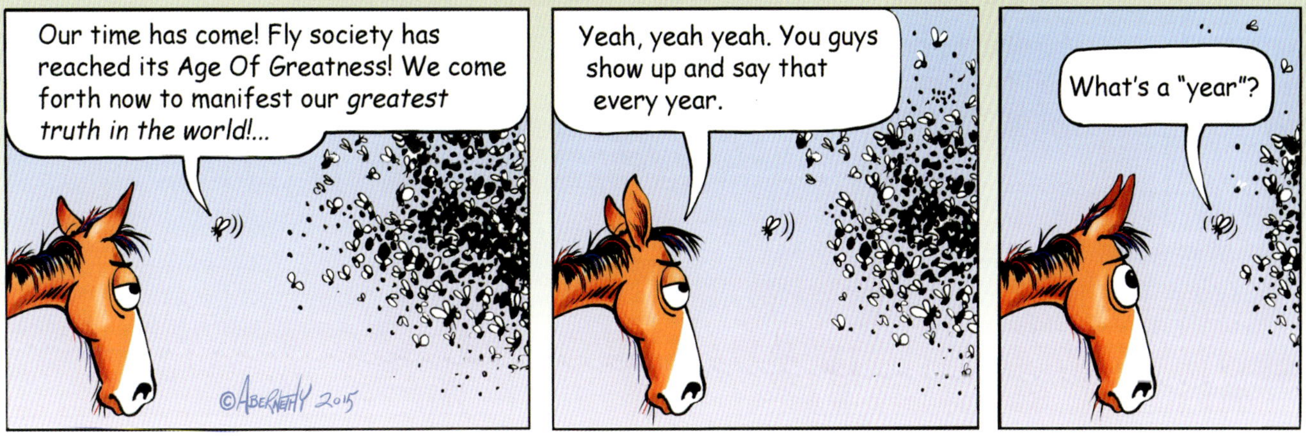
Our time has come! Fly society has reached its Age Of Greatness! We come forth now to manifest our *greatest truth in the world!...*
©ABERNETHY 2015
Yeah, yeah yeah. You guys show up and say that every year.
What's a "year"?

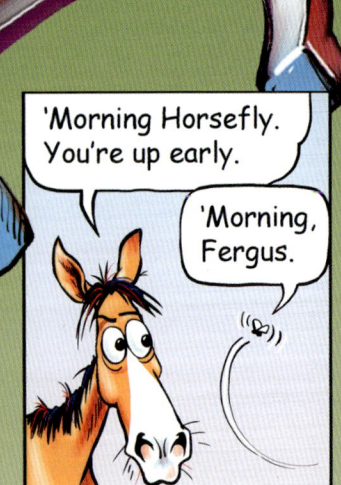

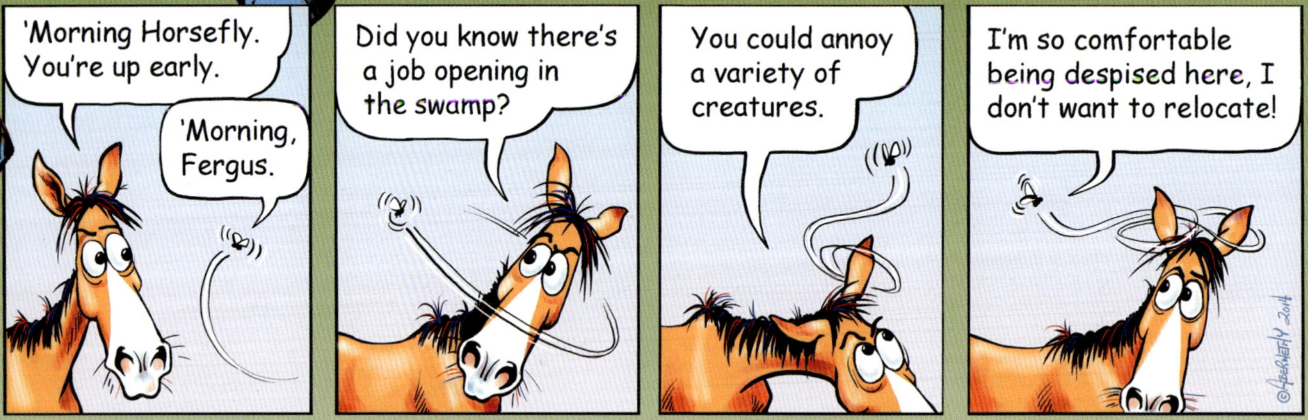
'Morning Horsefly. You're up early.
'Morning, Fergus.
Did you know there's a job opening in the swamp?
You could annoy a variety of creatures.
I'm so comfortable being despised here, I don't want to relocate!
©ABERNETHY 2014

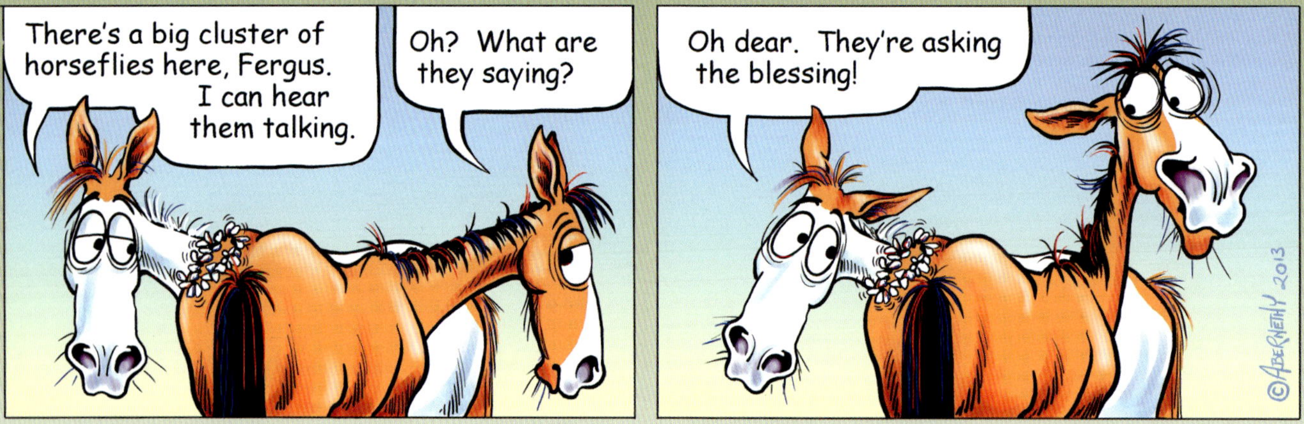
There's a big cluster of horseflies here, Fergus. I can hear them talking.
Oh? What are they saying?
Oh dear. They're asking the blessing!
©ABERNETHY 2013

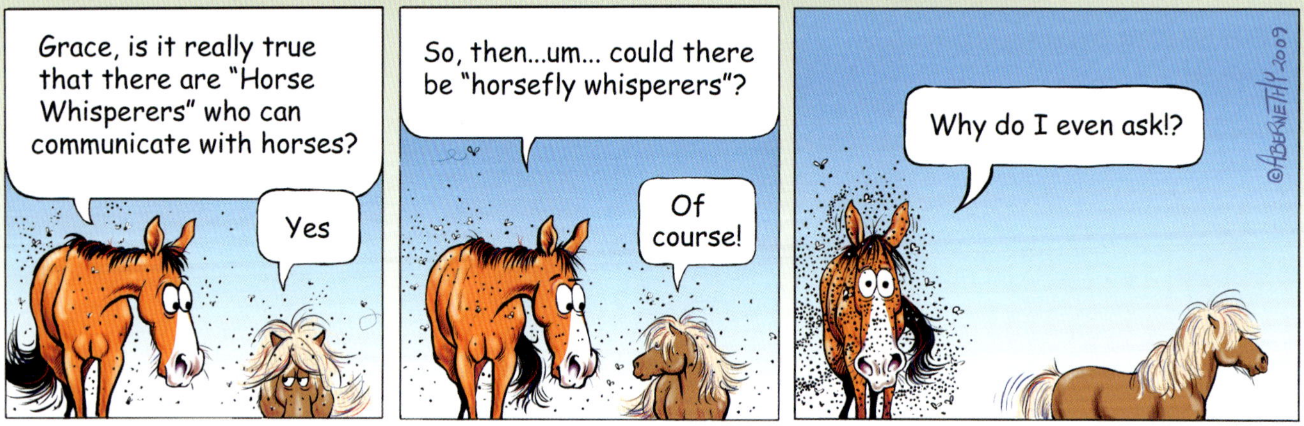
Grace, is it really true that there are "Horse Whisperers" who can communicate with horses?
Yes
So, then...um... could there be "horsefly whisperers"?
Of course!
Why do I even ask!?
©ABERNETHY 2009

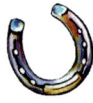

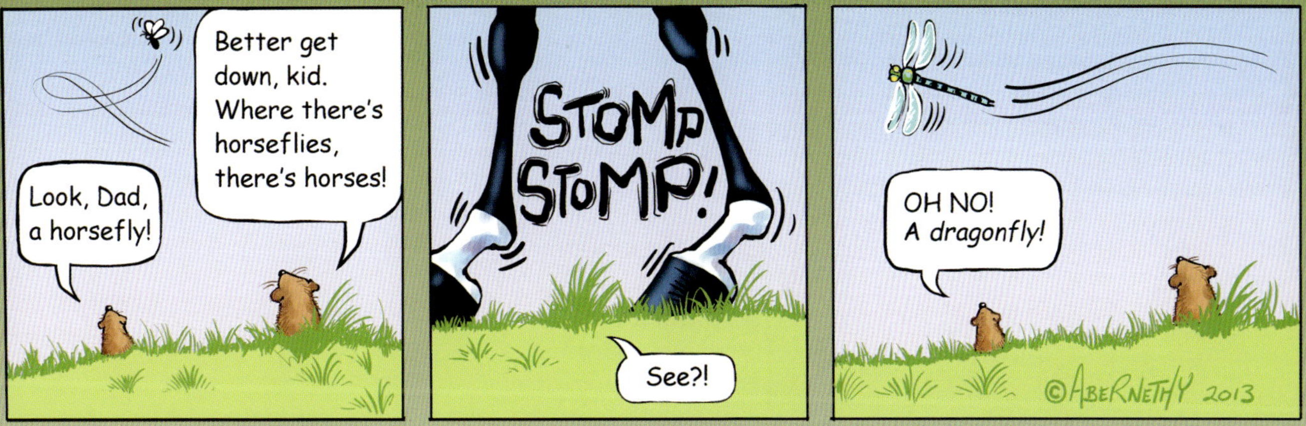
Look, Dad, a horsefly!
Better get down, kid. Where there's horseflies, there's horses!
STOMP STOMP!
See?!
OH NO! A *dragonfly*!
©ABERNETHY 2013

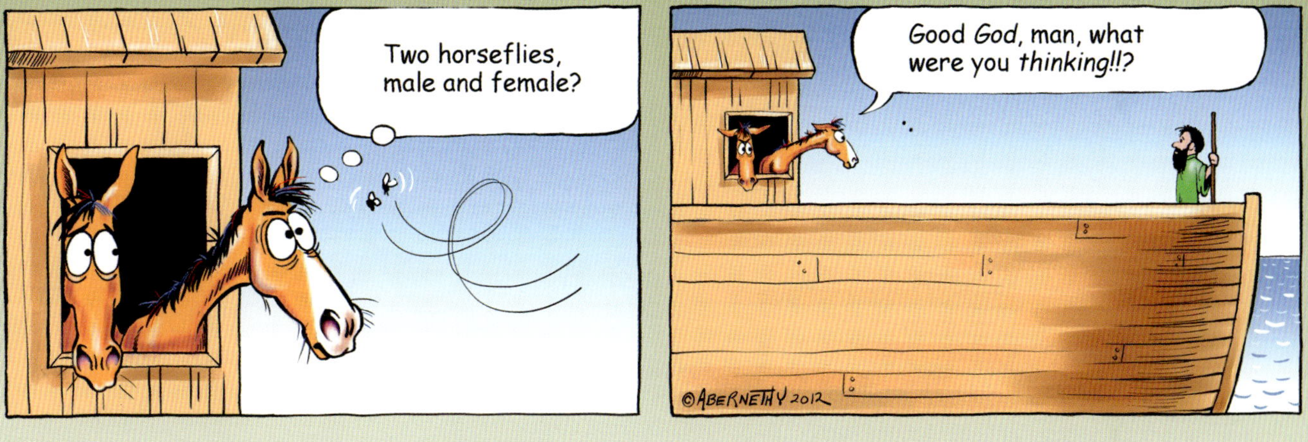
Two horseflies, male and female?
Good *God*, man, what were you *thinking*!!?
©ABERNETHY 2012

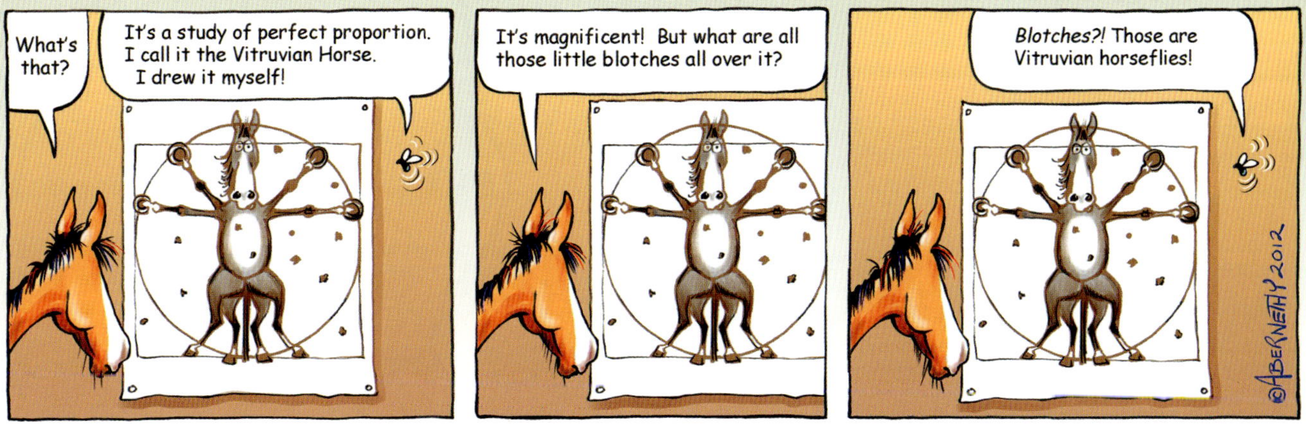
What's that?
It's a study of perfect proportion. I call it the Vitruvian Horse. I drew it myself!
It's magnificent! But what are all those little blotches all over it?
*Blotches?!* Those are Vitruvian horseflies!
©ABERNETHY 2012

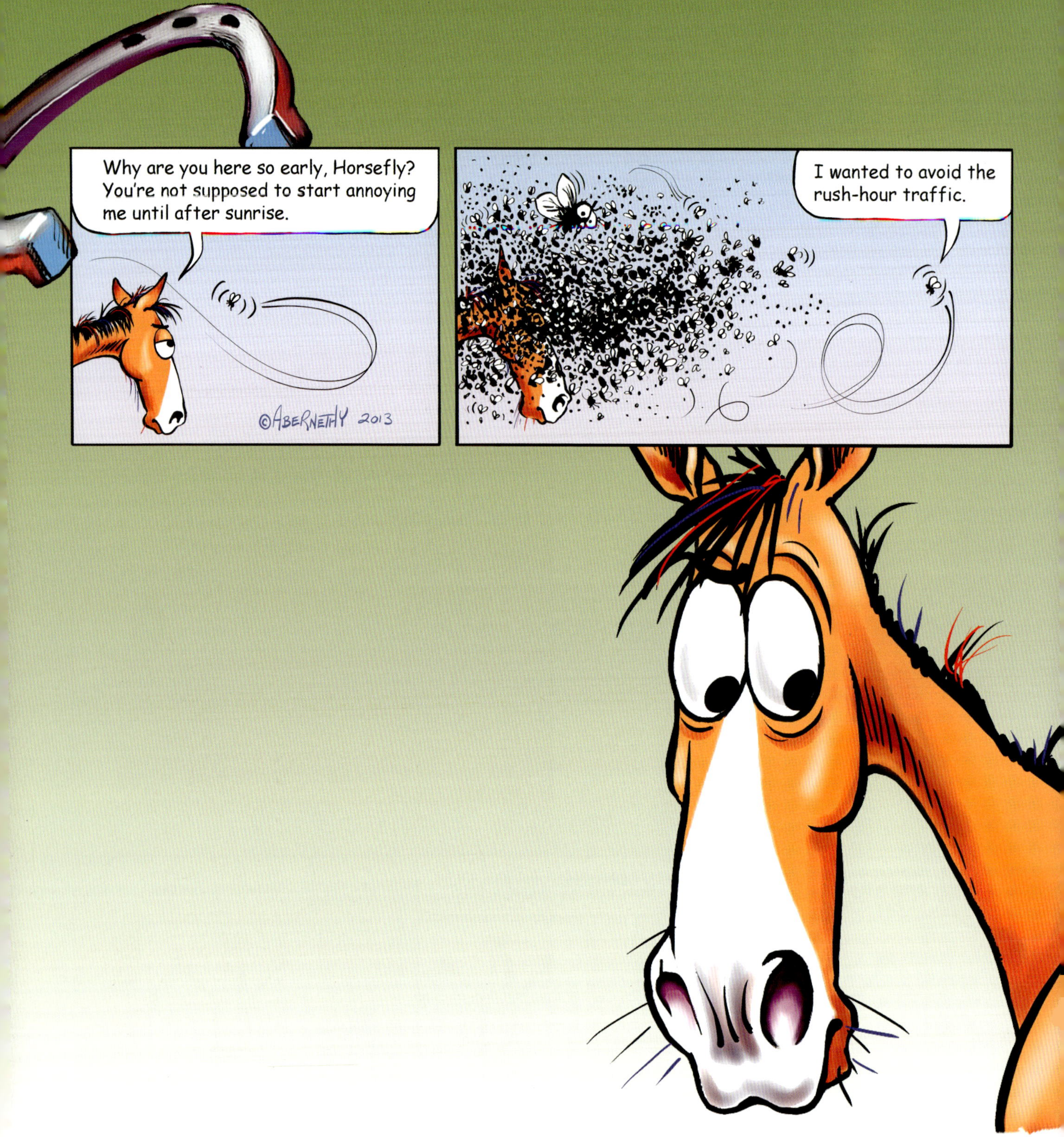
Why are you here so early, Horsefly? You're not supposed to start annoying me until after sunrise.
©ABERNETHY 2013
I wanted to avoid the rush-hour traffic.

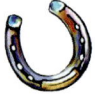

Horse
Wisdom

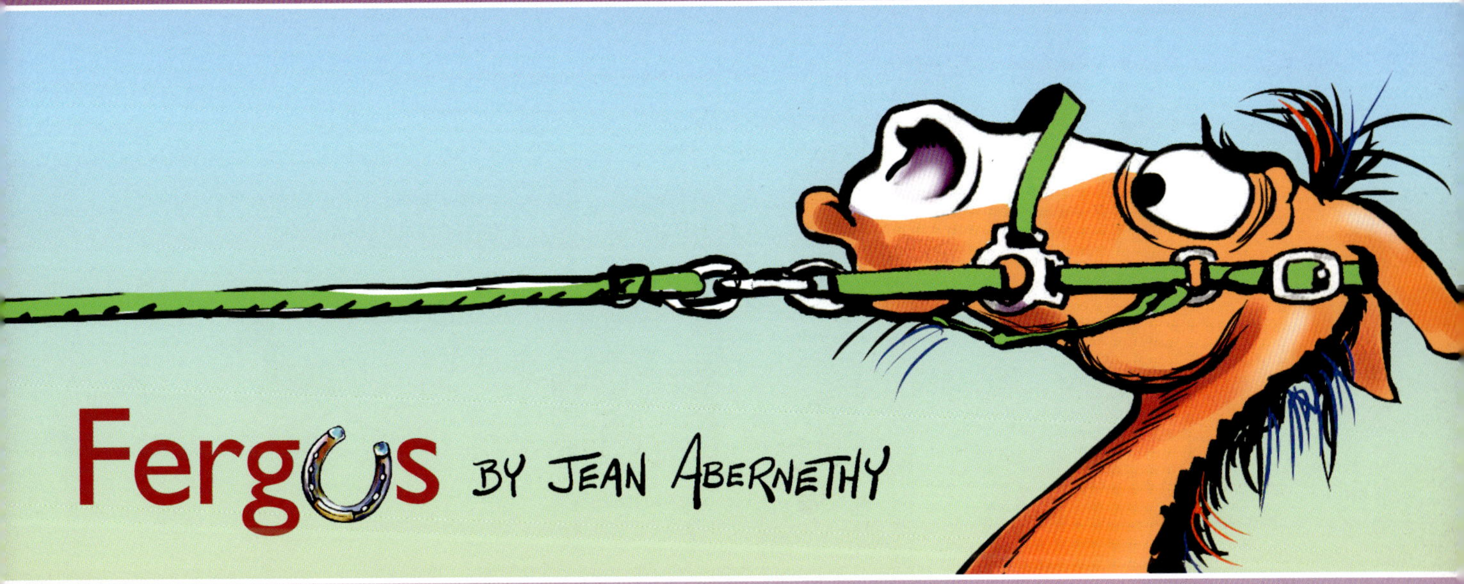
Fergus BY JEAN ABERNETHY

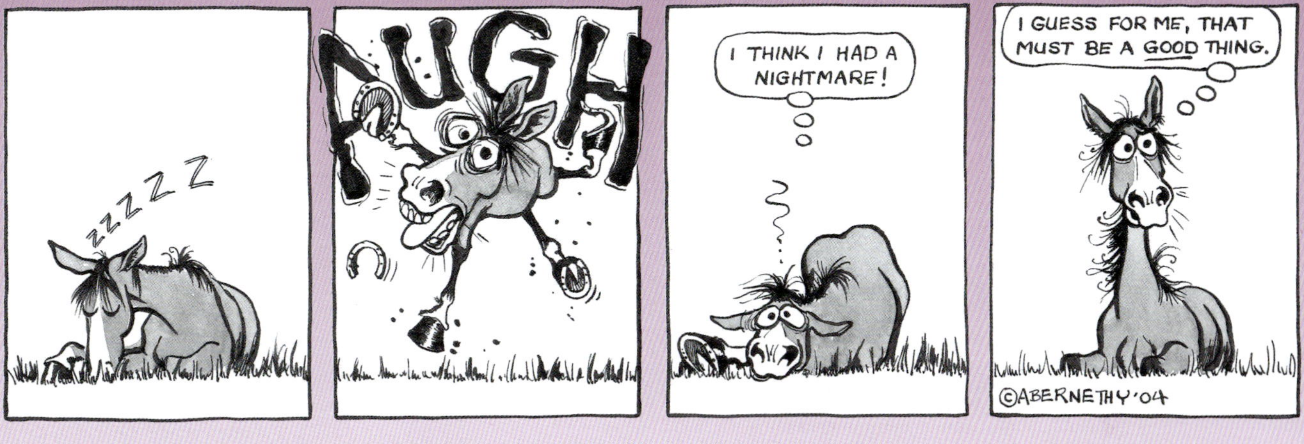
ZZZZZ Z
UGH
I THINK I HAD A NIGHTMARE!
I GUESS FOR ME, THAT MUST BE A GOOD THING.
©ABERNETHY '04

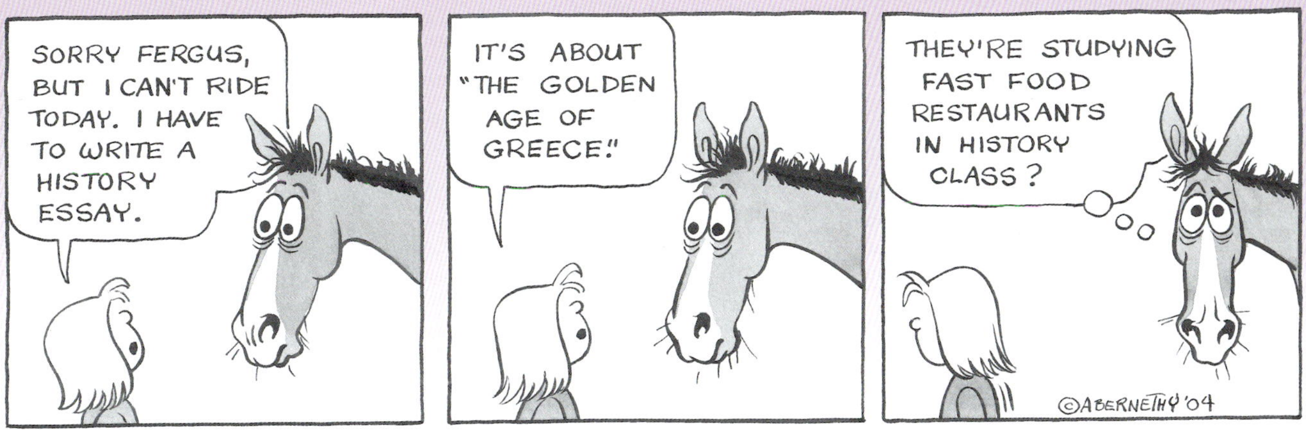
SORRY FERGUS, BUT I CAN'T RIDE TODAY. I HAVE TO WRITE A HISTORY ESSAY.
IT'S ABOUT "THE GOLDEN AGE OF GREECE."
THEY'RE STUDYING FAST FOOD RESTAURANTS IN HISTORY CLASS?
©ABERNETHY '04

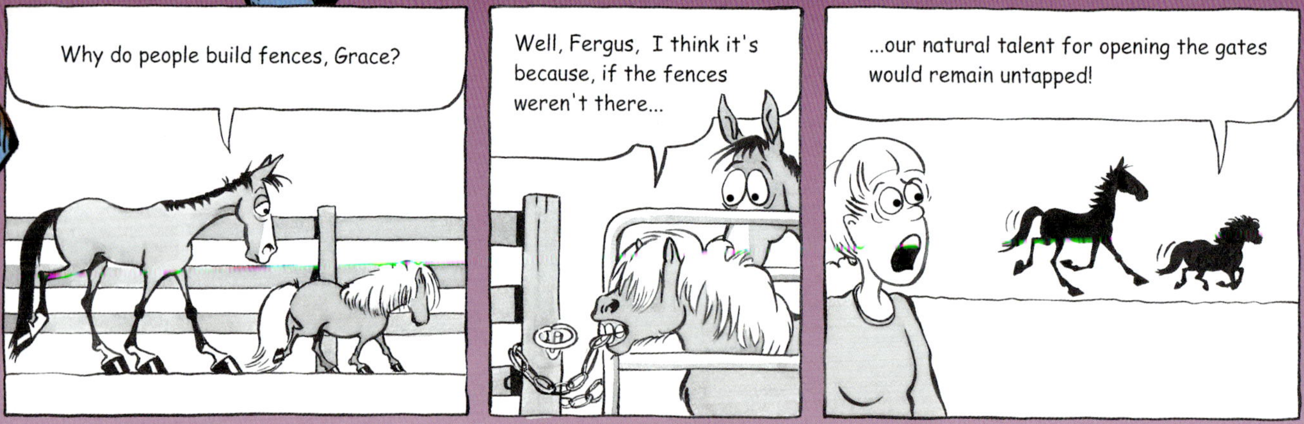
Why do people build fences, Grace?
Well, Fergus, I think it's because, if the fences weren't there...
...our natural talent for opening the gates would remain untapped!

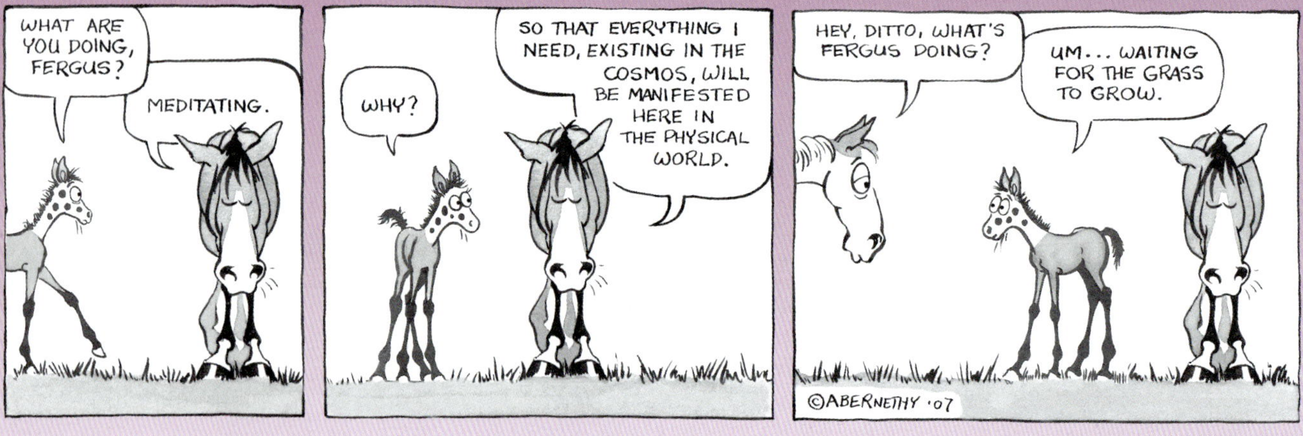
WHAT ARE YOU DOING, FERGUS?
MEDITATING.
WHY?
SO THAT EVERYTHING I NEED, EXISTING IN THE COSMOS, WILL BE MANIFESTED HERE IN THE PHYSICAL WORLD.
HEY, DITTO, WHAT'S FERGUS DOING?
UM... WAITING FOR THE GRASS TO GROW.
©ABERNETHY '07

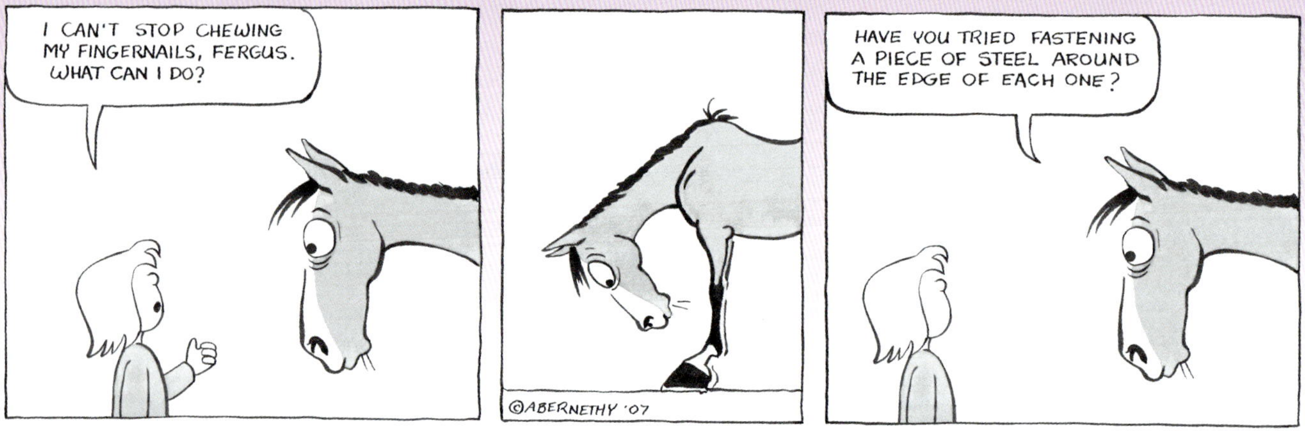
I CAN'T STOP CHEWING MY FINGERNAILS, FERGUS. WHAT CAN I DO?
©ABERNETHY '07
HAVE YOU TRIED FASTENING A PIECE OF STEEL AROUND THE EDGE OF EACH ONE?

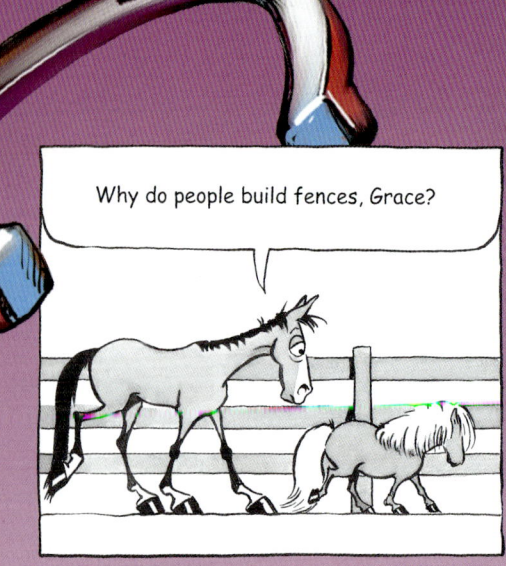

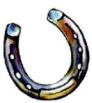

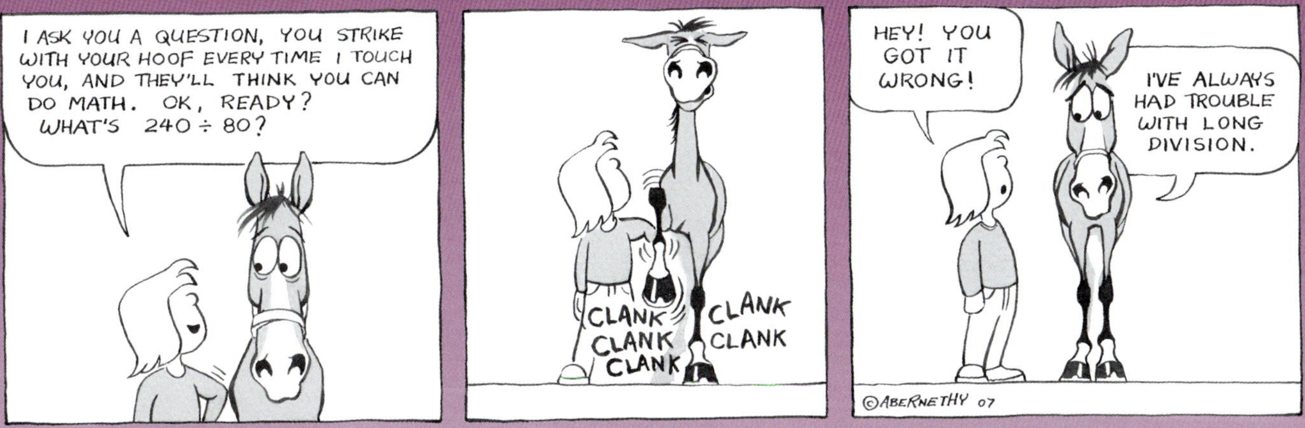
I ASK YOU A QUESTION, YOU STRIKE WITH YOUR HOOF EVERY TIME I TOUCH YOU, AND THEY'LL THINK YOU CAN DO MATH. OK, READY? WHAT'S 240 ÷ 80?
CLANK CLANK CLANK
CLANK CLANK
HEY! YOU GOT IT WRONG!
I'VE ALWAYS HAD TROUBLE WITH LONG DIVISION.
©ABERNETHY 07

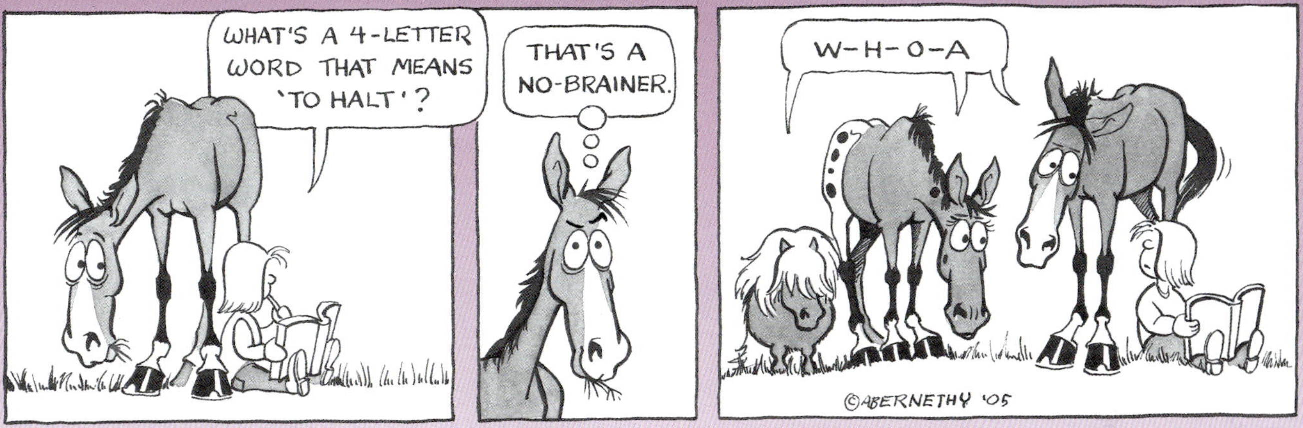
WHAT'S A 4-LETTER WORD THAT MEANS 'TO HALT'?
THAT'S A NO-BRAINER.
W-H-O-A
©ABERNETHY '05

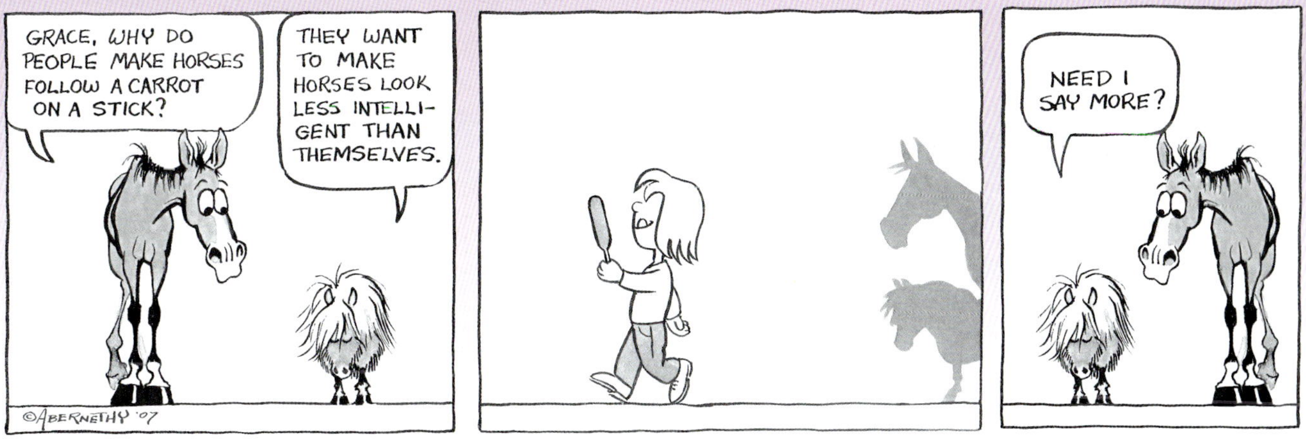
GRACE, WHY DO PEOPLE MAKE HORSES FOLLOW A CARROT ON A STICK?
THEY WANT TO MAKE HORSES LOOK LESS INTELLI-GENT THAN THEMSELVES.
NEED I SAY MORE?
©ABERNETHY '07

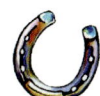

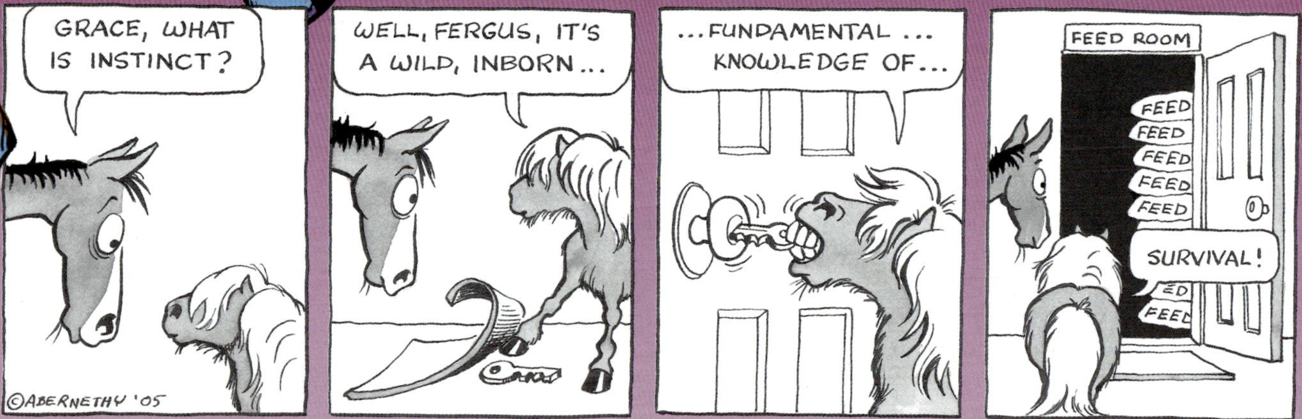
GRACE, WHAT IS INSTINCT?
©ABERNETHY '05
WELL, FERGUS, IT'S A WILD, INBORN...
...FUNDAMENTAL ... KNOWLEDGE OF...
FEED ROOM
FEED
FEED
FEED
FEED
FEED
SURVIVAL!

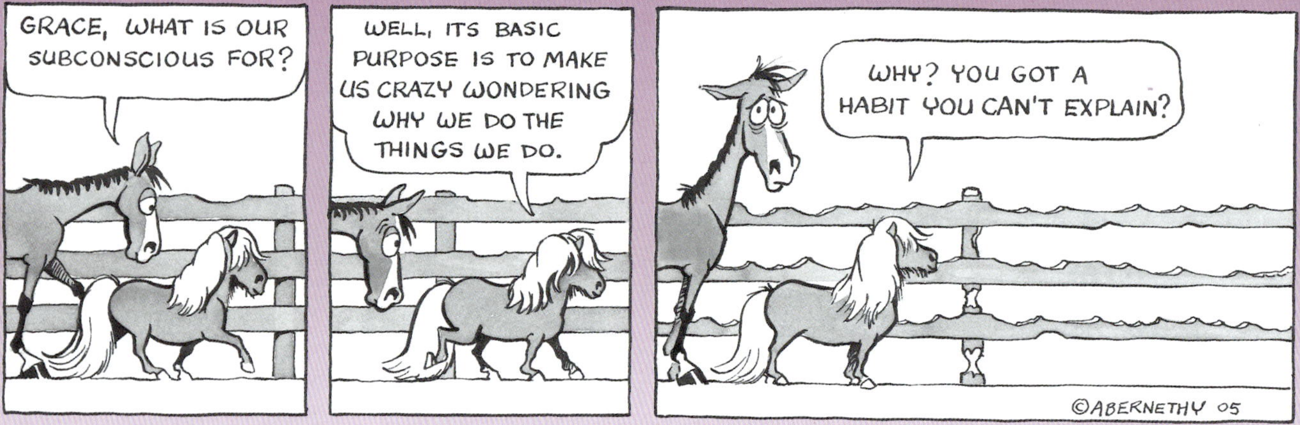
GRACE, WHAT IS OUR SUBCONSCIOUS FOR?
WELL, ITS BASIC PURPOSE IS TO MAKE US CRAZY WONDERING WHY WE DO THE THINGS WE DO.
WHY? YOU GOT A HABIT YOU CAN'T EXPLAIN?
©ABERNETHY 05

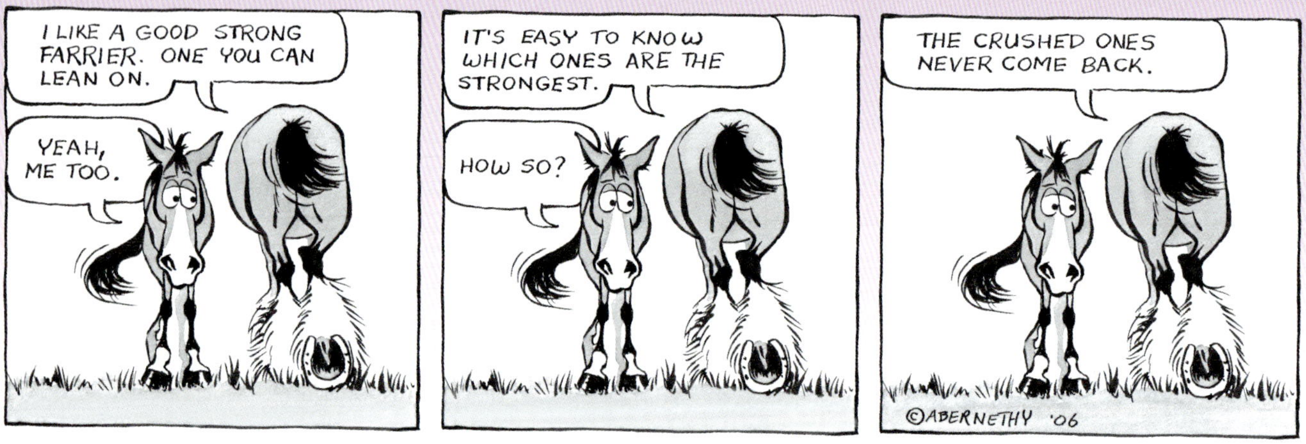
I LIKE A GOOD STRONG FARRIER. ONE YOU CAN LEAN ON.
YEAH, ME TOO.
IT'S EASY TO KNOW WHICH ONES ARE THE STRONGEST.
HOW SO?
THE CRUSHED ONES NEVER COME BACK.
©ABERNETHY '06

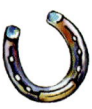

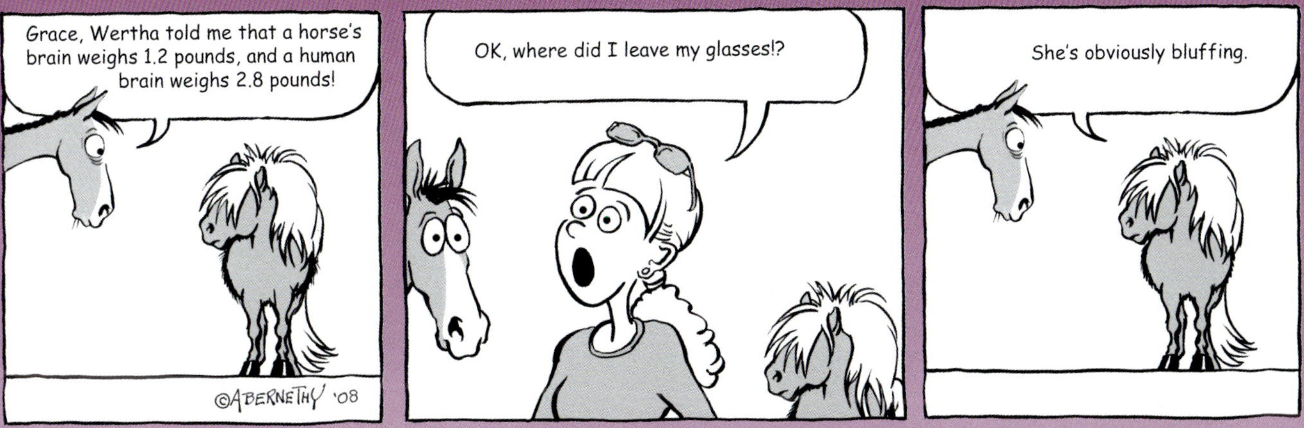
Grace, Wertha told me that a horse's brain weighs 1.2 pounds, and a human brain weighs 2.8 pounds!
©ABERNETHY '08
OK, where did I leave my glasses!?
She's obviously bluffing.

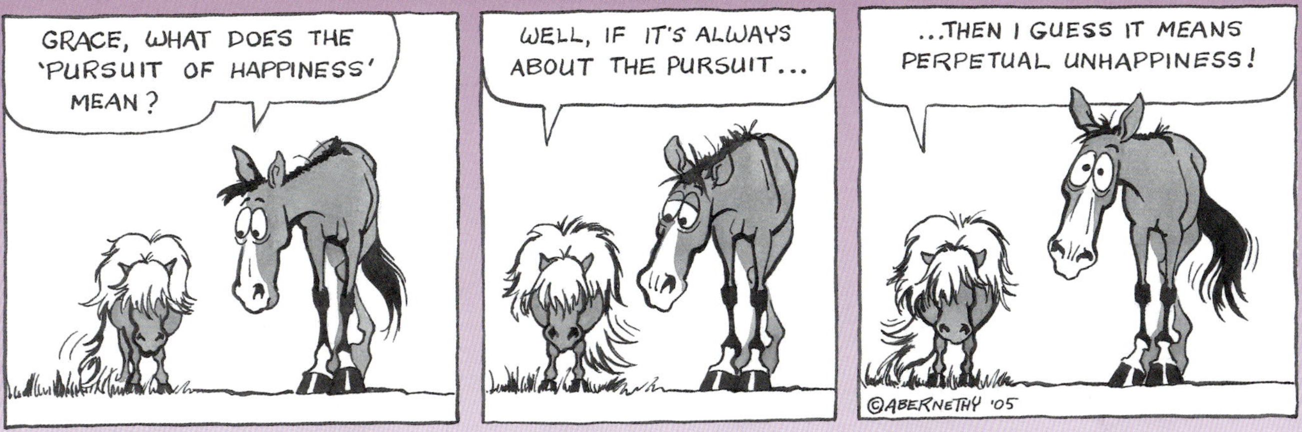
GRACE, WHAT DOES THE 'PURSUIT OF HAPPINESS' MEAN?
WELL, IF IT'S ALWAYS ABOUT THE PURSUIT...
...THEN I GUESS IT MEANS PERPETUAL UNHAPPINESS!
©ABERNETHY '05

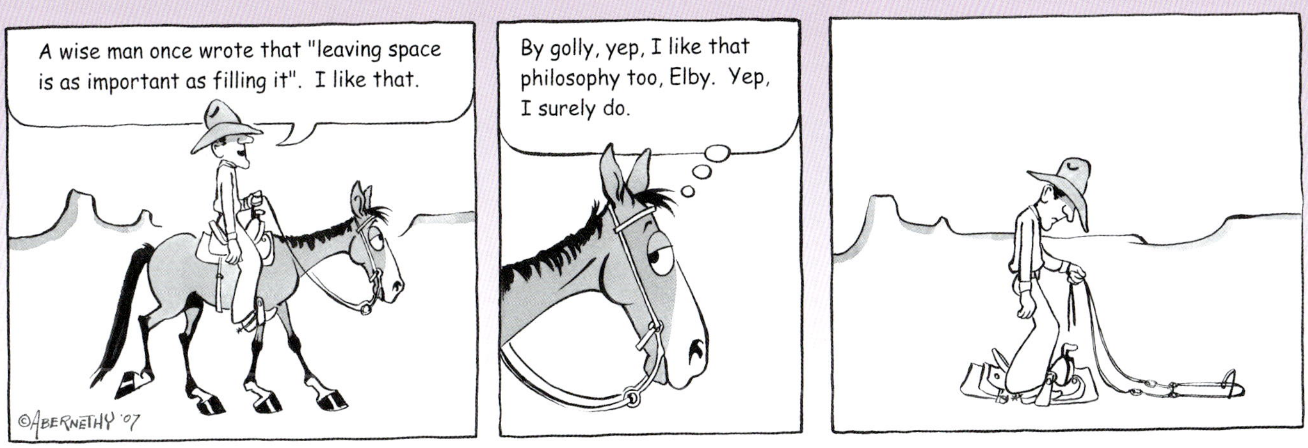
A wise man once wrote that "leaving space is as important as filling it". I like that.
©ABERNETHY '07
By golly, yep, I like that philosophy too, Elby. Yep, I surely do.

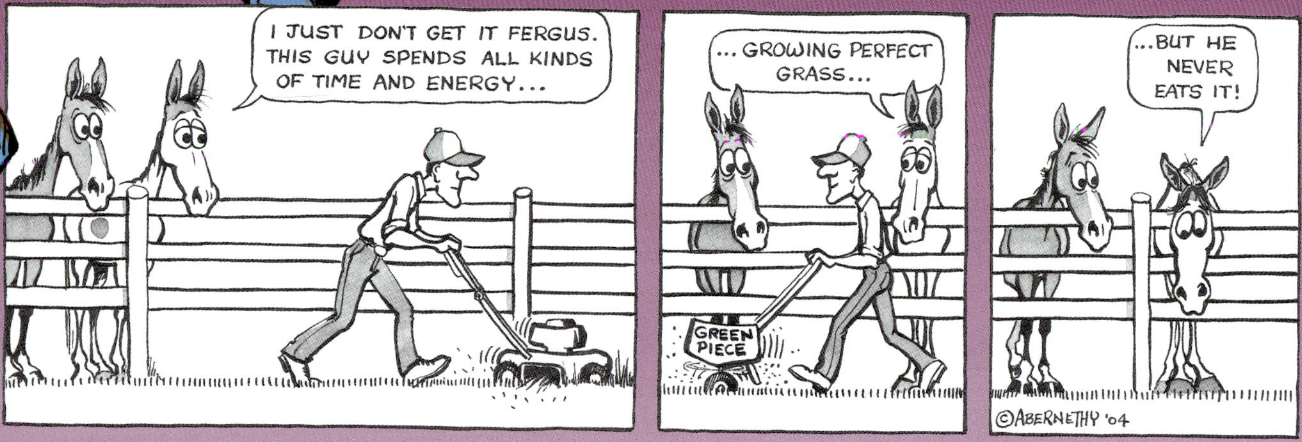
I JUST DON'T GET IT FERGUS. THIS GUY SPENDS ALL KINDS OF TIME AND ENERGY...
... GROWING PERFECT GRASS...
GREEN PIECE
...BUT HE NEVER EATS IT!
©ABERNETHY '04

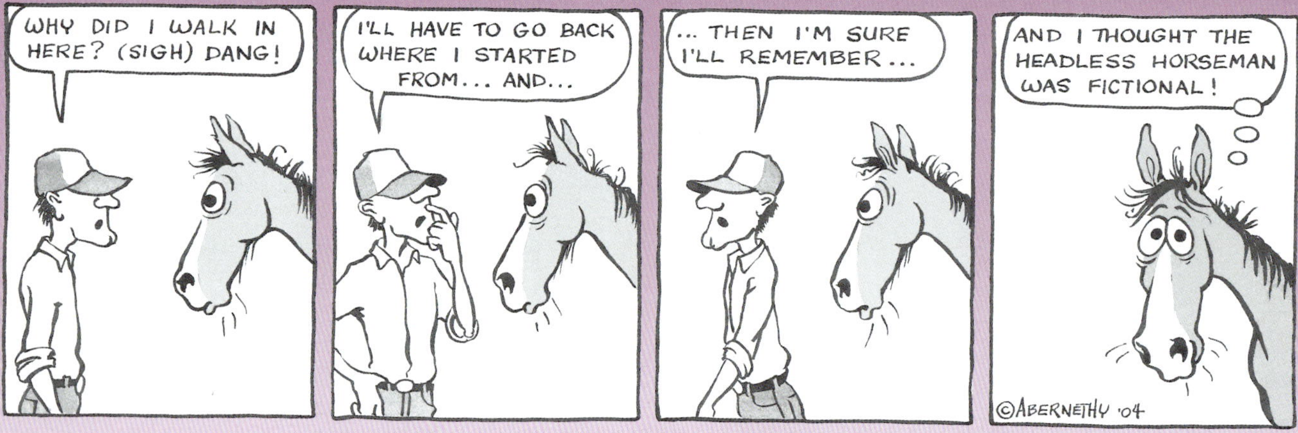
WHY DID I WALK IN HERE? (SIGH) DANG!
I'LL HAVE TO GO BACK WHERE I STARTED FROM... AND...
... THEN I'M SURE I'LL REMEMBER...
AND I THOUGHT THE HEADLESS HORSEMAN WAS FICTIONAL!
©ABERNETHY '04

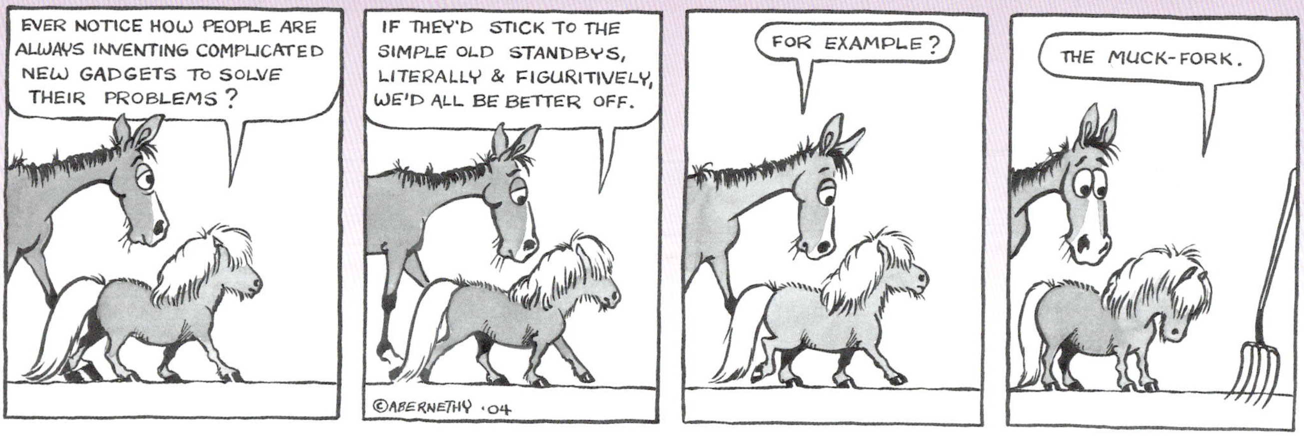
EVER NOTICE HOW PEOPLE ARE ALWAYS INVENTING COMPLICATED NEW GADGETS TO SOLVE THEIR PROBLEMS?
IF THEY'D STICK TO THE SIMPLE OLD STANDBYS, LITERALLY & FIGURITIVELY, WE'D ALL BE BETTER OFF.
©ABERNETHY '04
FOR EXAMPLE?
THE MUCK-FORK.

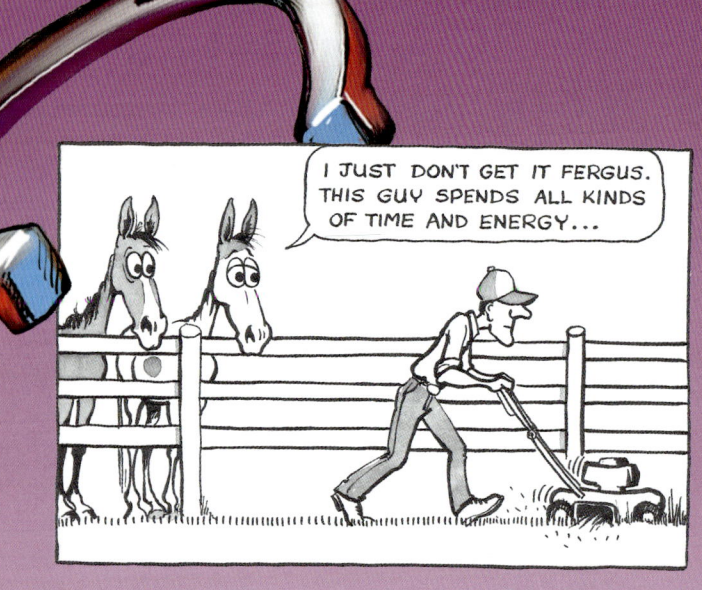

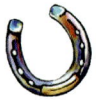

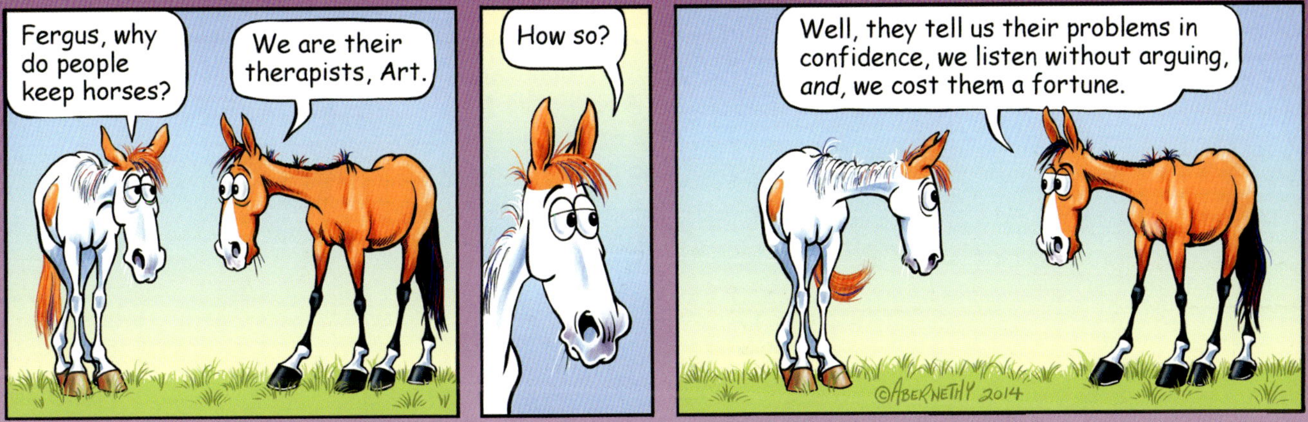

Fergus, why do people keep horses?
We are their therapists, Art.
How so?
Well, they tell us their problems in confidence, we listen without arguing, *and,* we cost them a fortune.
©ABERNETHY 2014


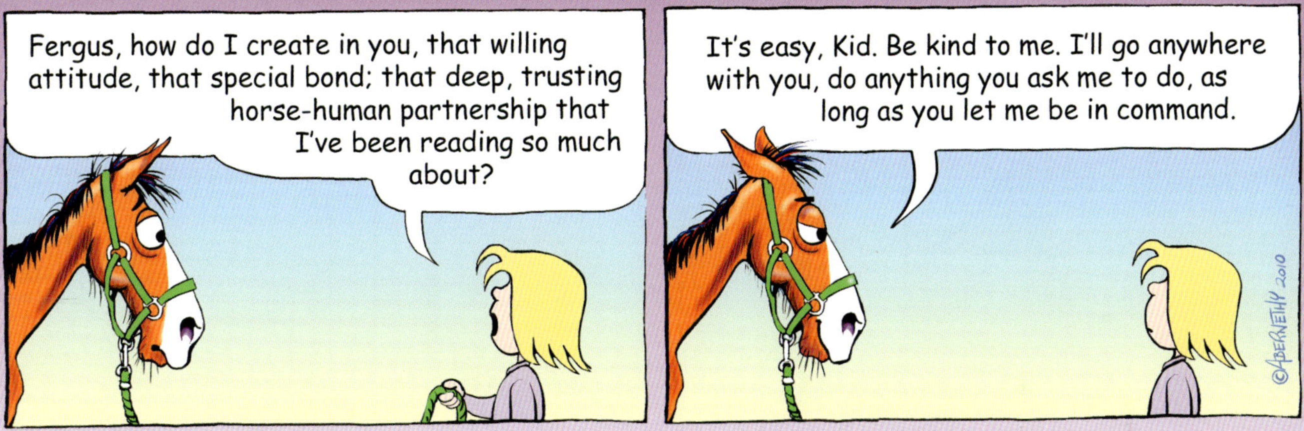

Fergus, how do I create in you, that willing attitude, that special bond; that deep, trusting horse-human partnership that I've been reading so much about?
It's easy, Kid. Be kind to me. I'll go anywhere with you, do anything you ask me to do, as long as you let me be in command.
©ABERNETHY 2010


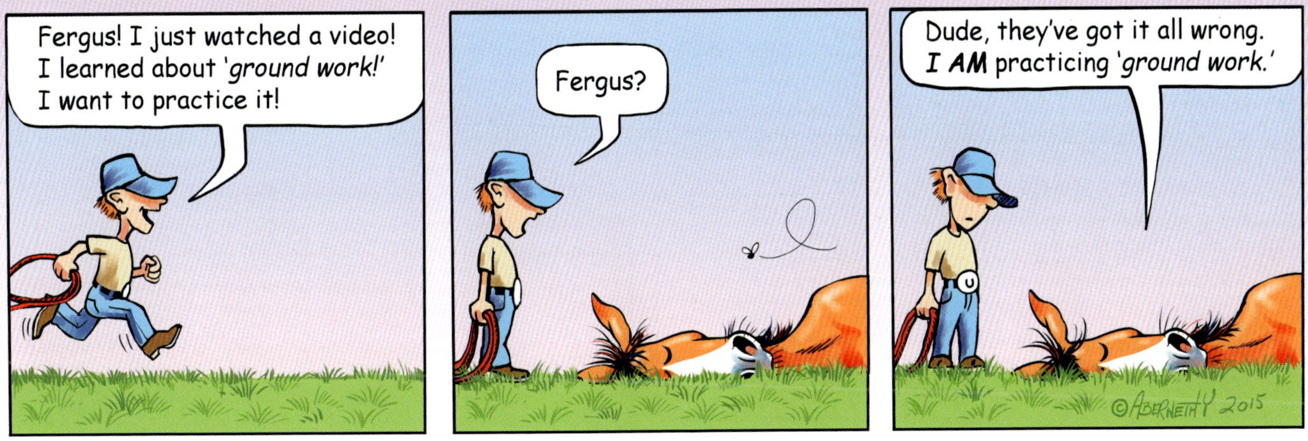

Fergus! I just watched a video! I learned about *'ground work!'* I want to practice it!
Fergus?
Dude, they've got it all wrong. ***I AM*** practicing *'ground work.'*
©ABERNETHY 2015

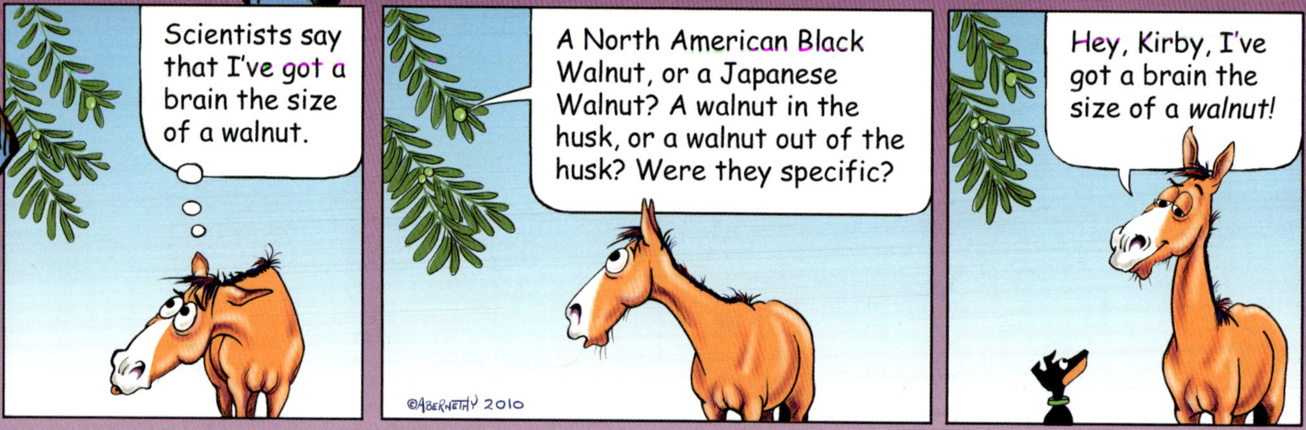
Scientists say that I've got a brain the size of a walnut.
A North American Black Walnut, or a Japanese Walnut? A walnut in the husk, or a walnut out of the husk? Were they specific?
©ABERNETHY 2010
Hey, Kirby, I've got a brain the size of a *walnut*!

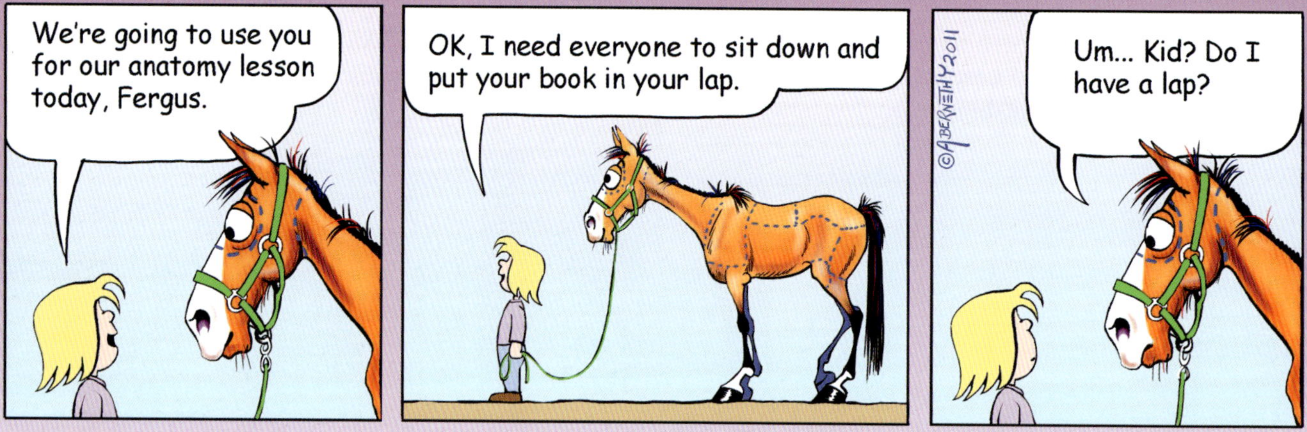
We're going to use you for our anatomy lesson today, Fergus.
OK, I need everyone to sit down and put your book in your lap.
©ABERNETHY 2011
Um... Kid? Do I have a lap?

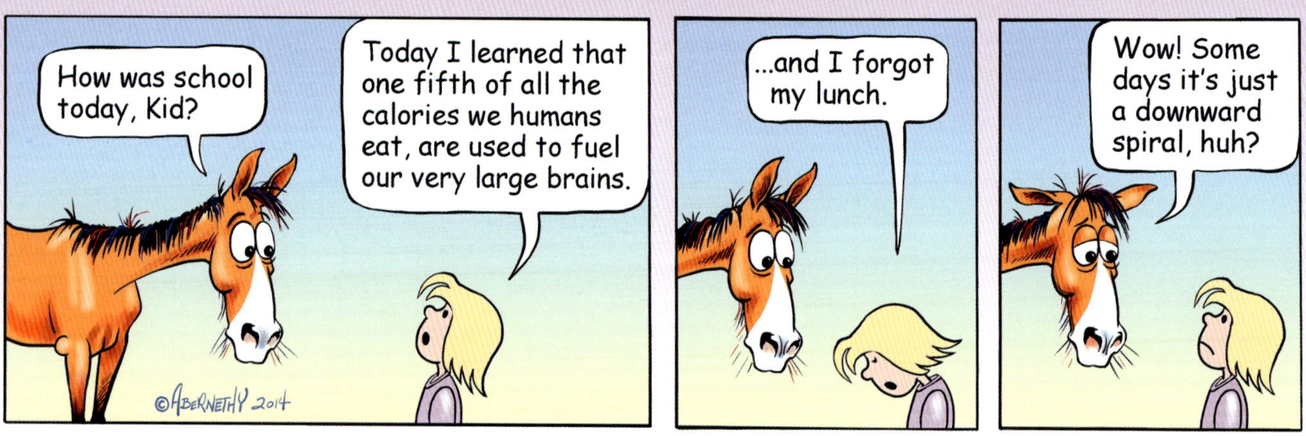
How was school today, Kid?
Today I learned that one fifth of all the calories we humans eat, are used to fuel our very large brains.
©ABERNETHY 2014
...and I forgot my lunch.
Wow! Some days it's just a downward spiral, huh?

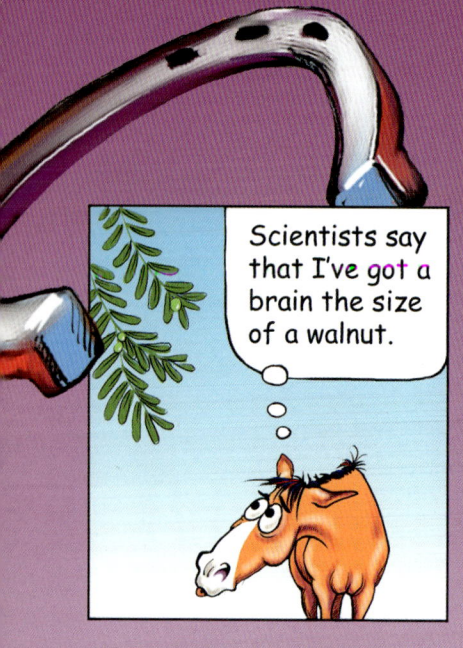

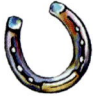

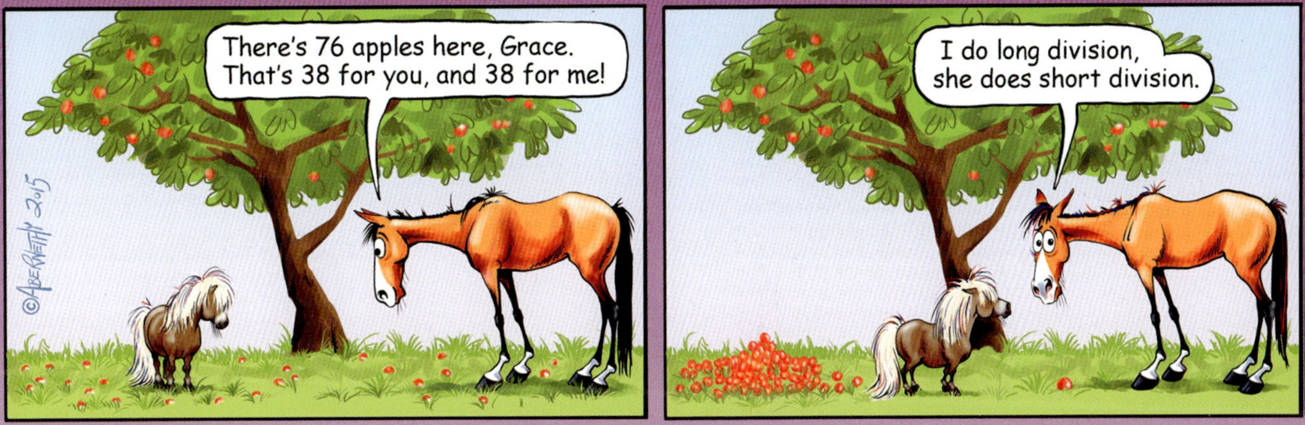
©ABERNETHY 2015
There's 76 apples here, Grace. That's 38 for you, and 38 for me!
I do long division, she does short division.

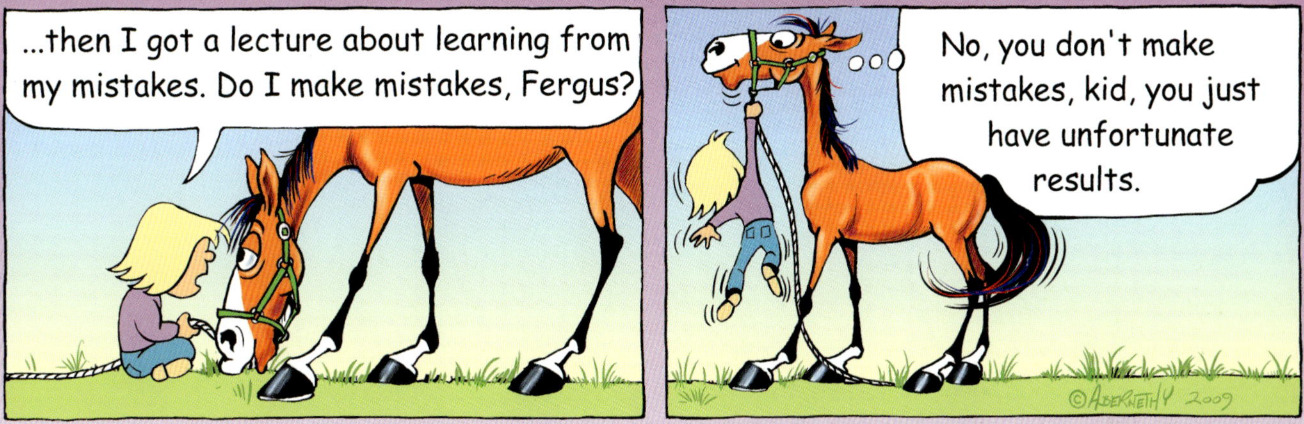
...then I got a lecture about learning from my mistakes. Do I make mistakes, Fergus?
No, you don't make mistakes, kid, you just have unfortunate results.
©ABERNETHY 2009

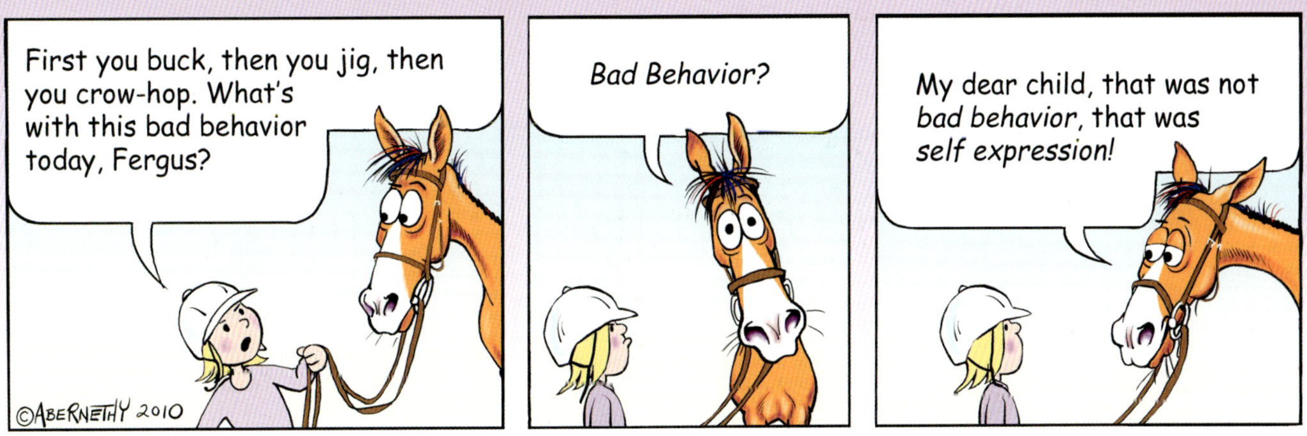
First you buck, then you jig, then you crow-hop. What's with this bad behavior today, Fergus?
©ABERNETHY 2010
*Bad Behavior?*
My dear child, that was not *bad behavior*, that was *self expression!*

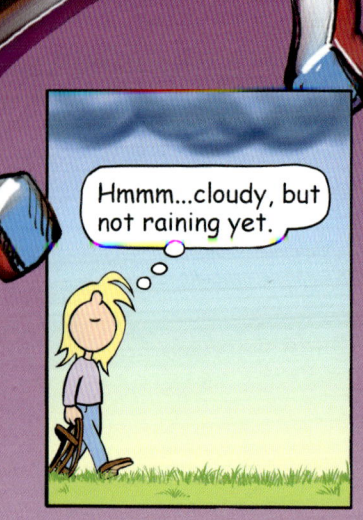

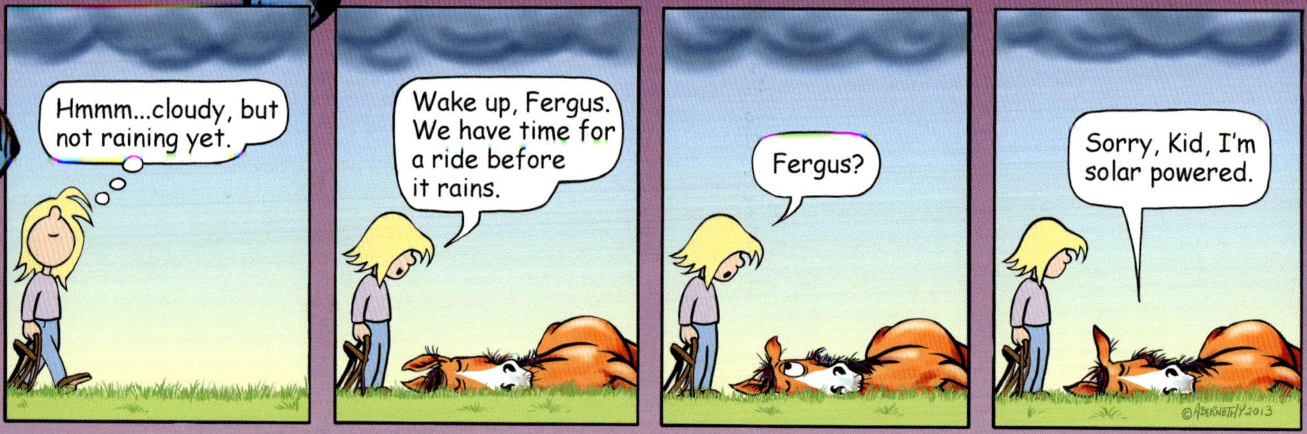
Hmmm...cloudy, but not raining yet.
Wake up, Fergus. We have time for a ride before it rains.
Fergus?
Sorry, Kid, I'm solar powered.

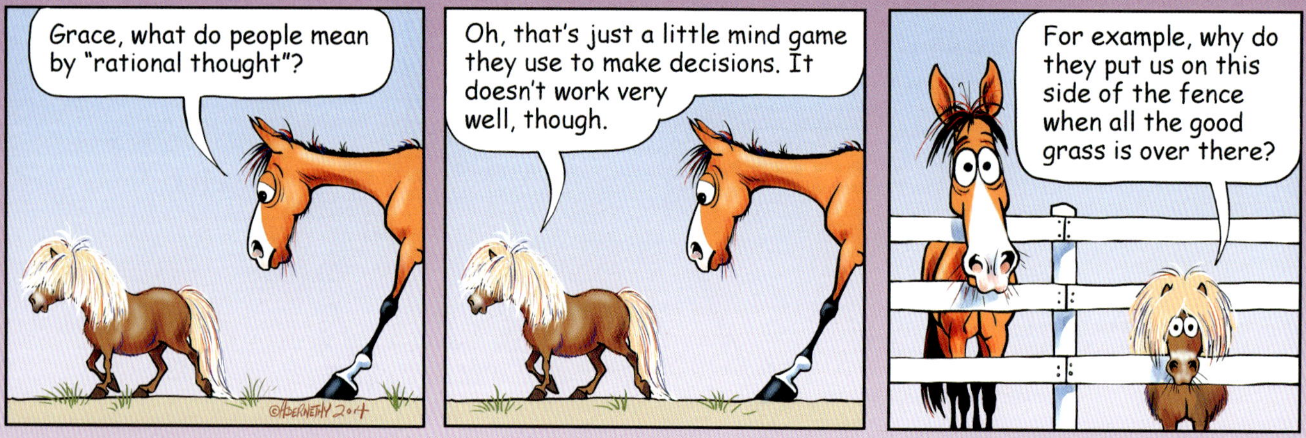
Grace, what do people mean by "rational thought"?
©ABERNETHY 2014
Oh, that's just a little mind game they use to make decisions. It doesn't work very well, though.
For example, why do they put us on this side of the fence when all the good grass is over there?

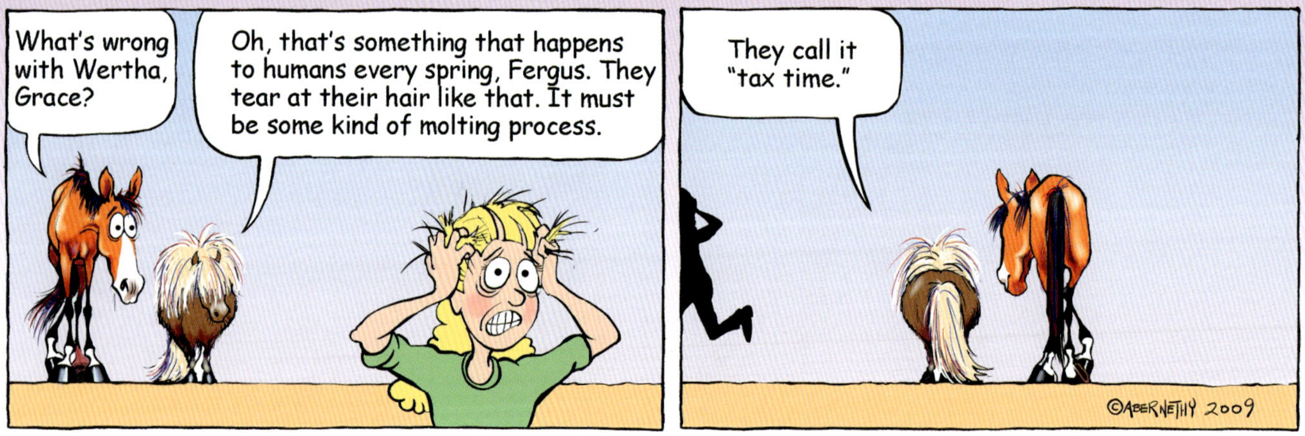
What's wrong with Wertha, Grace?
Oh, that's something that happens to humans every spring, Fergus. They tear at their hair like that. It must be some kind of molting process.
They call it "tax time."
©ABERNETHY 2009

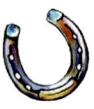

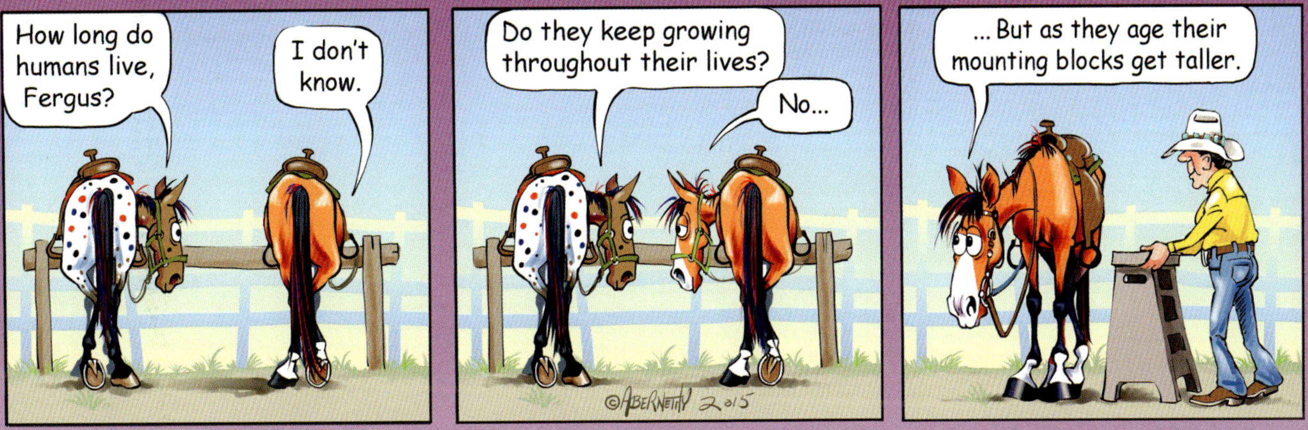
How long do humans live, Fergus?
I don't know.
Do they keep growing throughout their lives?
No...
... But as they age their mounting blocks get taller.
©ABERNETHY 2015

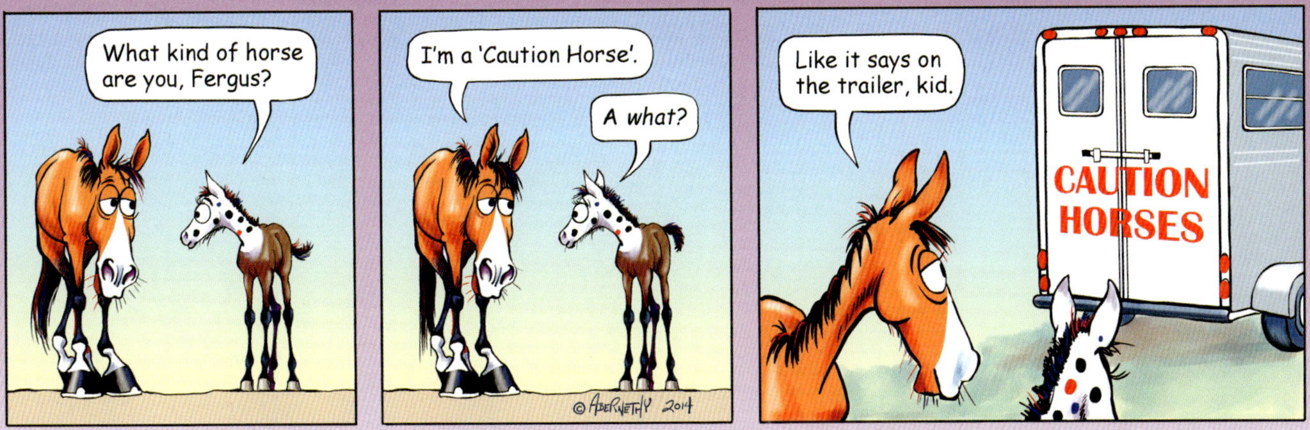
What kind of horse are you, Fergus?
I'm a 'Caution Horse'.
A what?
©ABERNETHY 2014
Like it says on the trailer, kid.
CAUTION HORSES

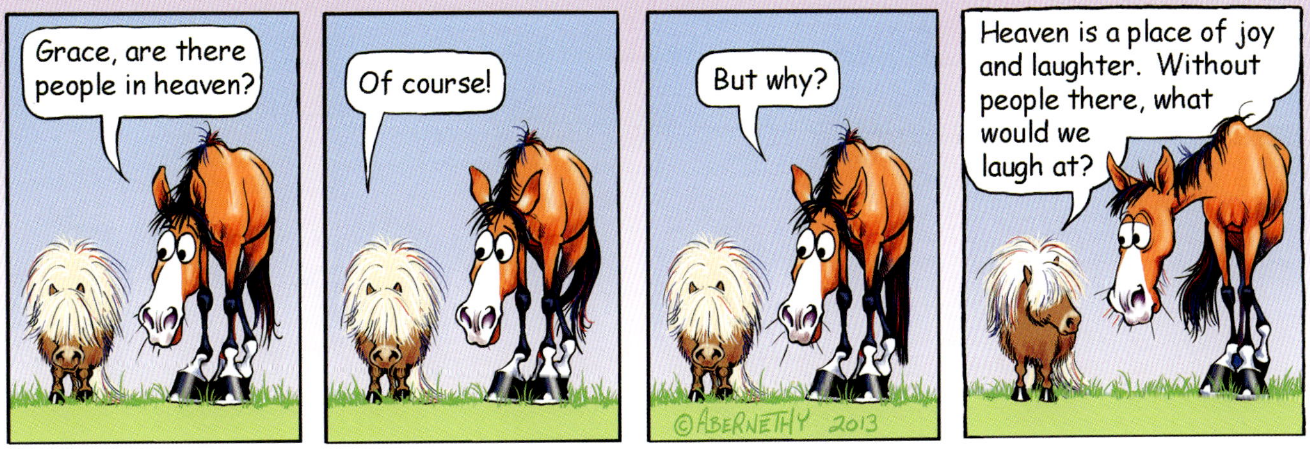
Grace, are there people in heaven?
Of course!
But why?
©ABERNETHY 2013
Heaven is a place of joy and laughter. Without people there, what would we laugh at?

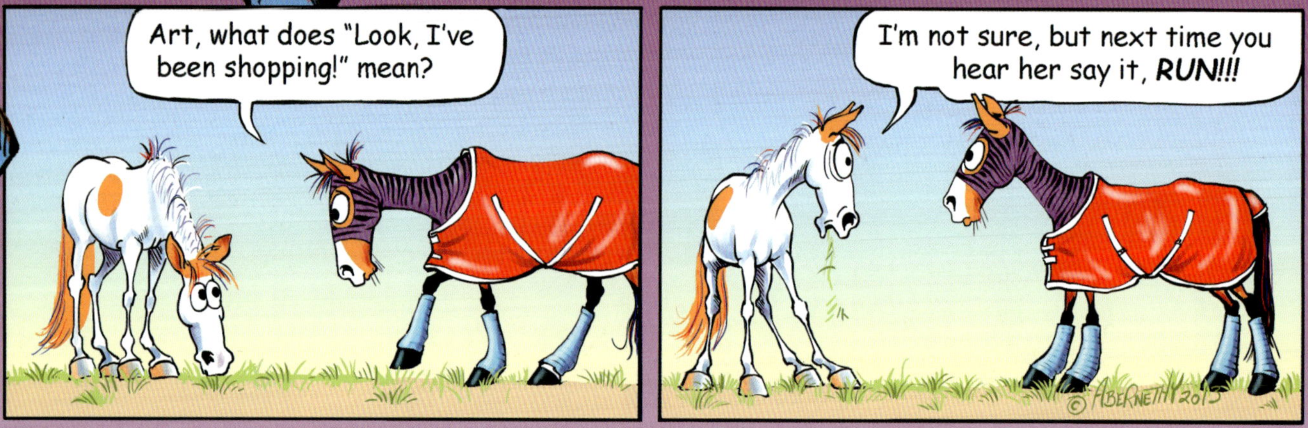
Art, what does "Look, I've been shopping!" mean?
I'm not sure, but next time you hear her say it, **RUN!!!**
© ABERNETHY 2013

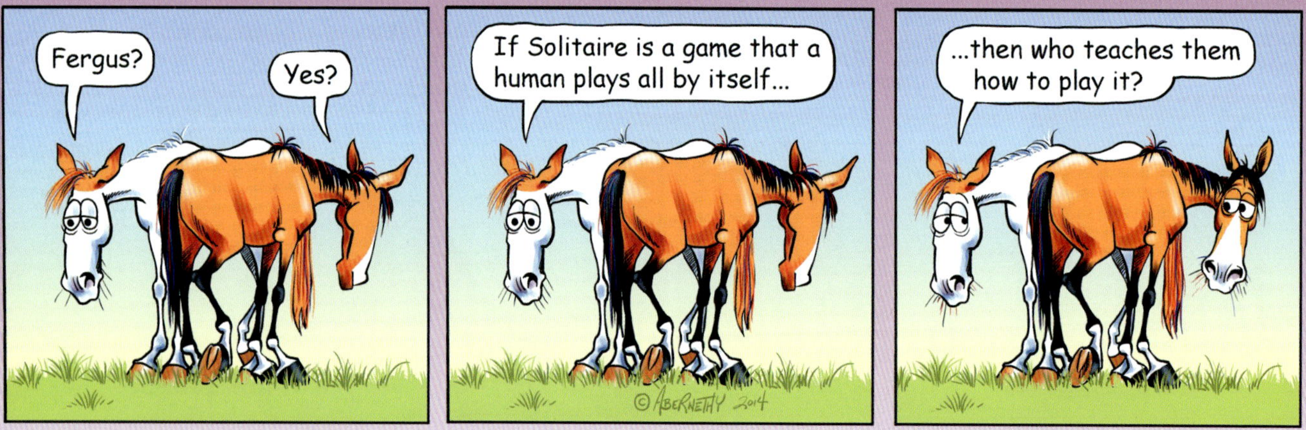
Fergus?
Yes?
If Solitaire is a game that a human plays all by itself...
...then who teaches them how to play it?
© ABERNETHY 2014

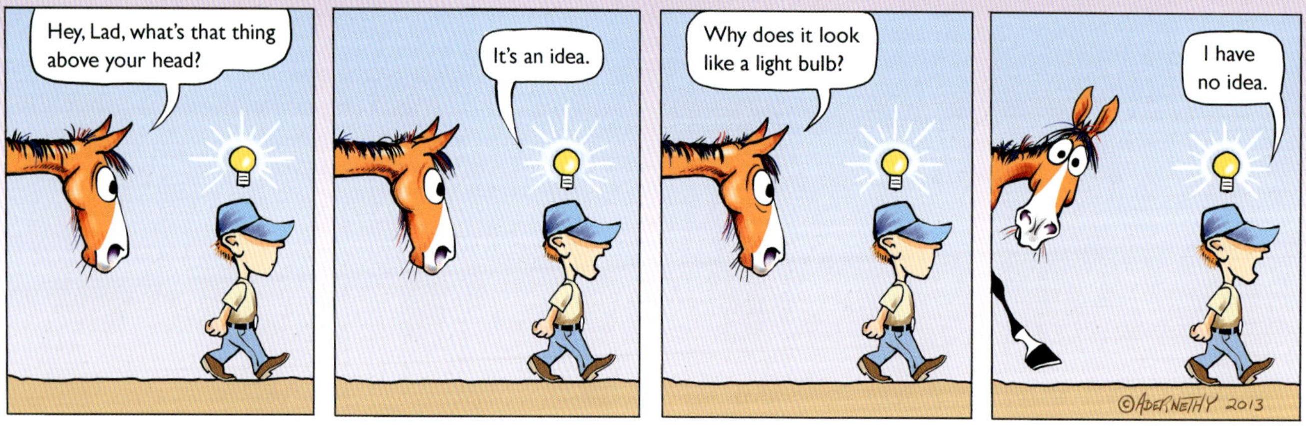
Hey, Lad, what's that thing above your head?
It's an idea.
Why does it look like a light bulb?
I have no idea.
© ABERNETHY 2013

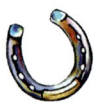

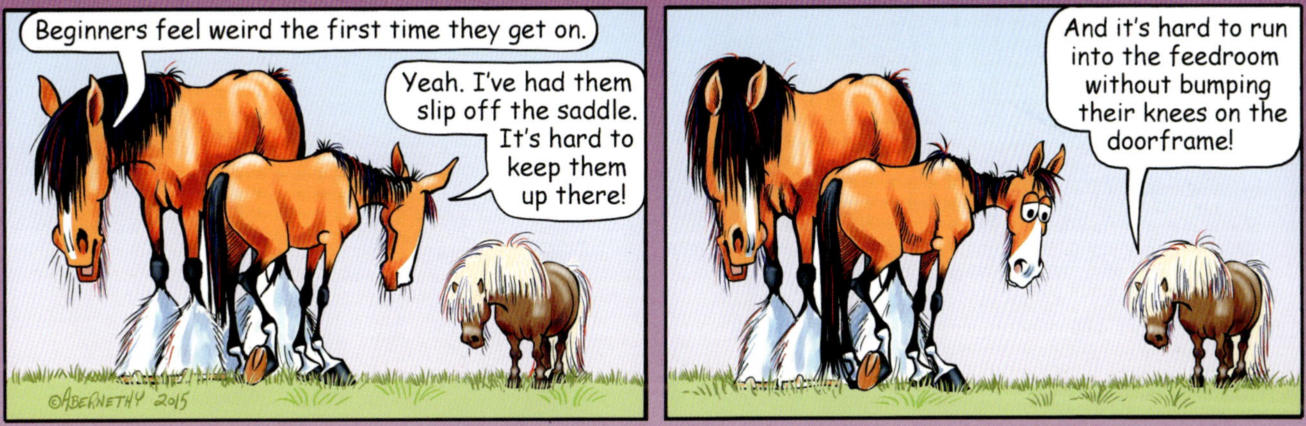
Beginners feel weird the first time they get on.
Yeah. I've had them slip off the saddle. It's hard to keep them up there!
And it's hard to run into the feedroom without bumping their knees on the doorframe!
©ABERNETHY 2015

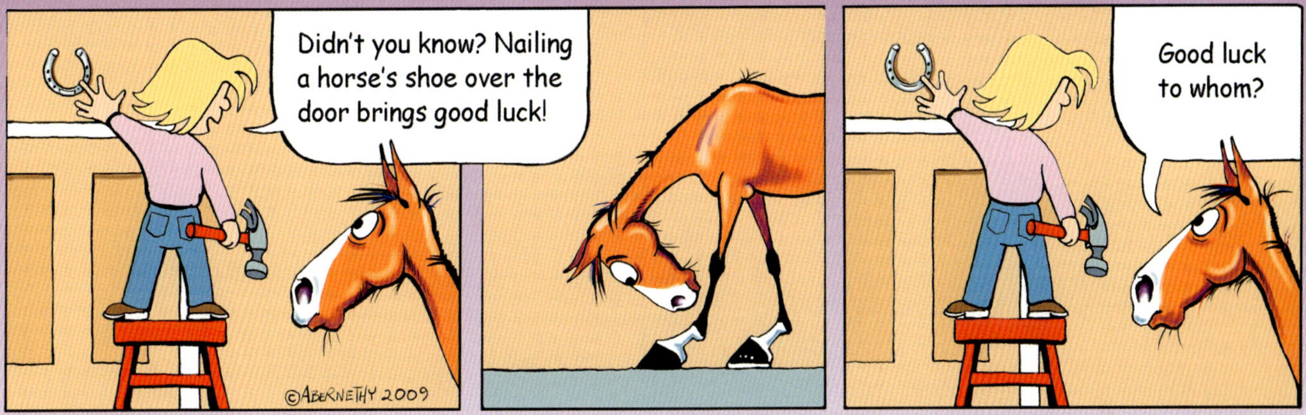
Didn't you know? Nailing a horse's shoe over the door brings good luck!
Good luck to whom?
©ABERNETHY 2009

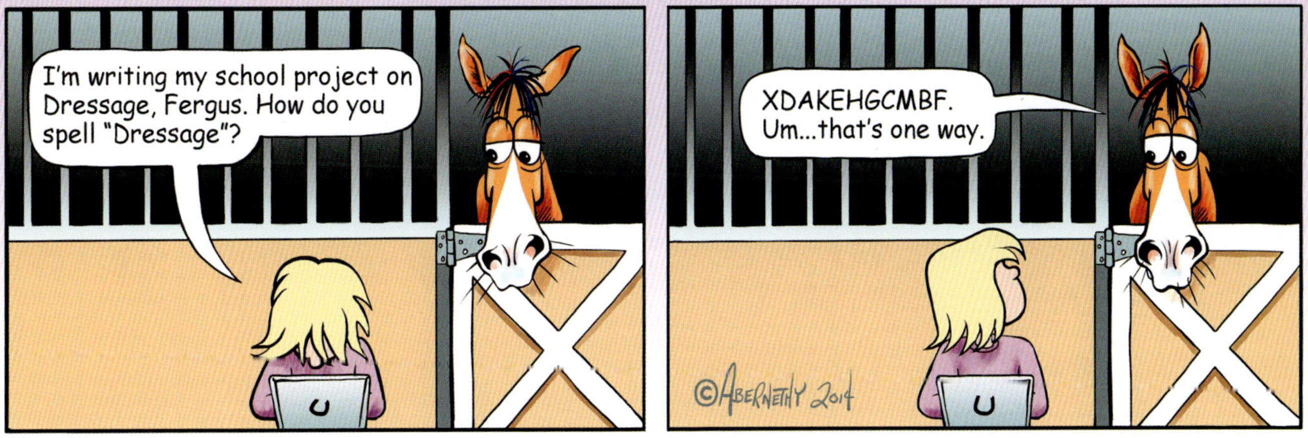
I'm writing my school project on Dressage, Fergus. How do you spell "Dressage"?
XDAKEHGCMBF. Um...that's one way.
©ABERNETHY 2014

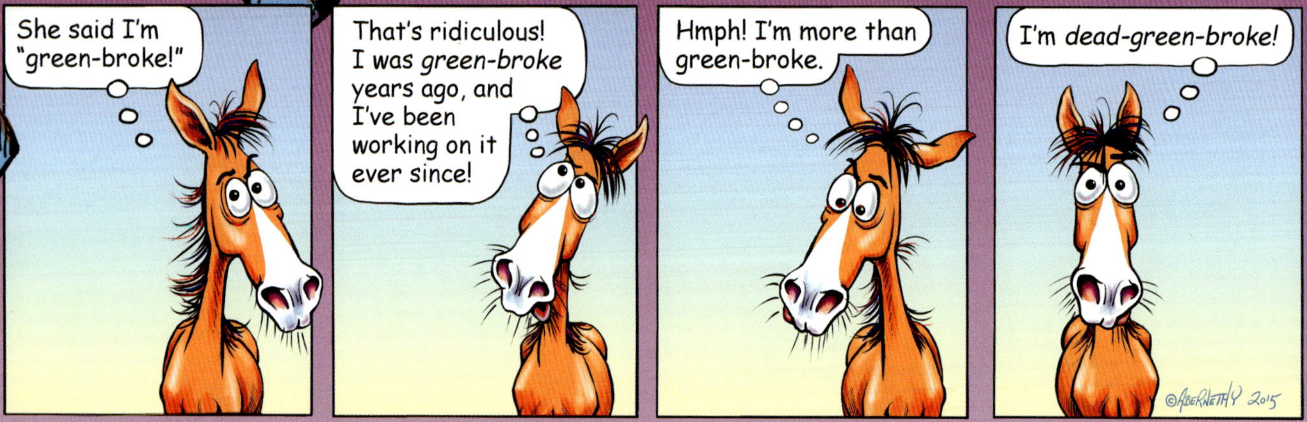
She said I'm "green-broke!"
That's ridiculous! I was *green-broke* years ago, and I've been working on it ever since!
Hmph! I'm more than green-broke.
I'm *dead-green-broke*!
©ABERNETHY 2015

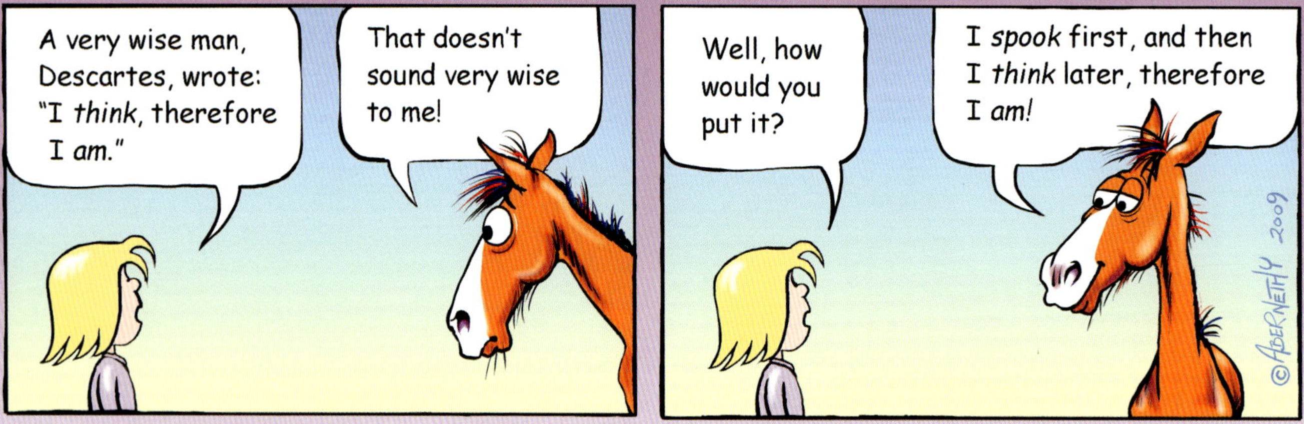
A very wise man, Descartes, wrote: "I *think*, therefore I *am*."
That doesn't sound very wise to me!
Well, how would you put it?
I *spook* first, and then I *think* later, therefore I *am*!
©ABERNETHY 2009

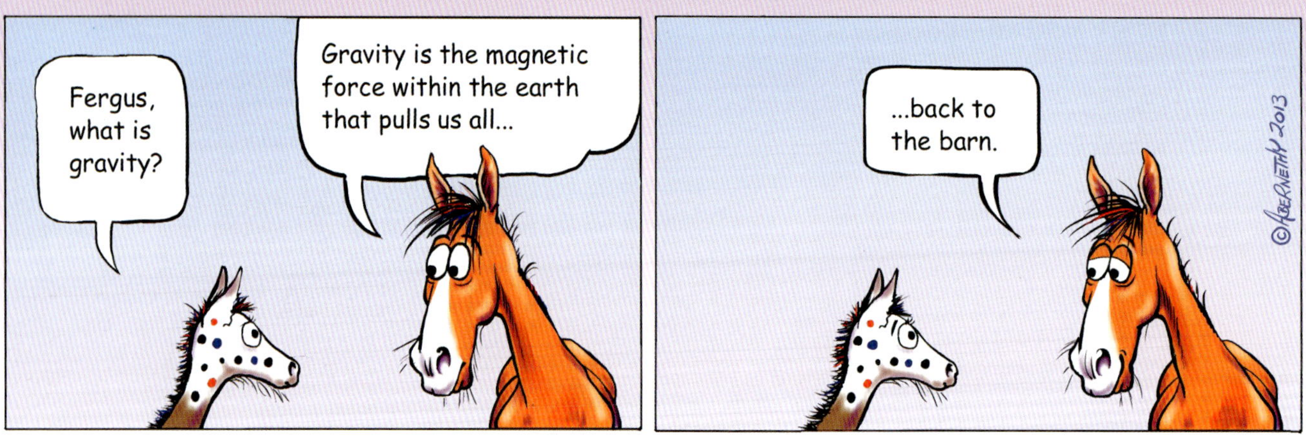
Fergus, what is gravity?
Gravity is the magnetic force within the earth that pulls us all...
...back to the barn.
©ABERNETHY 2013

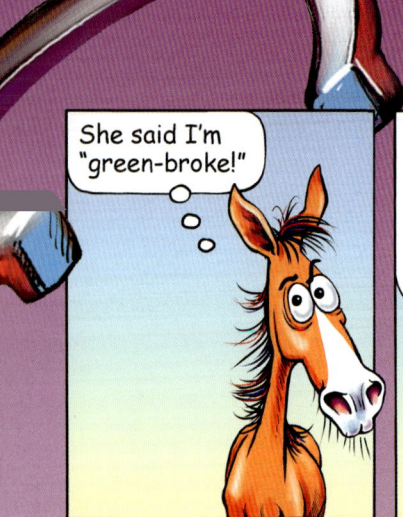

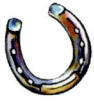

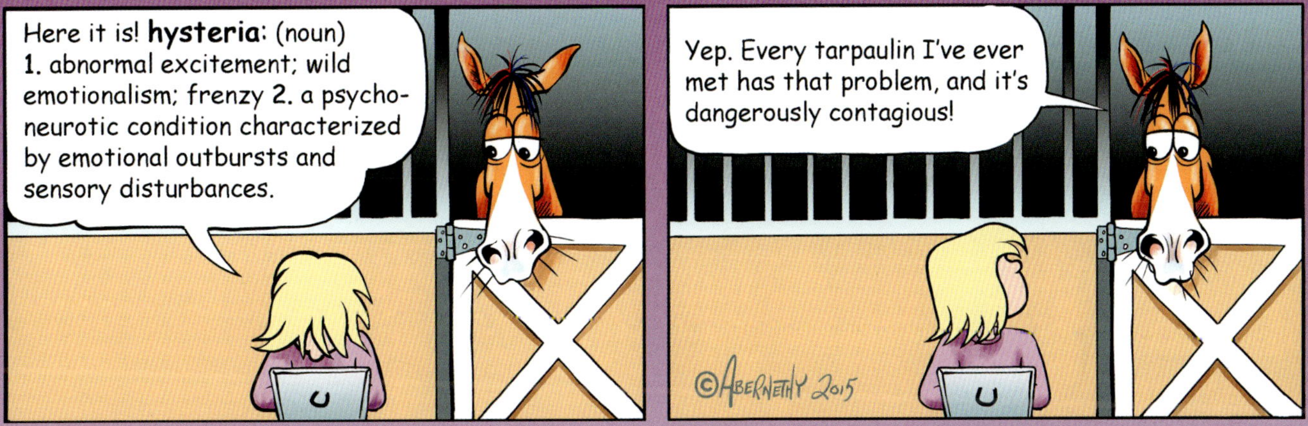
Here it is! **hysteria**: (noun) **1.** abnormal excitement; wild emotionalism; frenzy **2.** a psychoneurotic condition characterized by emotional outbursts and sensory disturbances.
Yep. Every tarpaulin I've ever met has that problem, and it's dangerously contagious!
©ABERNETHY 2015

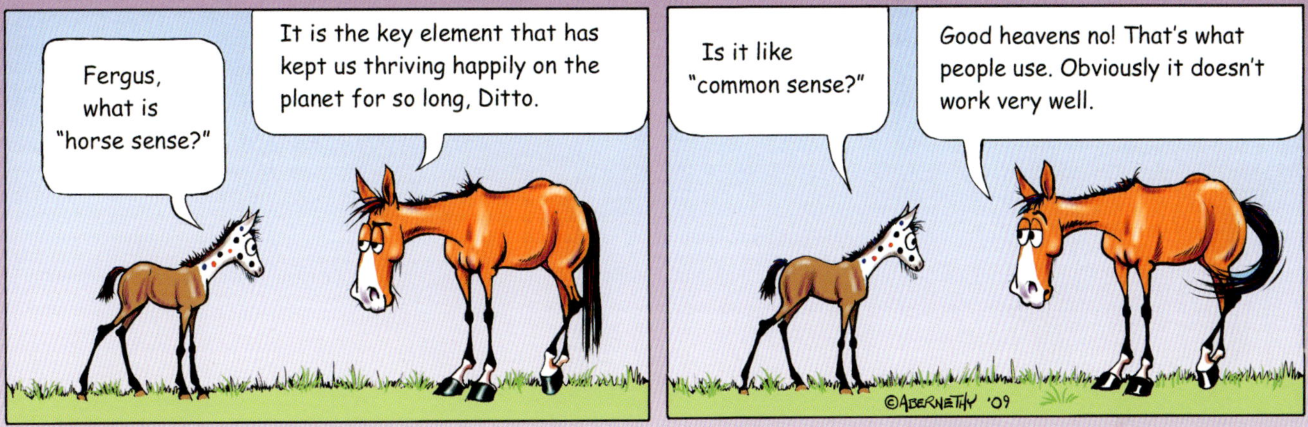
Fergus, what is "horse sense?"
It is the key element that has kept us thriving happily on the planet for so long, Ditto.
Is it like "common sense?"
Good heavens no! That's what people use. Obviously it doesn't work very well.
©ABERNETHY '09

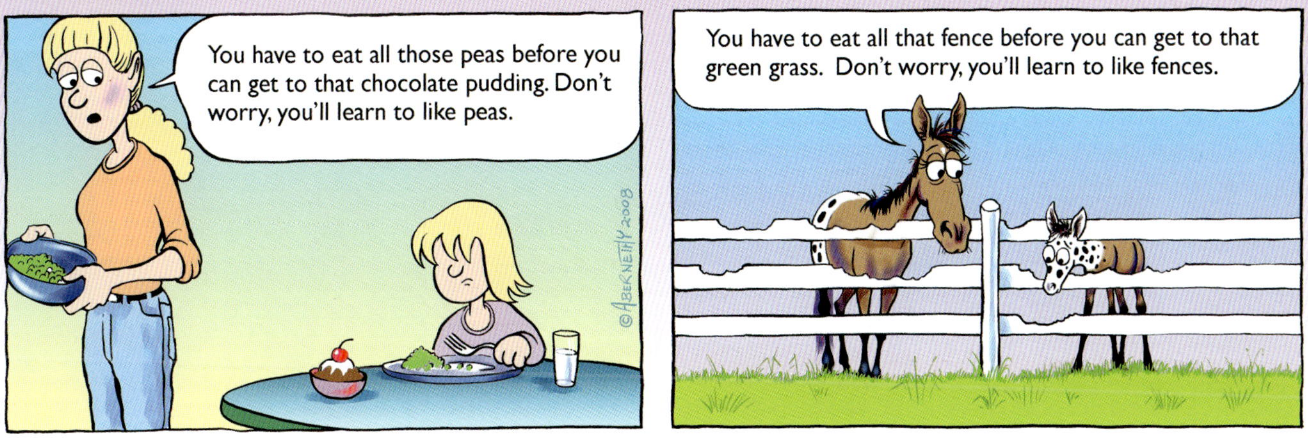
You have to eat all those peas before you can get to that chocolate pudding. Don't worry, you'll learn to like peas.
©ABERNETHY 2008
You have to eat all that fence before you can get to that green grass. Don't worry, you'll learn to like fences.

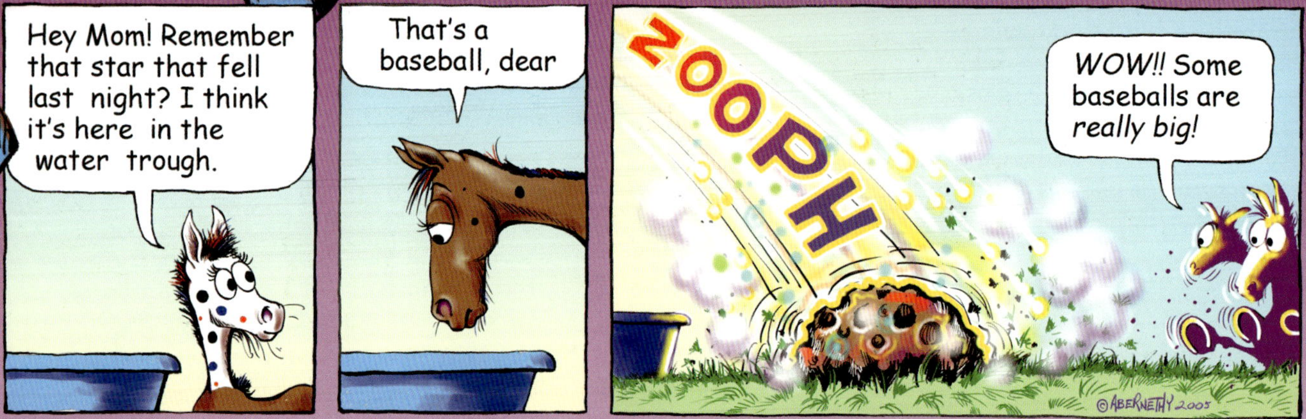
Hey Mom! Remember that star that fell last night? I think it's here in the water trough.
That's a baseball, dear
ZOOPH
WOW!! Some baseballs are really big!
©ABERNETHY 2005

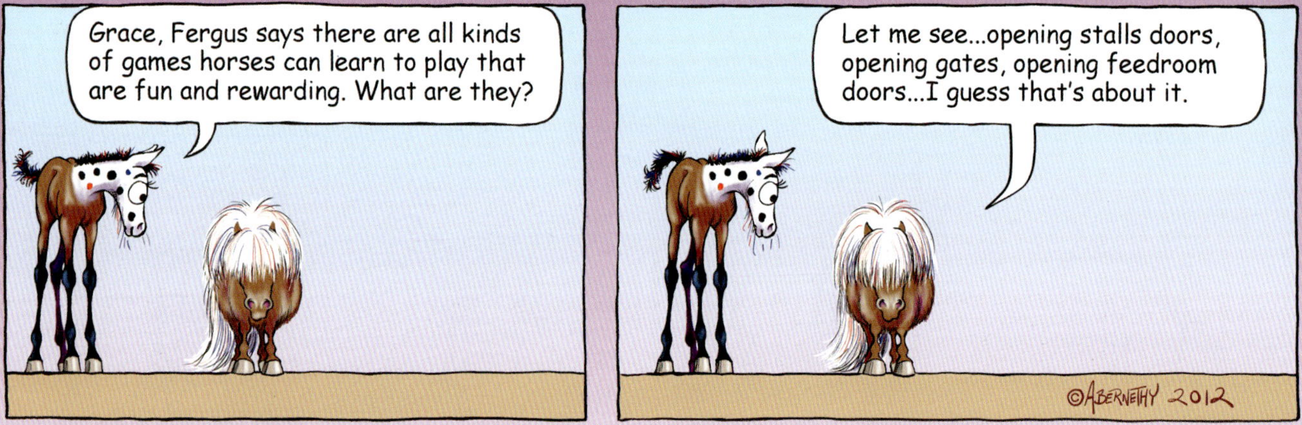
Grace, Fergus says there are all kinds of games horses can learn to play that are fun and rewarding. What are they?
Let me see...opening stalls doors, opening gates, opening feedroom doors...I guess that's about it.
©ABERNETHY 2012

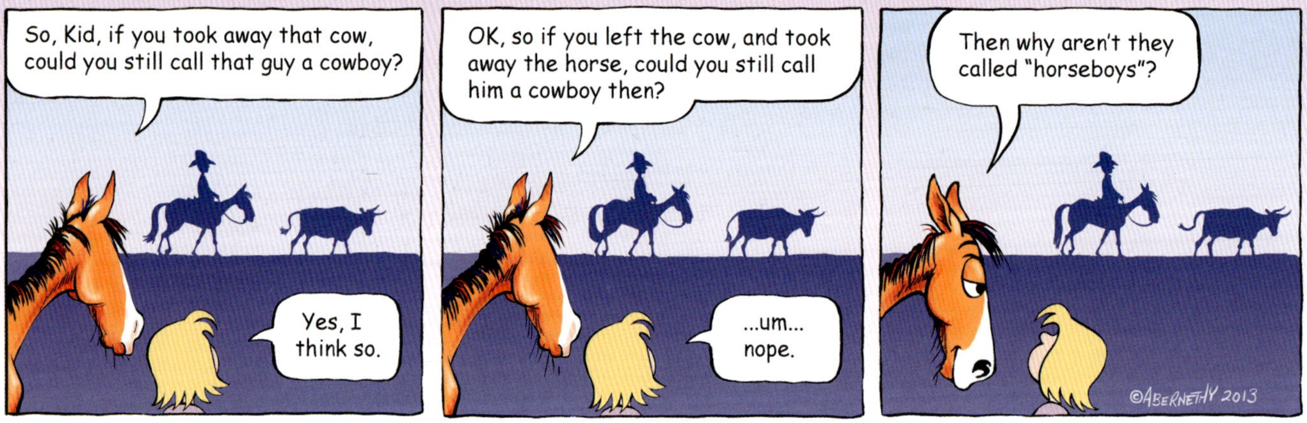
So, Kid, if you took away that cow, could you still call that guy a cowboy?
Yes, I think so.
OK, so if you left the cow, and took away the horse, could you still call him a cowboy then?
...um... nope.
Then why aren't they called "horseboys"?
©ABERNETHY 2013

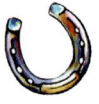

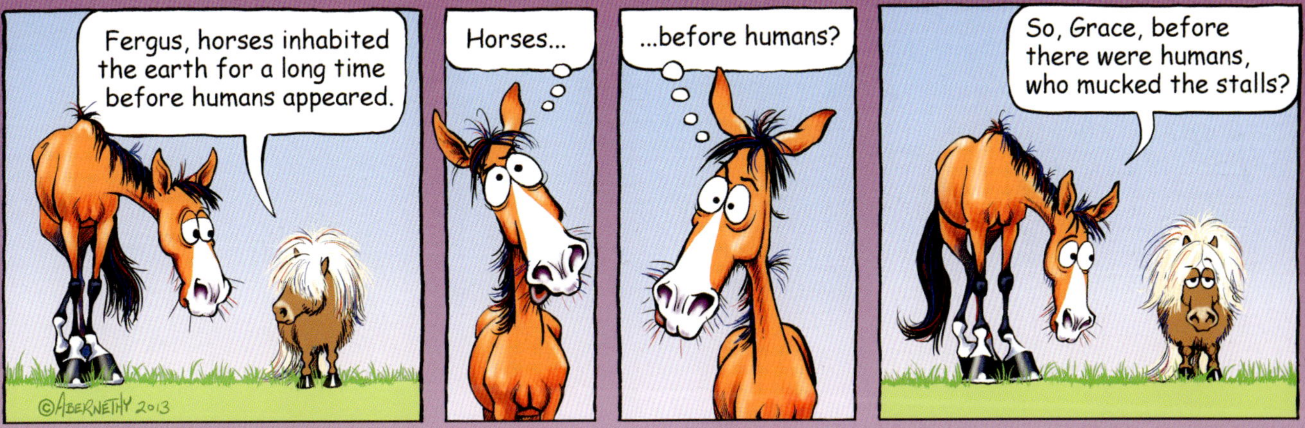
Fergus, horses inhabited the earth for a long time before humans appeared.
Horses...
...before humans?
So, Grace, before there were humans, who mucked the stalls?
©ABERNETHY 2013

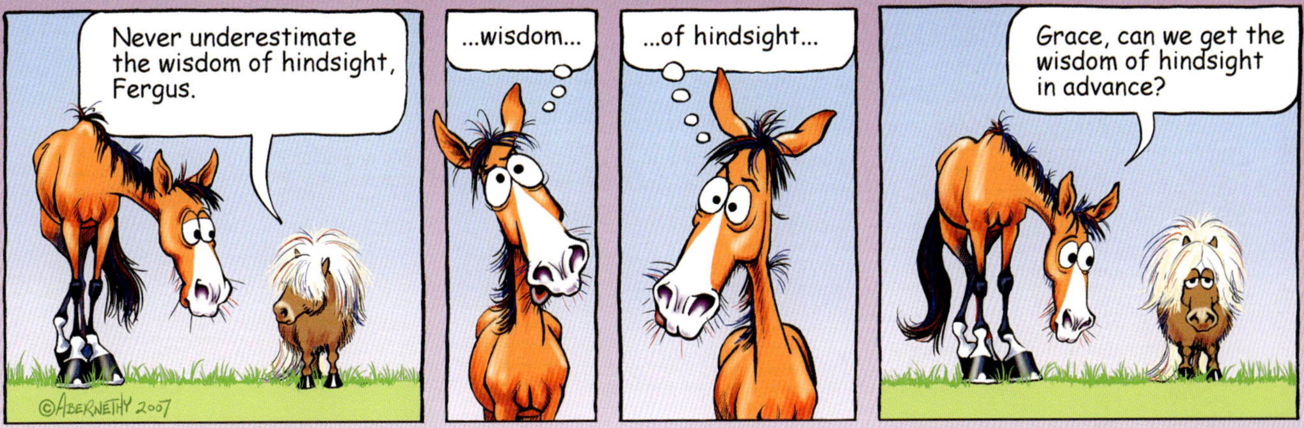
Never underestimate the wisdom of hindsight, Fergus.
...wisdom...
...of hindsight...
Grace, can we get the wisdom of hindsight in advance?
©ABERNETHY 2007

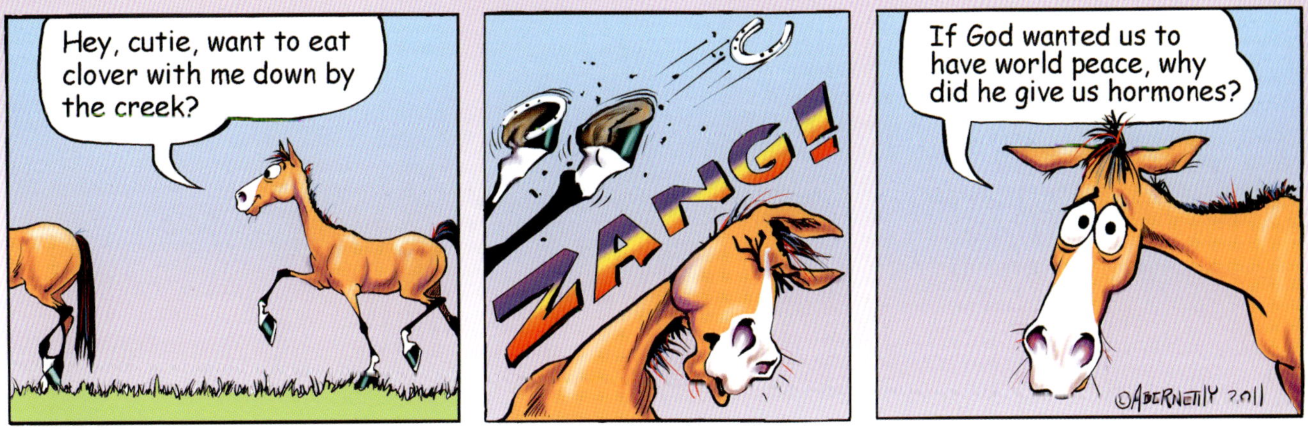
Hey, cutie, want to eat clover with me down by the creek?
ZANG!
If God wanted us to have world peace, why did he give us hormones?
©ABERNETHY 2011

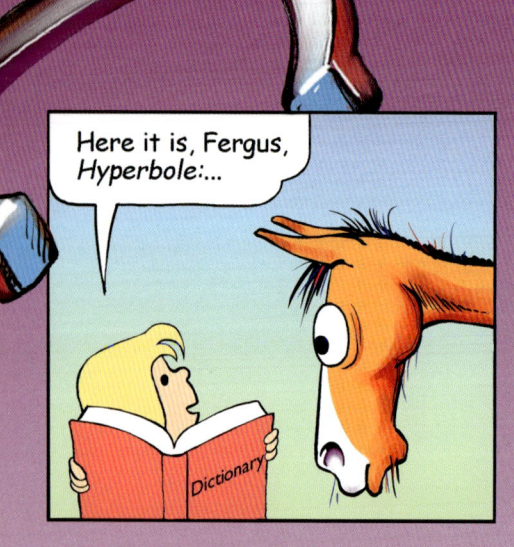

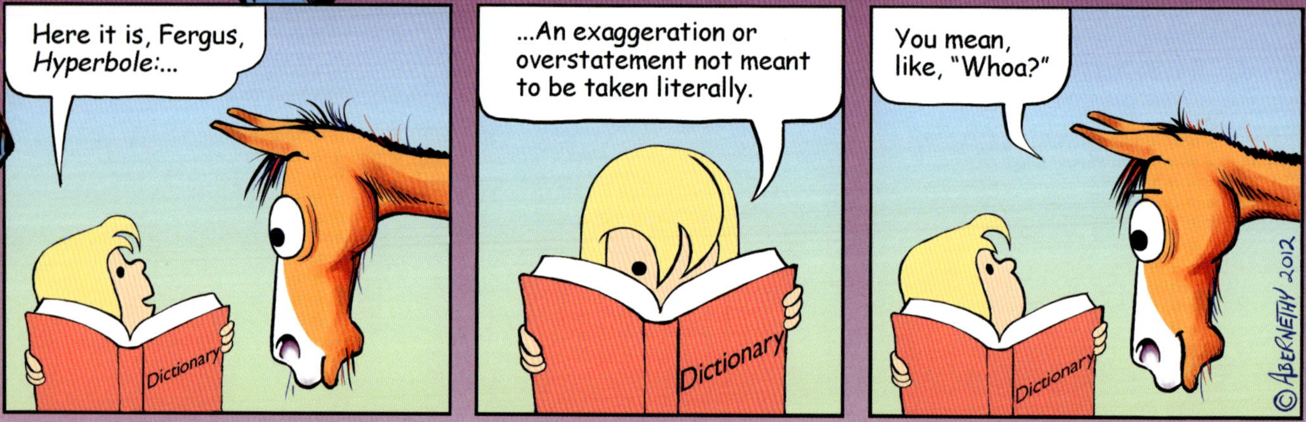
Here it is, Fergus, *Hyperbole*:...
Dictionary
...An exaggeration or overstatement not meant to be taken literally.
Dictionary
You mean, like, "Whoa?"
Dictionary
©ABERNETHY 2012

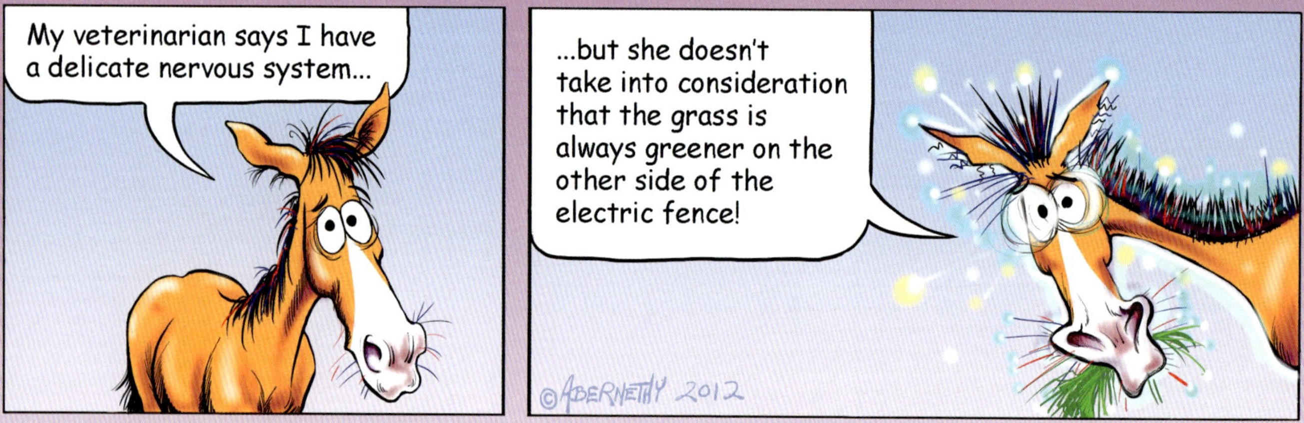
My veterinarian says I have a delicate nervous system...
...but she doesn't take into consideration that the grass is always greener on the other side of the electric fence!
©ABERNETHY 2012

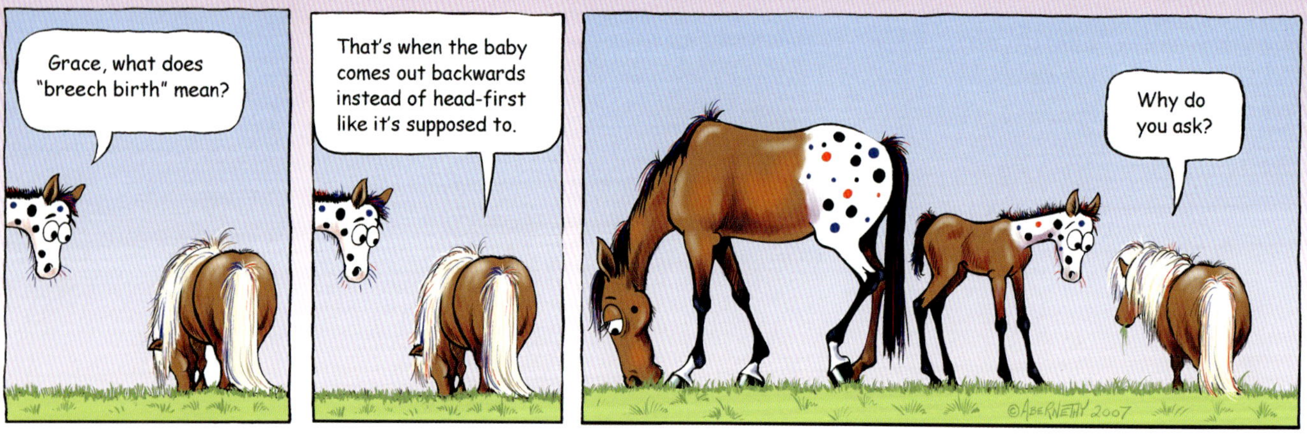
Grace, what does "breech birth" mean?
That's when the baby comes out backwards instead of head-first like it's supposed to.
Why do you ask?
©ABERNETHY 2007

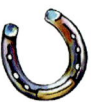

Barn
Smarts

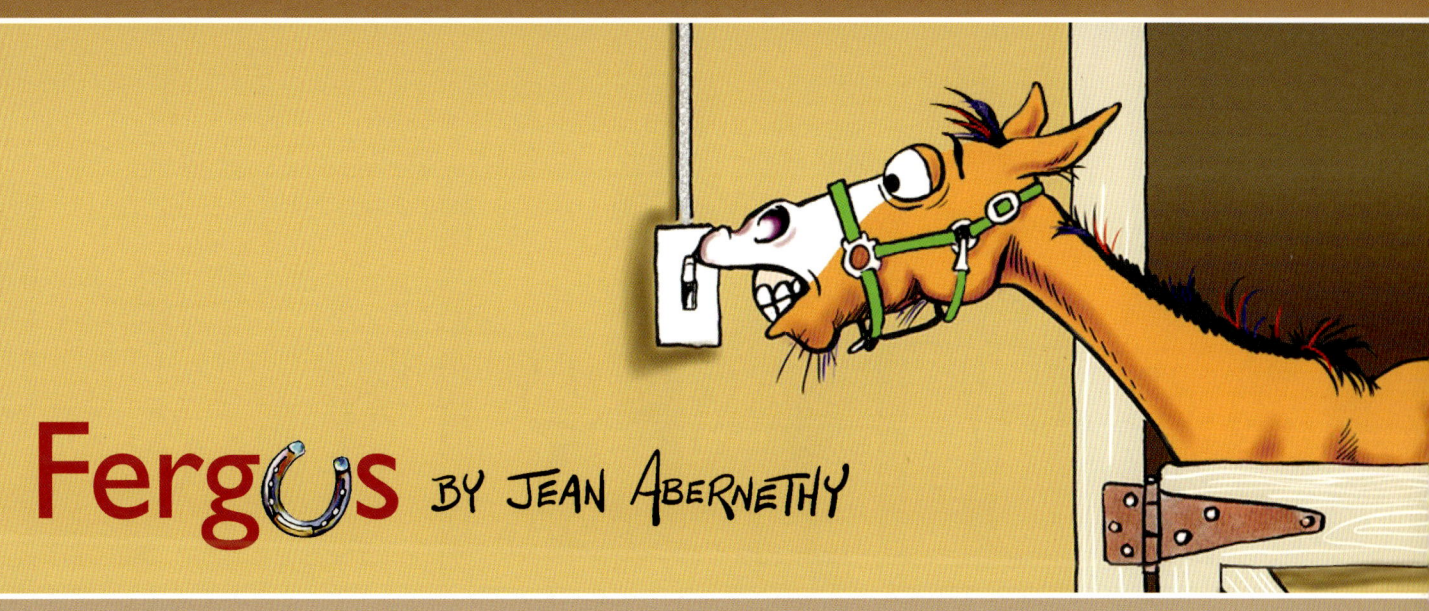

# Fergus BY JEAN ABERNETHY

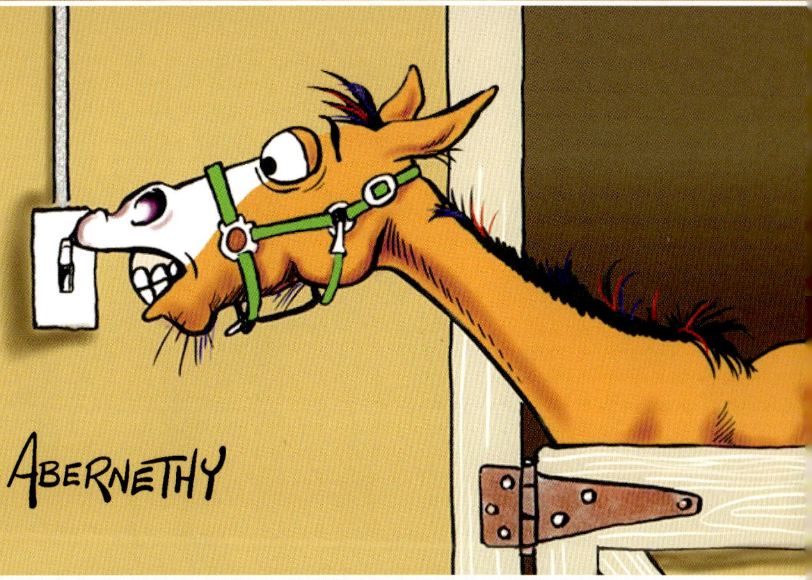

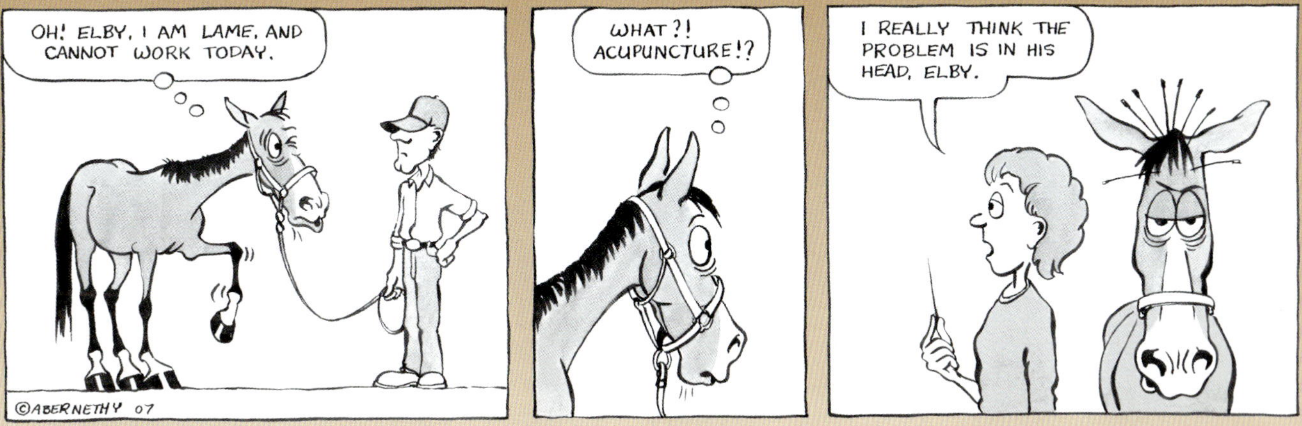
OH! ELBY, I AM LAME, AND CANNOT WORK TODAY.
©ABERNETHY 07
WHAT?! ACUPUNCTURE!?
I REALLY THINK THE PROBLEM IS IN HIS HEAD, ELBY.

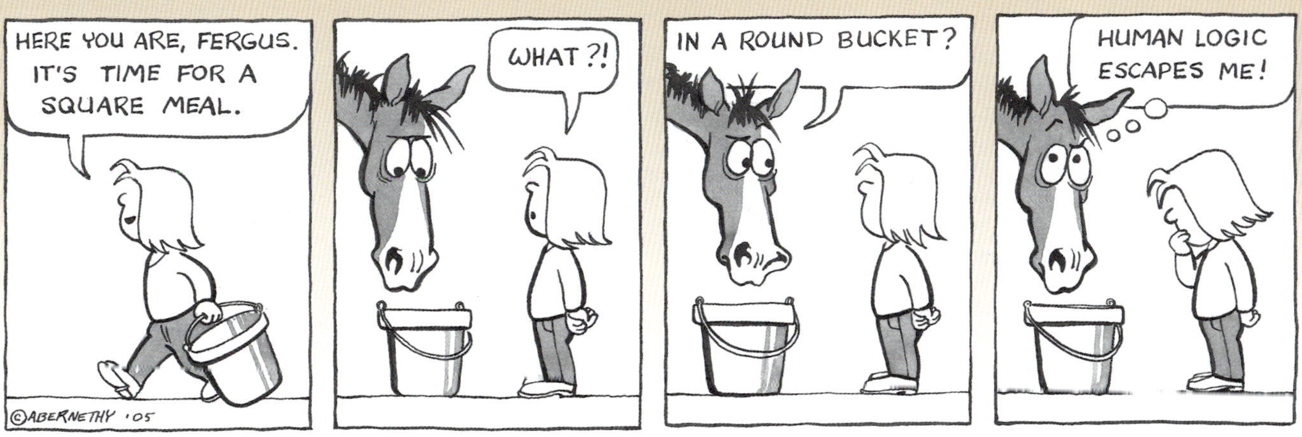
HERE YOU ARE, FERGUS. IT'S TIME FOR A SQUARE MEAL.
©ABERNETHY '05
WHAT?!
IN A ROUND BUCKET?
HUMAN LOGIC ESCAPES ME!

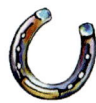

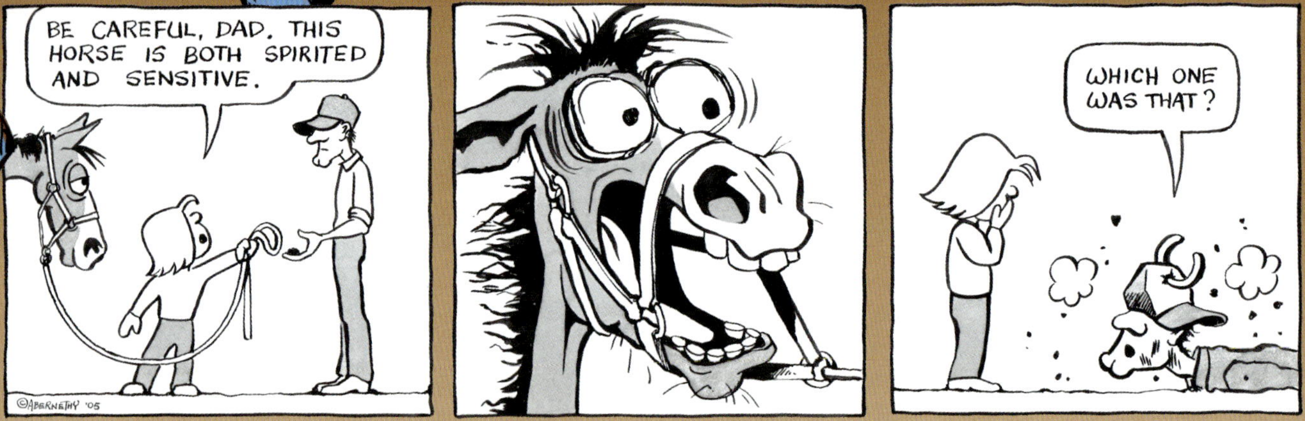
BE CAREFUL, DAD. THIS HORSE IS BOTH SPIRITED AND SENSITIVE.
©ABERNETHY '05
WHICH ONE WAS THAT?

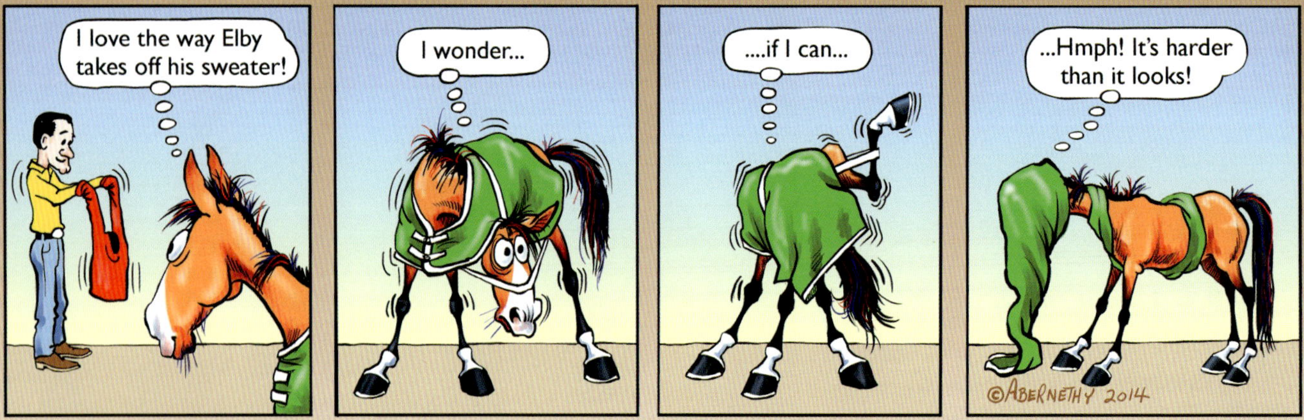
I love the way Elby takes off his sweater!
I wonder...
....if I can...
...Hmph! It's harder than it looks!
©ABERNETHY 2014

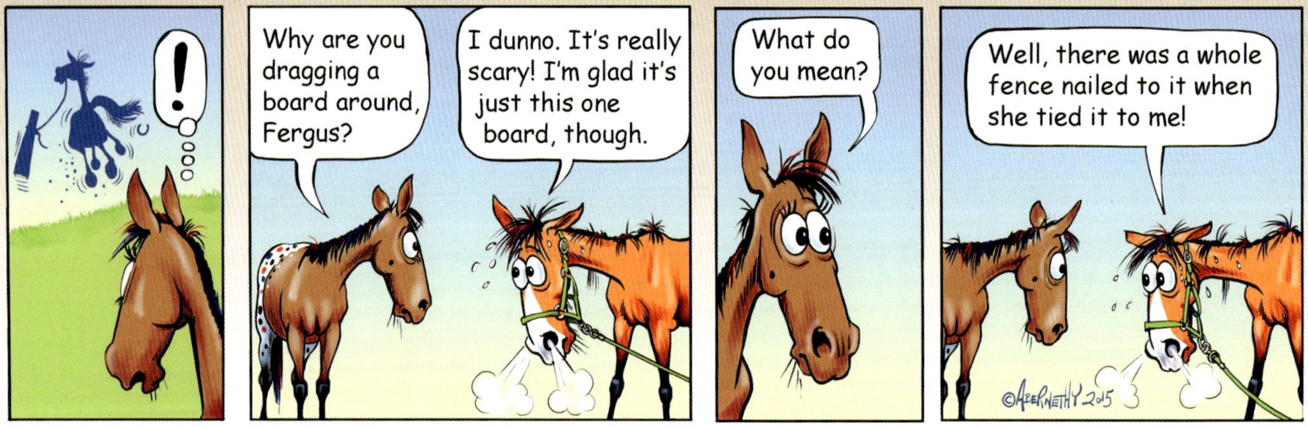
!
Why are you dragging a board around, Fergus?
I dunno. It's really scary! I'm glad it's just this one board, though.
What do you mean?
Well, there was a whole fence nailed to it when she tied it to me!
©ABERNETHY 2015

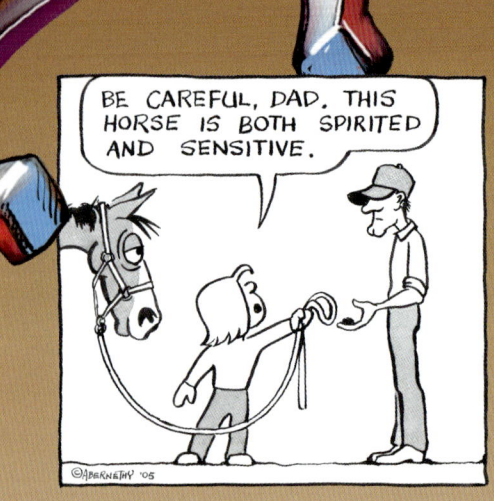

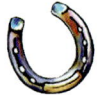

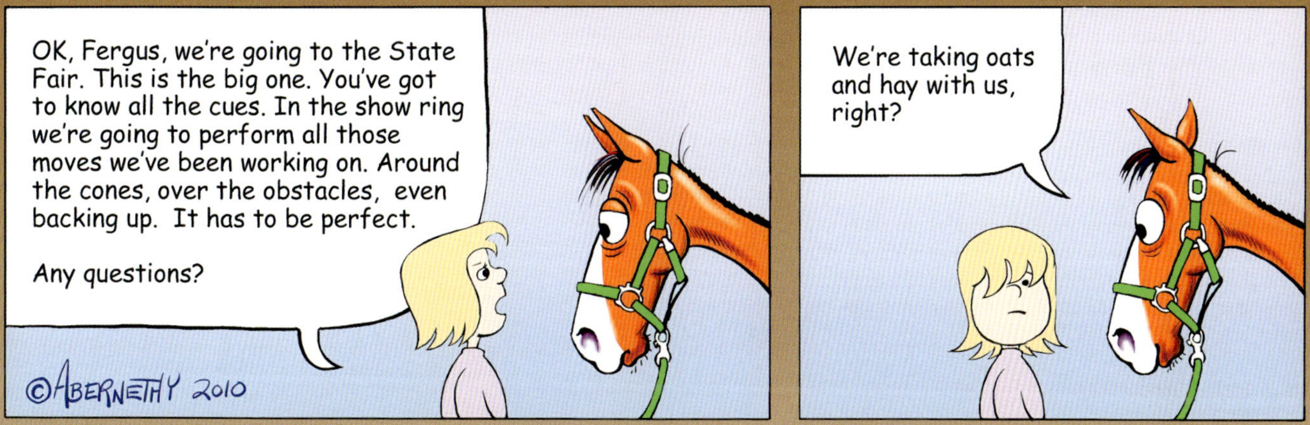
OK, Fergus, we're going to the State Fair. This is the big one. You've got to know all the cues. In the show ring we're going to perform all those moves we've been working on. Around the cones, over the obstacles, even backing up. It has to be perfect.
Any questions?
©ABERNETHY 2010
We're taking oats and hay with us, right?

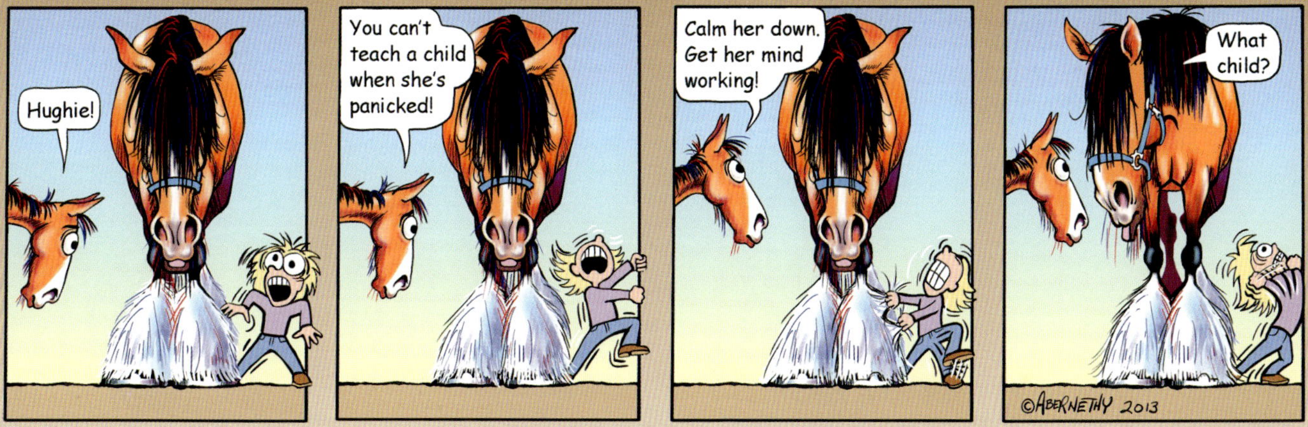
Hughie!
You can't teach a child when she's panicked!
Calm her down. Get her mind working!
What child?
©ABERNETHY 2013

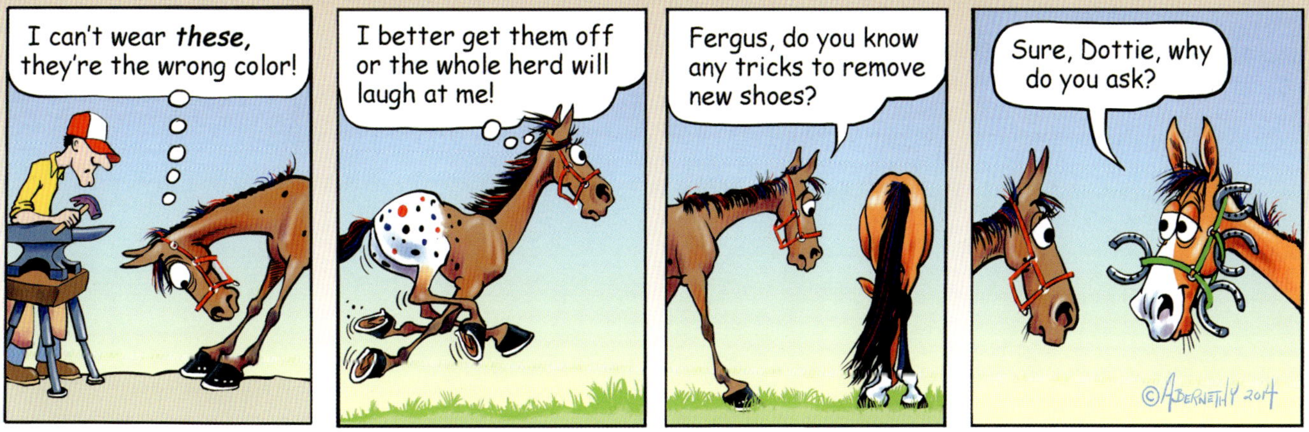
I can't wear *these,* they're the wrong color!
I better get them off or the whole herd will laugh at me!
Fergus, do you know any tricks to remove new shoes?
Sure, Dottie, why do you ask?
©ABERNETHY 2014

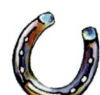

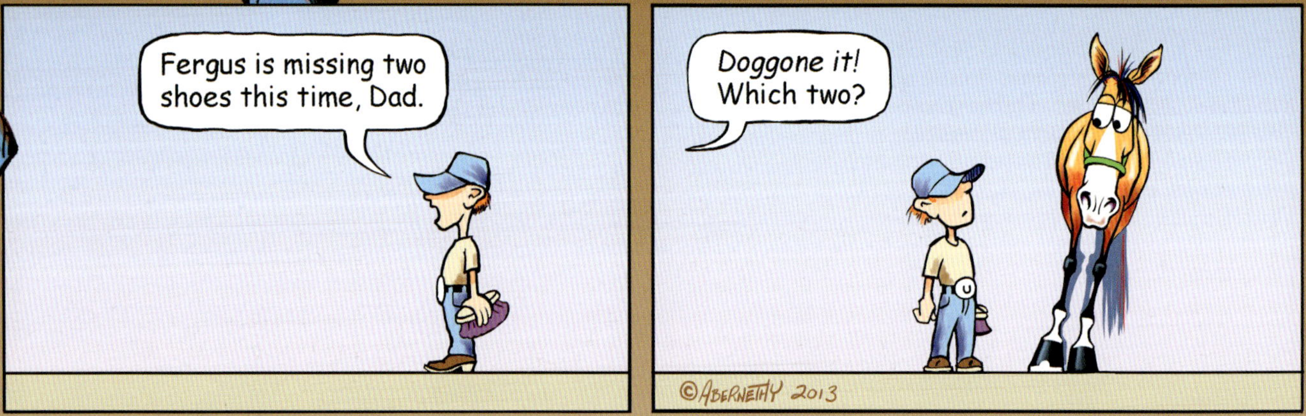
Fergus is missing two shoes this time, Dad.
Doggone it! Which two?
©ABERNETHY 2013

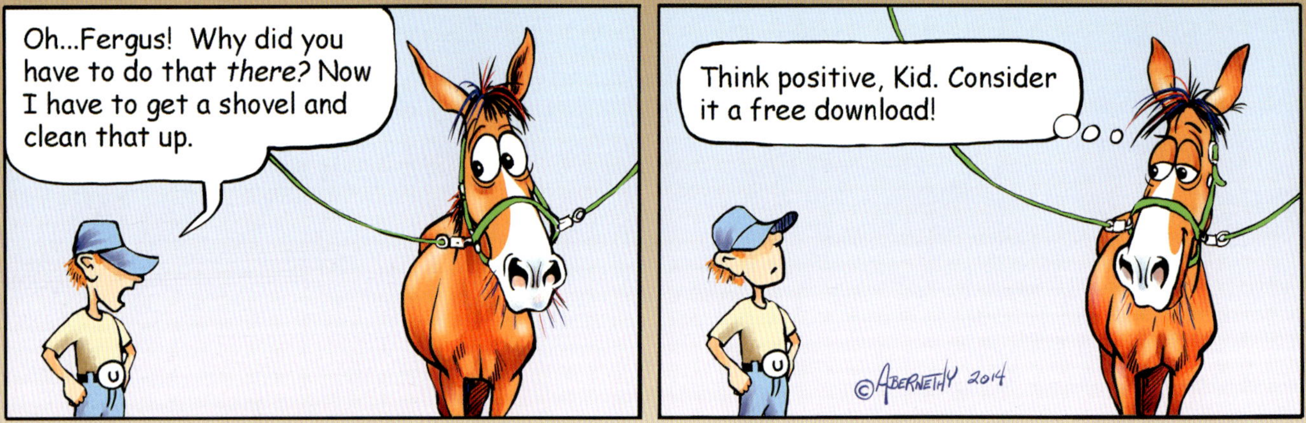
Oh...Fergus! Why did you have to do that *there*? Now I have to get a shovel and clean that up.
Think positive, Kid. Consider it a free download!
©ABERNETHY 2014

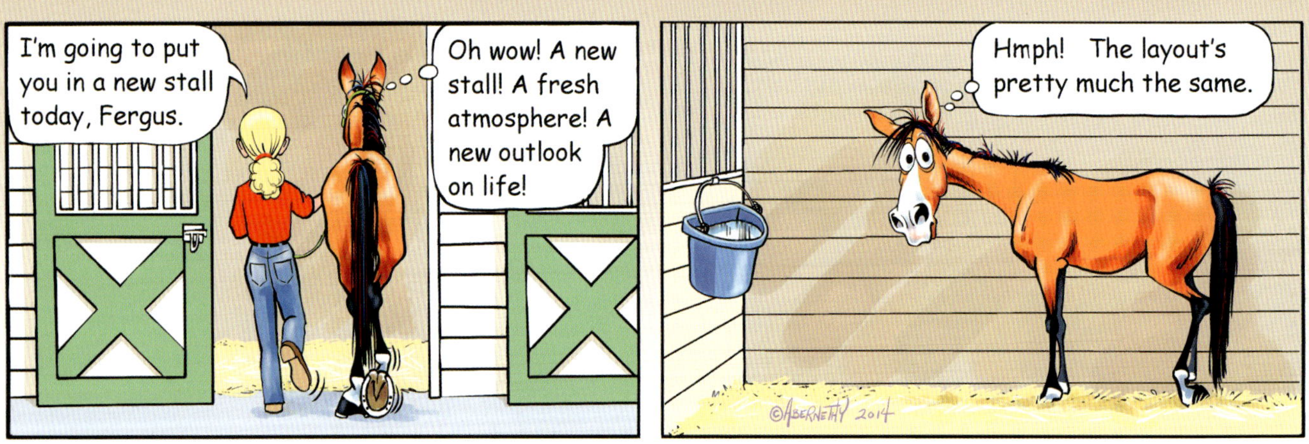
I'm going to put you in a new stall today, Fergus.
Oh wow! A new stall! A fresh atmosphere! A new outlook on life!
Hmph! The layout's pretty much the same.
©ABERNETHY 2014

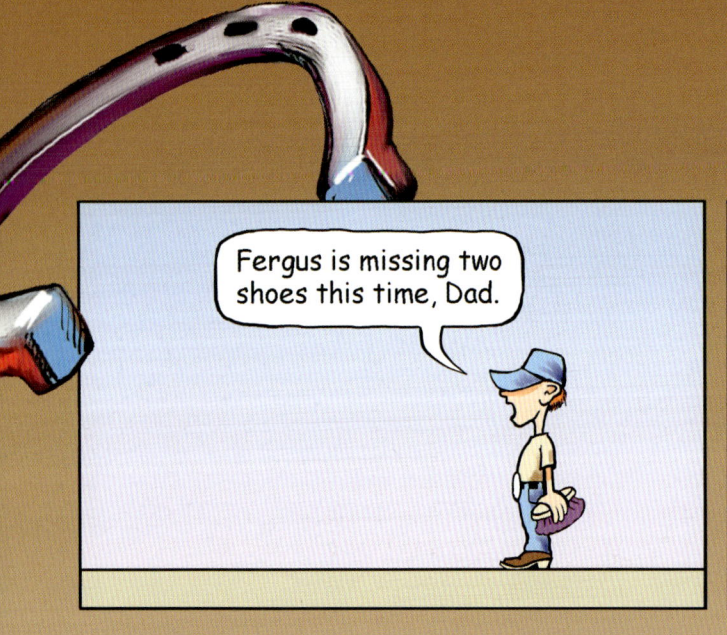

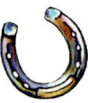

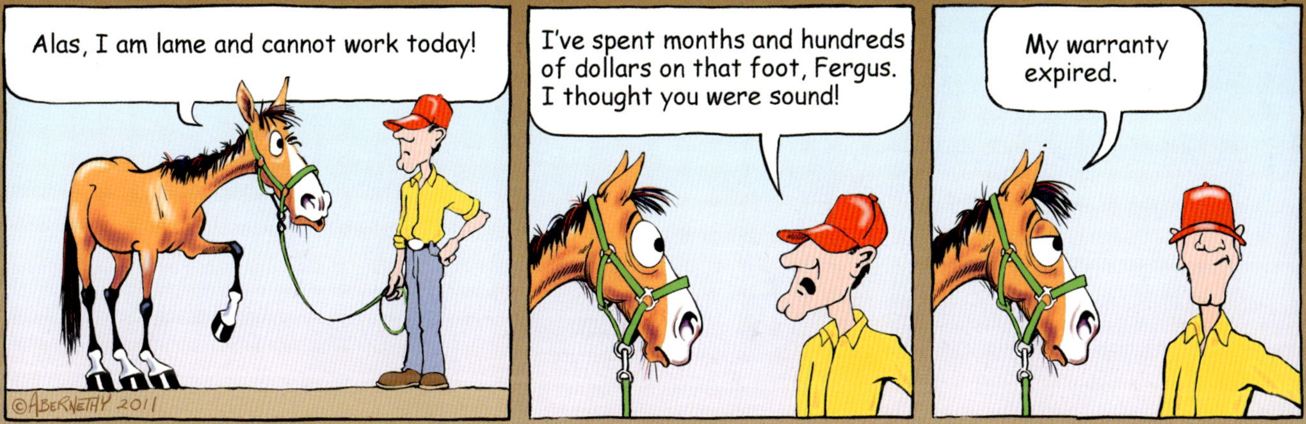
Alas, I am lame and cannot work today!
I've spent months and hundreds of dollars on that foot, Fergus. I thought you were sound!
My warranty expired.
©ABERNETHY 2011

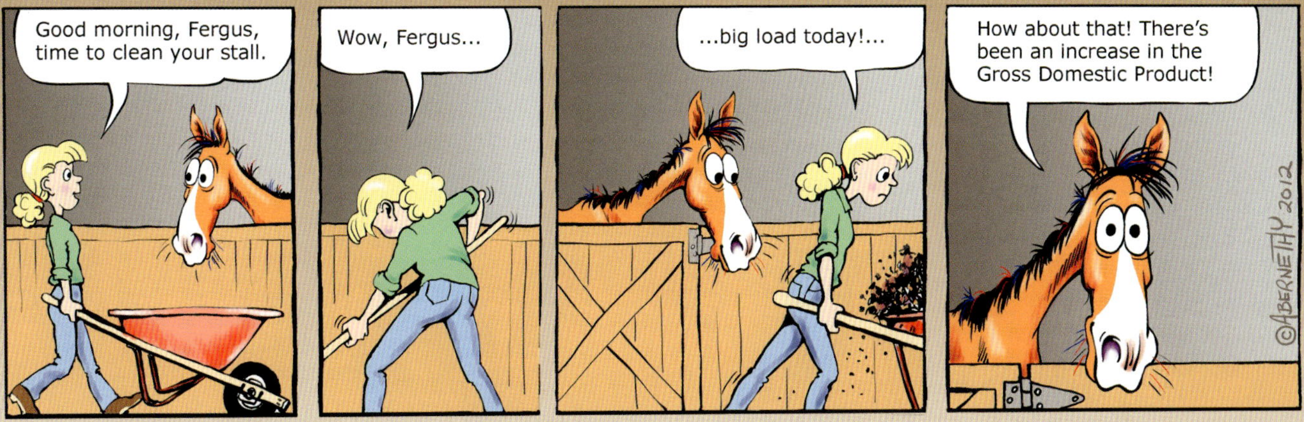
Good morning, Fergus, time to clean your stall.
Wow, Fergus...
...big load today!...
How about that! There's been an increase in the Gross Domestic Product!
©ABERNETHY 2012

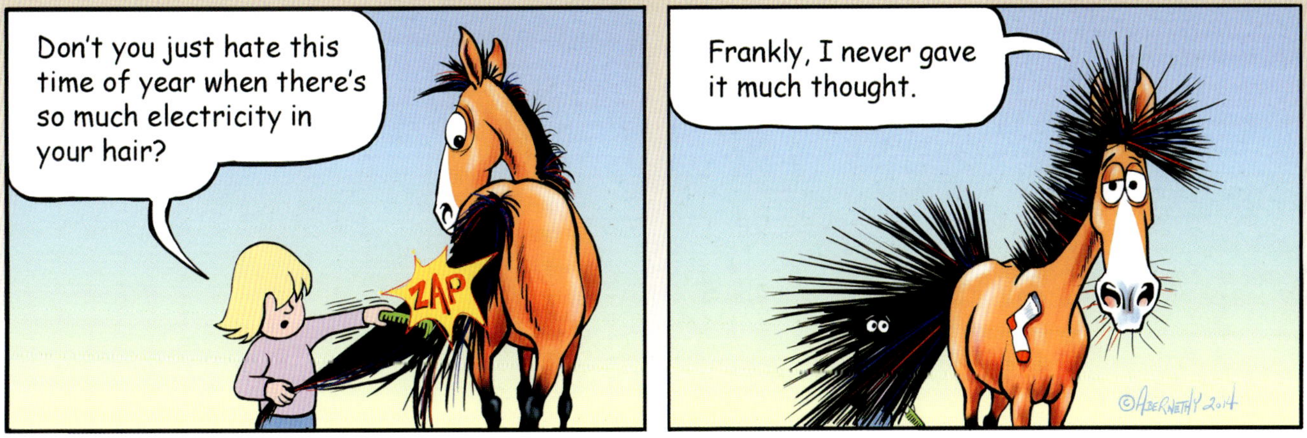
Don't you just hate this time of year when there's so much electricity in your hair?
ZAP
Frankly, I never gave it much thought.
©ABERNETHY 2014

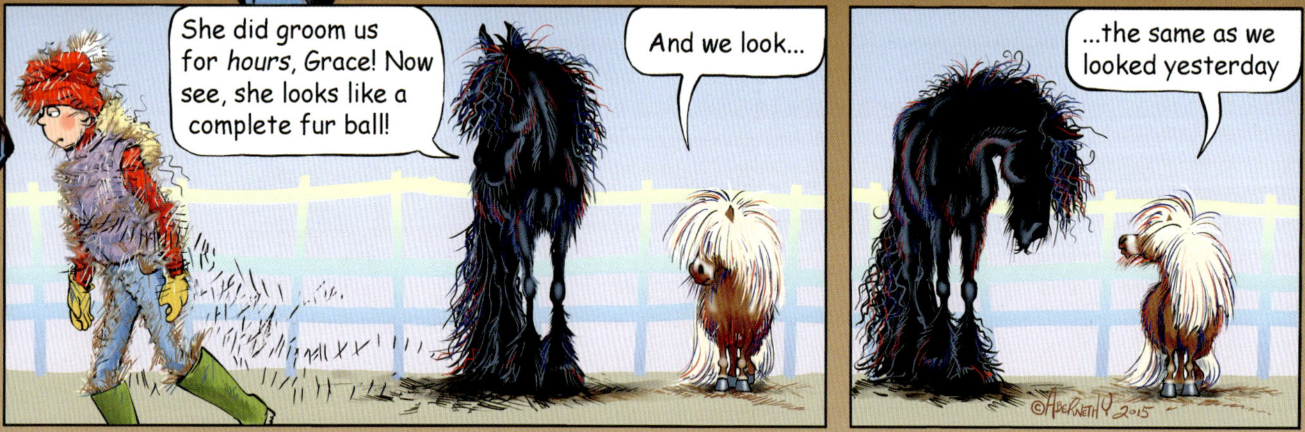
She did groom us for *hours*, Grace! Now see, she looks like a complete fur ball!
And we look...
...the same as we looked yesterday
©ABERNETHY 2015

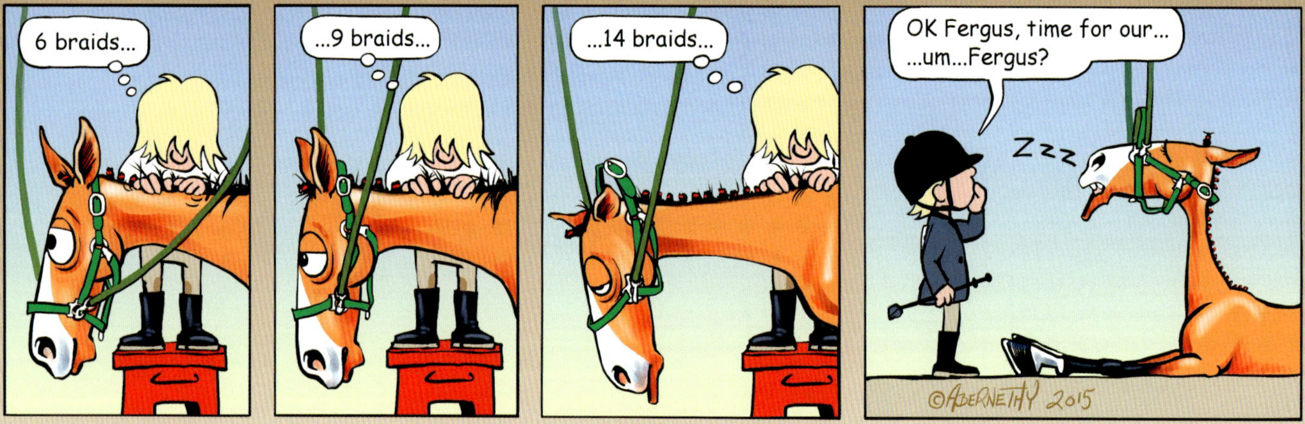
6 braids...
...9 braids...
...14 braids...
OK Fergus, time for our... ...um...Fergus?
ZZZ
©ABERNETHY 2015

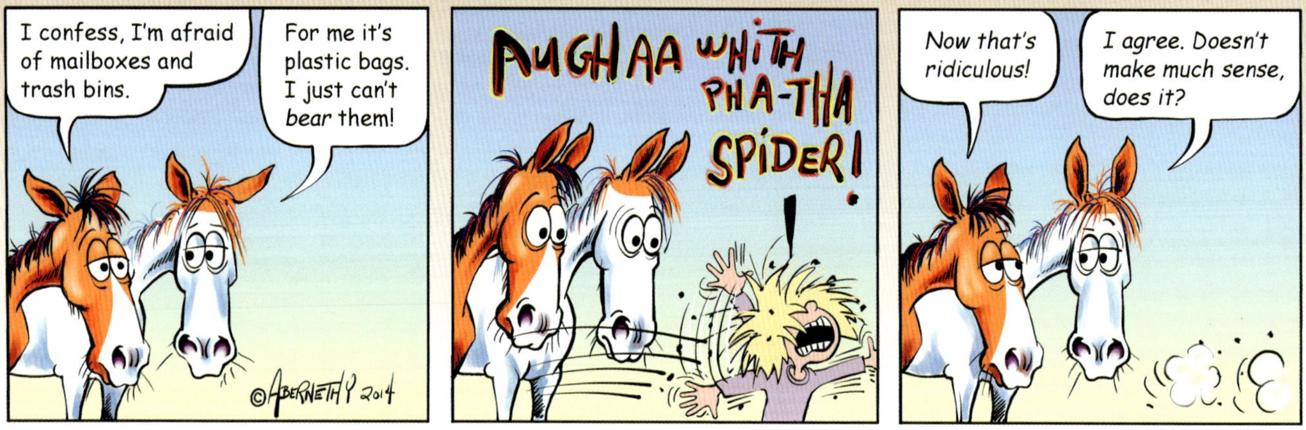
I confess, I'm afraid of mailboxes and trash bins.
For me it's plastic bags. I just can't *bear* them!
©ABERNETHY 2014
AUGHAA WHITH PHA-THA SPIDER!
!
Now that's ridiculous!
I agree. Doesn't make much sense, does it?

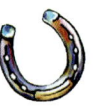

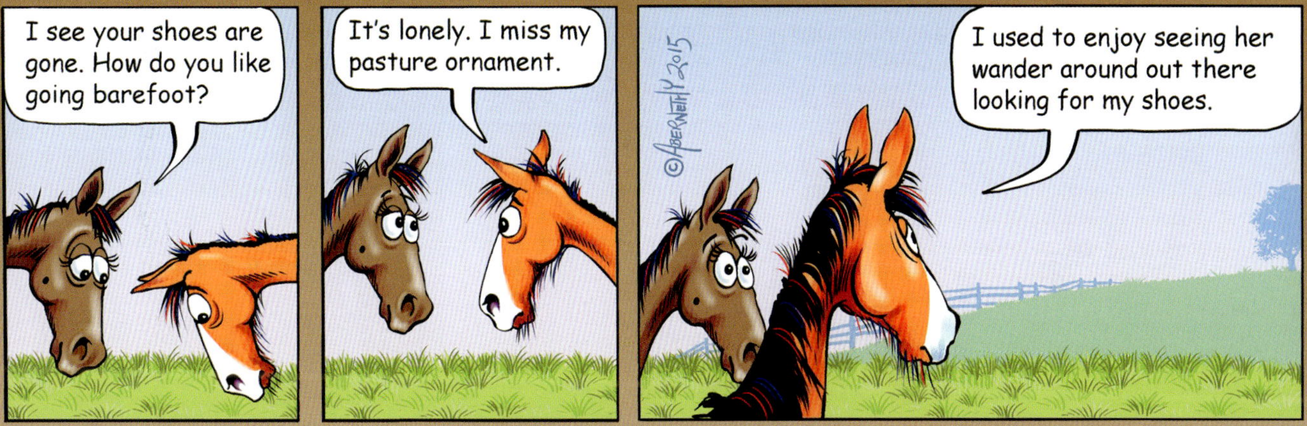
I see your shoes are gone. How do you like going barefoot?
It's lonely. I miss my pasture ornament.
I used to enjoy seeing her wander around out there looking for my shoes.

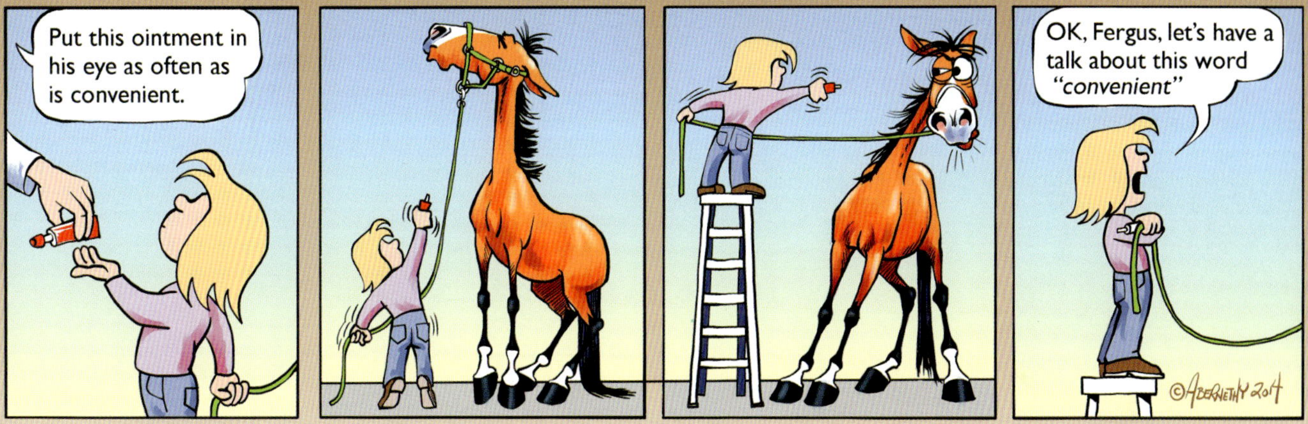
Put this ointment in his eye as often as is convenient.
OK, Fergus, let's have a talk about this word *"convenient"*

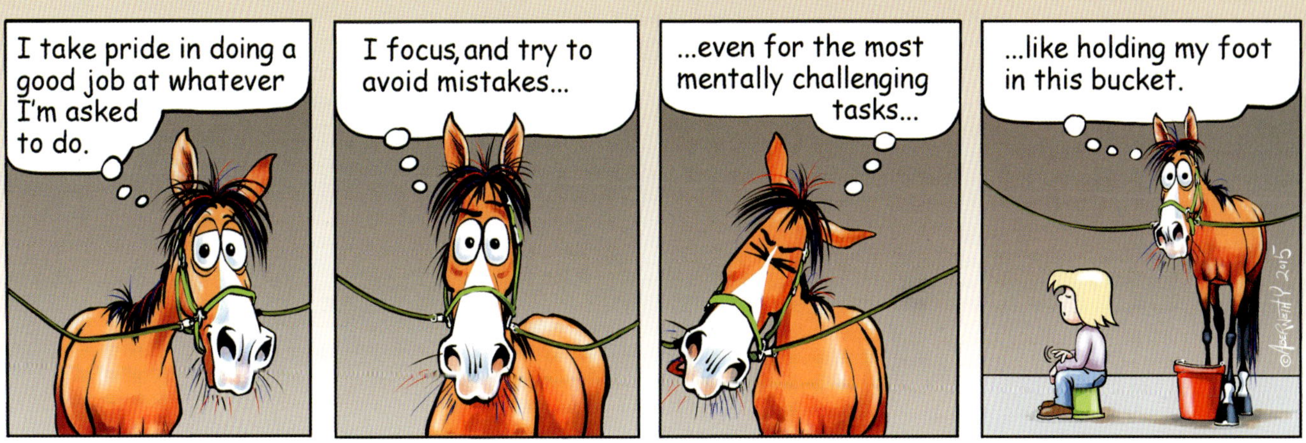
I take pride in doing a good job at whatever I'm asked to do.
I focus, and try to avoid mistakes...
...even for the most mentally challenging tasks...
...like holding my foot in this bucket.

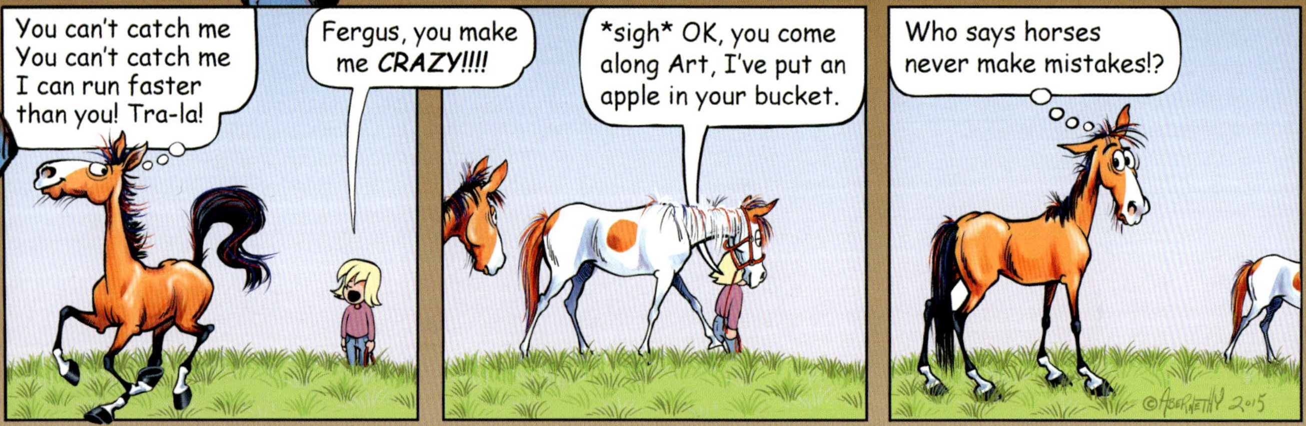
You can't catch me
You can't catch me
I can run faster
than you! Tra-la!
Fergus, you make me *CRAZY!!!!*
*sigh* OK, you come along Art, I've put an apple in your bucket.
Who says horses never make mistakes!?
©ABERNETHY 2015

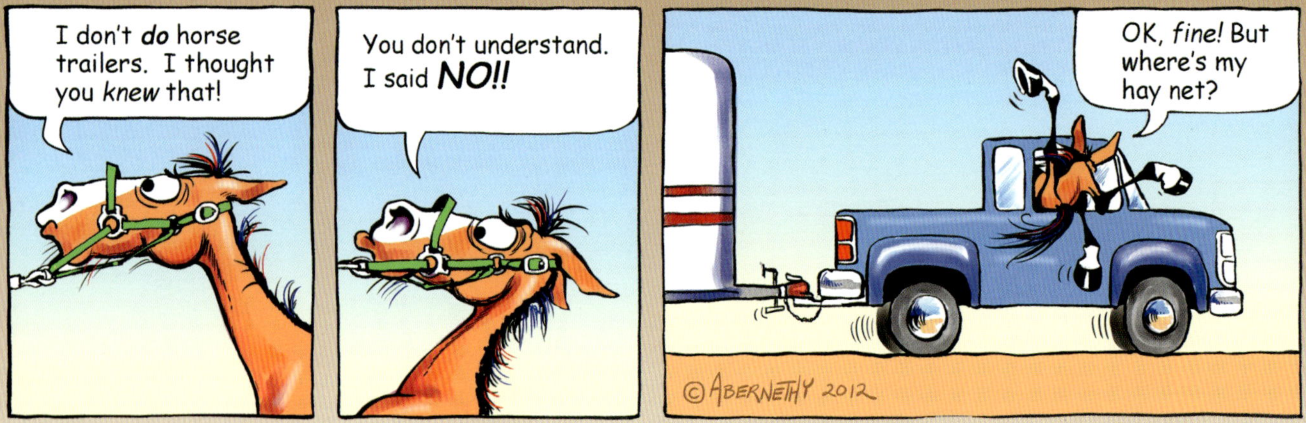
I don't **do** horse trailers. I thought you *knew* that!
You don't understand. I said **NO!!**
OK, *fine!* But where's my hay net?
©ABERNETHY 2012

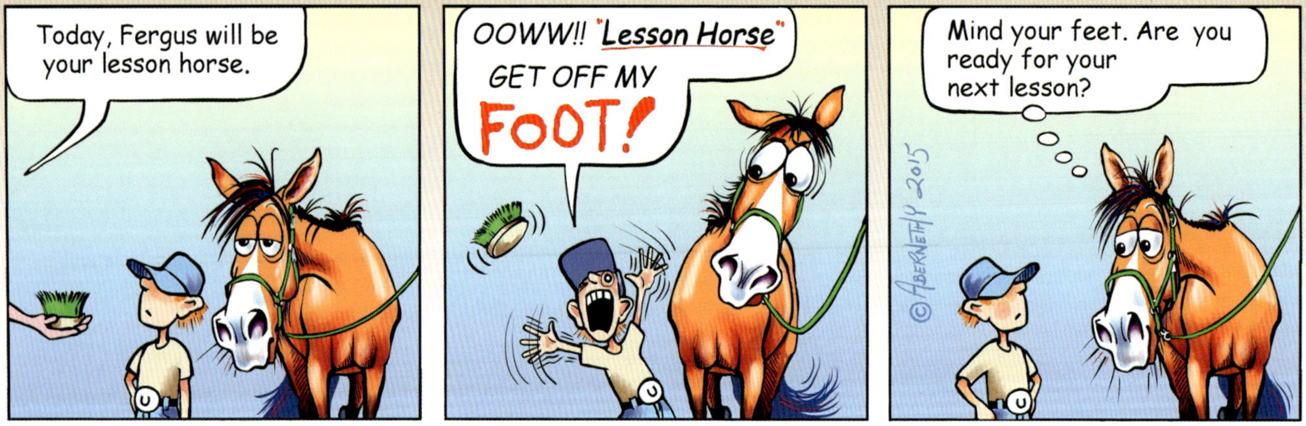
Today, Fergus will be your lesson horse.
OOWW!! "Lesson Horse"
GET OFF MY
FOOT!
Mind your feet. Are you ready for your next lesson?
©ABERNETHY 2015

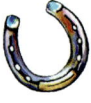

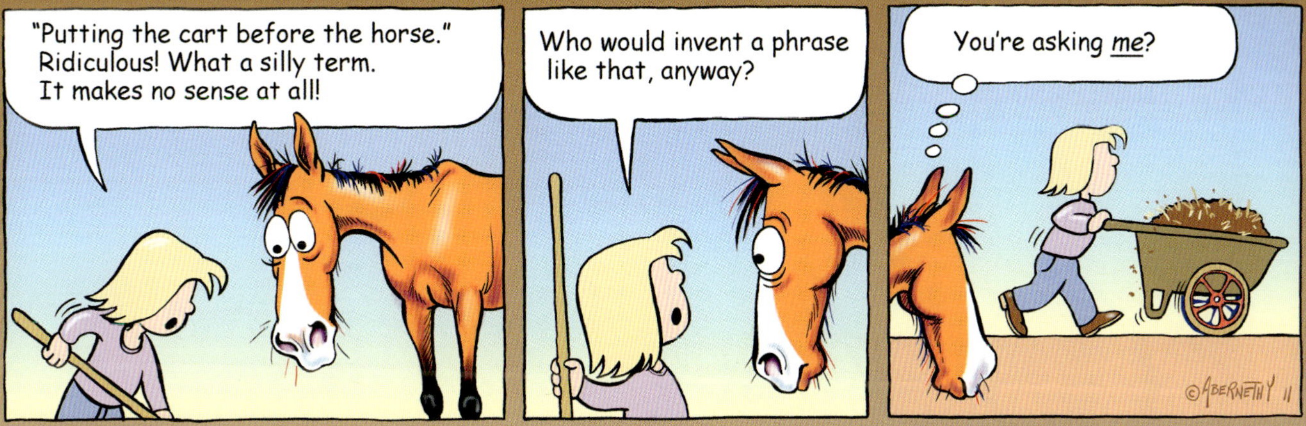
"Putting the cart before the horse." Ridiculous! What a silly term. It makes no sense at all!
Who would invent a phrase like that, anyway?
You're asking me?
©ABERNETHY 11

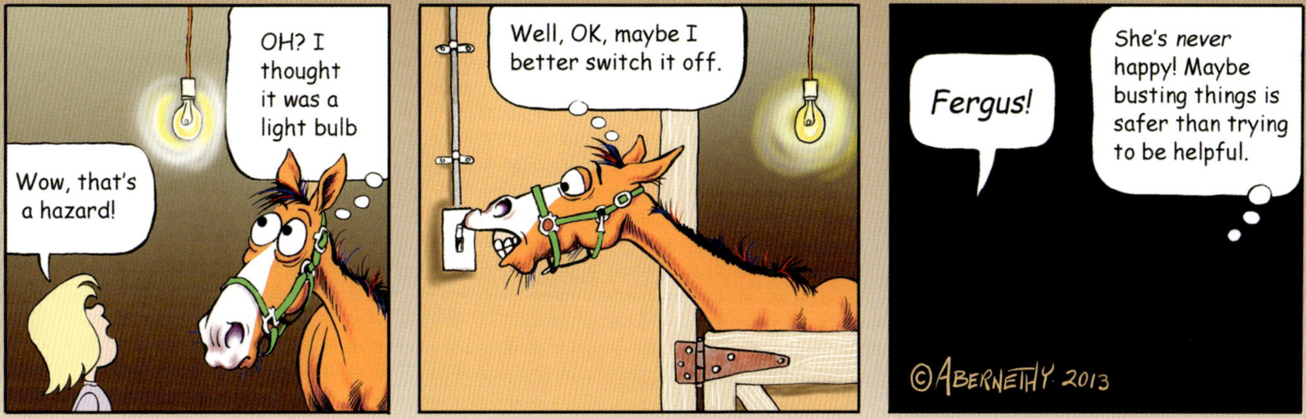
Wow, that's a hazard!
OH? I thought it was a light bulb
Well, OK, maybe I better switch it off.
Fergus!
She's never happy! Maybe busting things is safer than trying to be helpful.
©ABERNETHY 2013

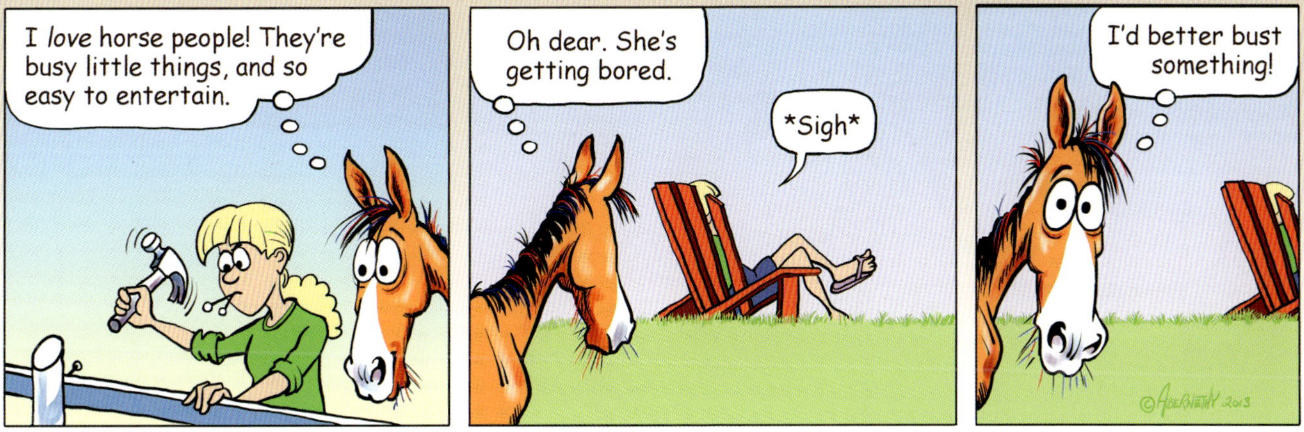
I love horse people! They're busy little things, and so easy to entertain.
Oh dear. She's getting bored.
*Sigh*
I'd better bust something!
©ABERNETHY 2013

I repeat: *I DON'T DO HORSE TRAILERS!!*

Duct tape, huh?

OK, he gets points for creativity, but he forgot my hay net again!

©ABERNETHY 2012

# Sweet Companions

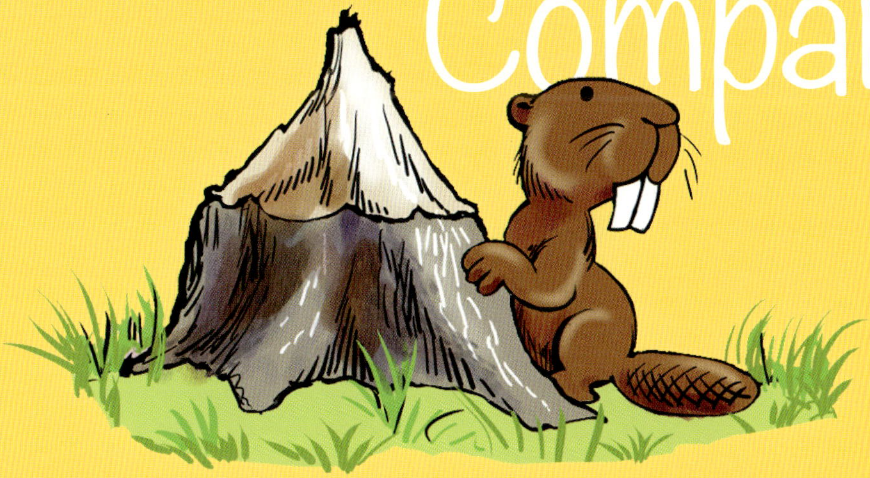

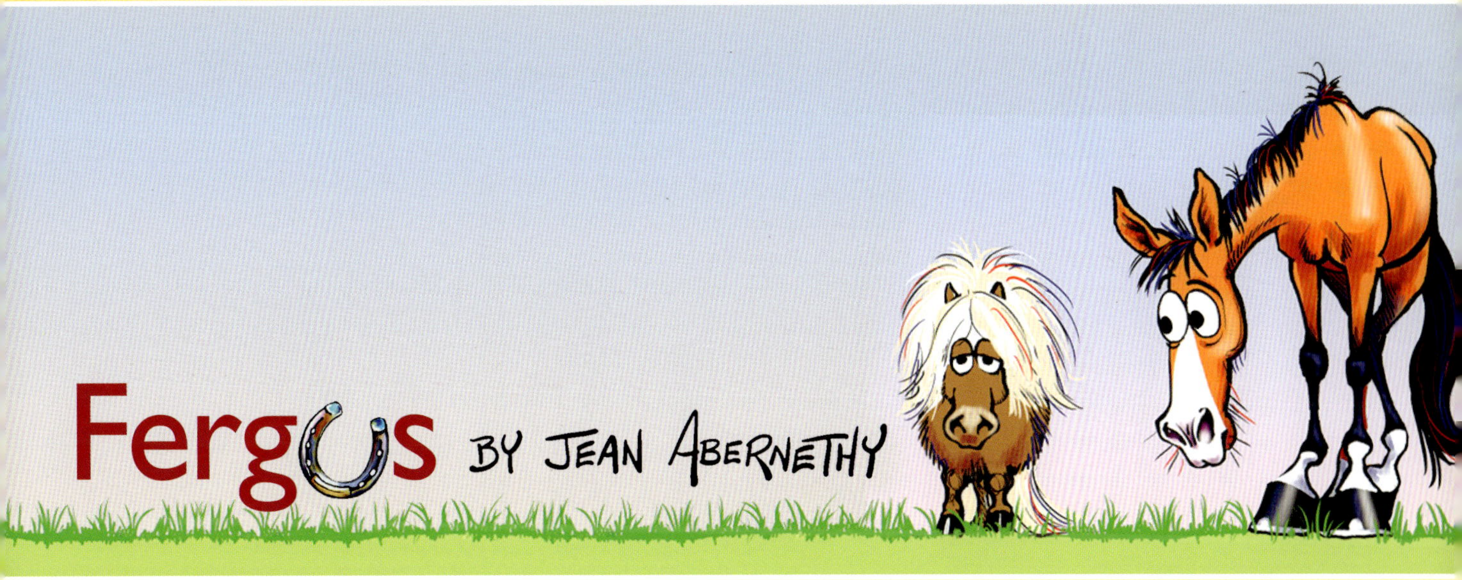
Fergus
BY JEAN ABERNETHY

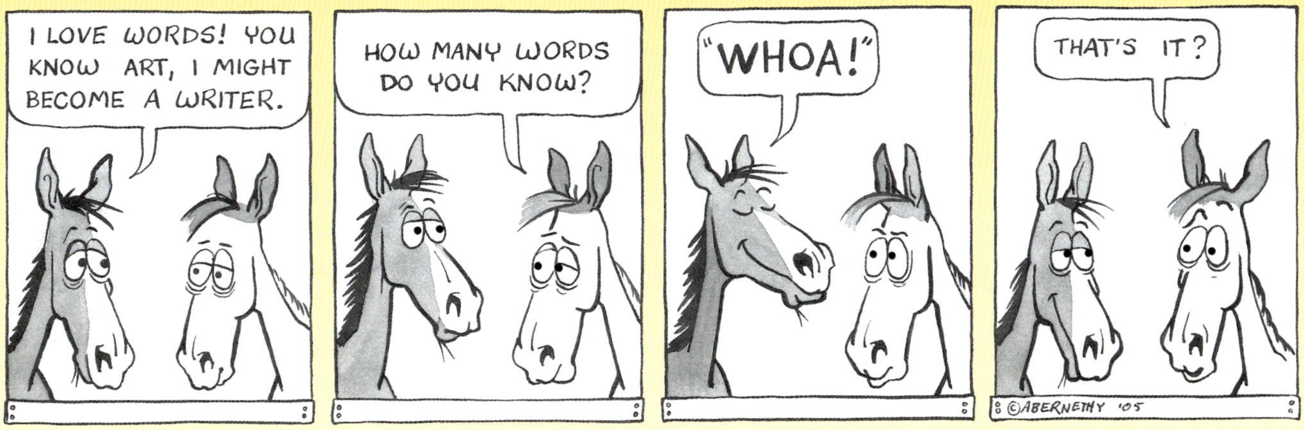
I LOVE WORDS! YOU KNOW ART, I MIGHT BECOME A WRITER.
HOW MANY WORDS DO YOU KNOW?
"WHOA!"
THAT'S IT?
©ABERNETHY '05

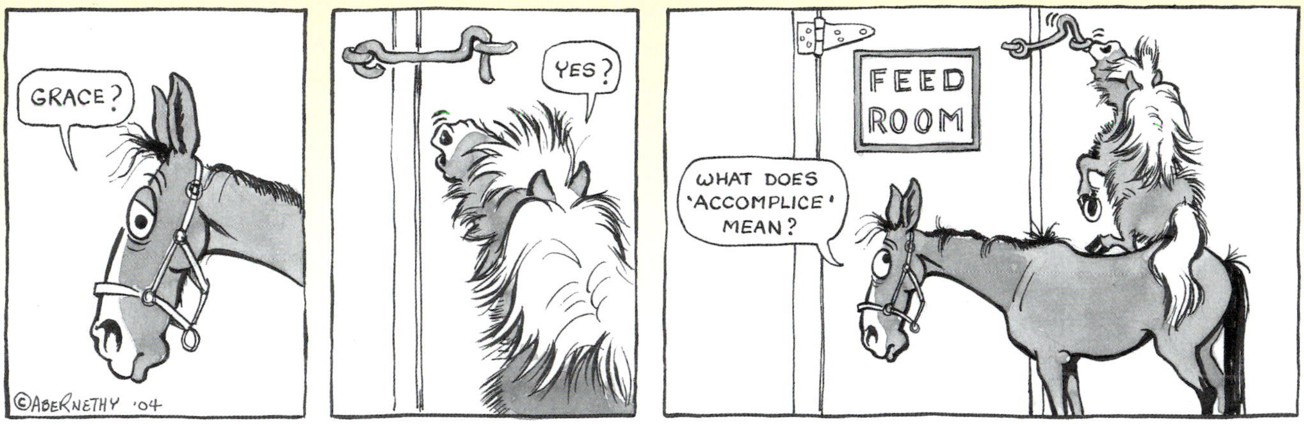
GRACE?
©ABERNETHY '04
YES?
FEED ROOM
WHAT DOES 'ACCOMPLICE' MEAN?

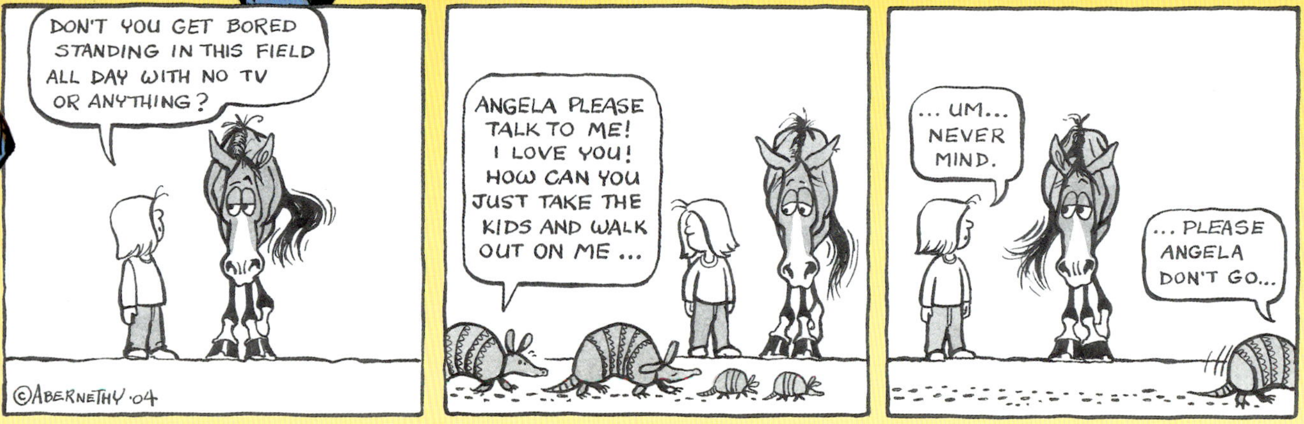
DON'T YOU GET BORED STANDING IN THIS FIELD ALL DAY WITH NO TV OR ANYTHING?
ANGELA PLEASE TALK TO ME! I LOVE YOU! HOW CAN YOU JUST TAKE THE KIDS AND WALK OUT ON ME...
... UM... NEVER MIND.
... PLEASE ANGELA DON'T GO...
©ABERNETHY '04

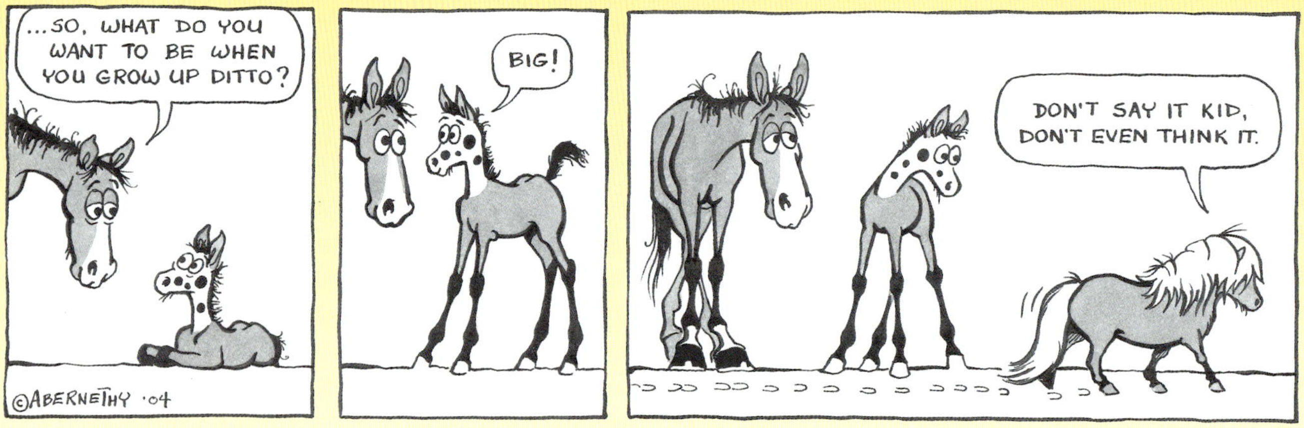
...SO, WHAT DO YOU WANT TO BE WHEN YOU GROW UP DITTO?
BIG!
DON'T SAY IT KID, DON'T EVEN THINK IT.
©ABERNETHY '04

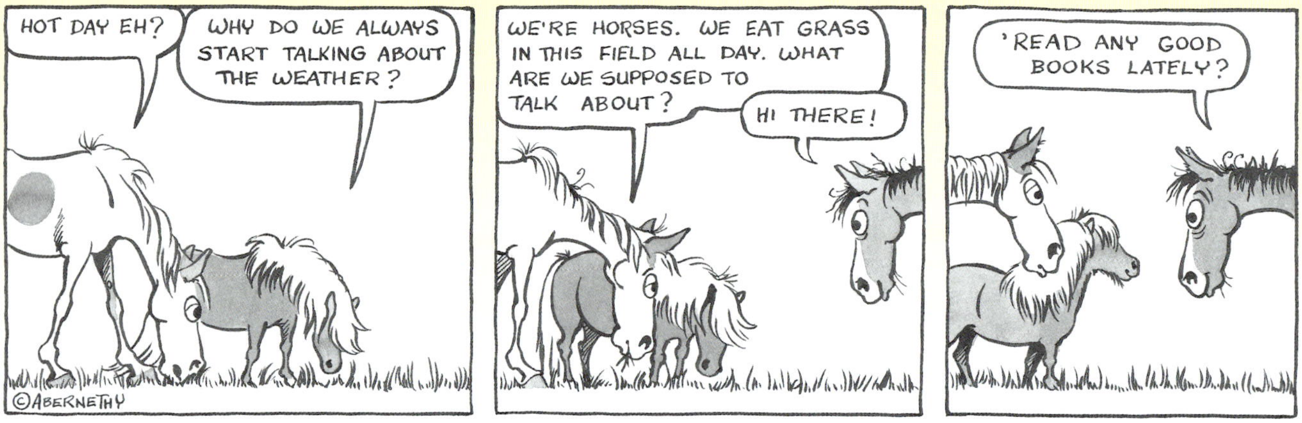
HOT DAY EH?
WHY DO WE ALWAYS START TALKING ABOUT THE WEATHER?
WE'RE HORSES. WE EAT GRASS IN THIS FIELD ALL DAY. WHAT ARE WE SUPPOSED TO TALK ABOUT?
HI THERE!
'READ ANY GOOD BOOKS LATELY?
©ABERNETHY

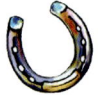

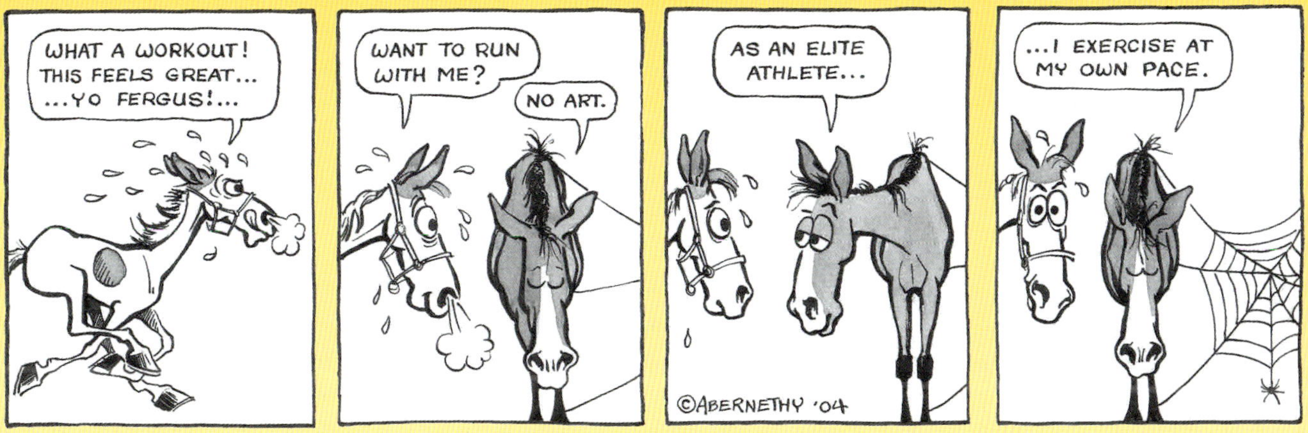
WHAT A WORKOUT! THIS FEELS GREAT... ...YO FERGUS!...
WANT TO RUN WITH ME?
NO ART.
AS AN ELITE ATHLETE...
...I EXERCISE AT MY OWN PACE.
©ABERNETHY '04

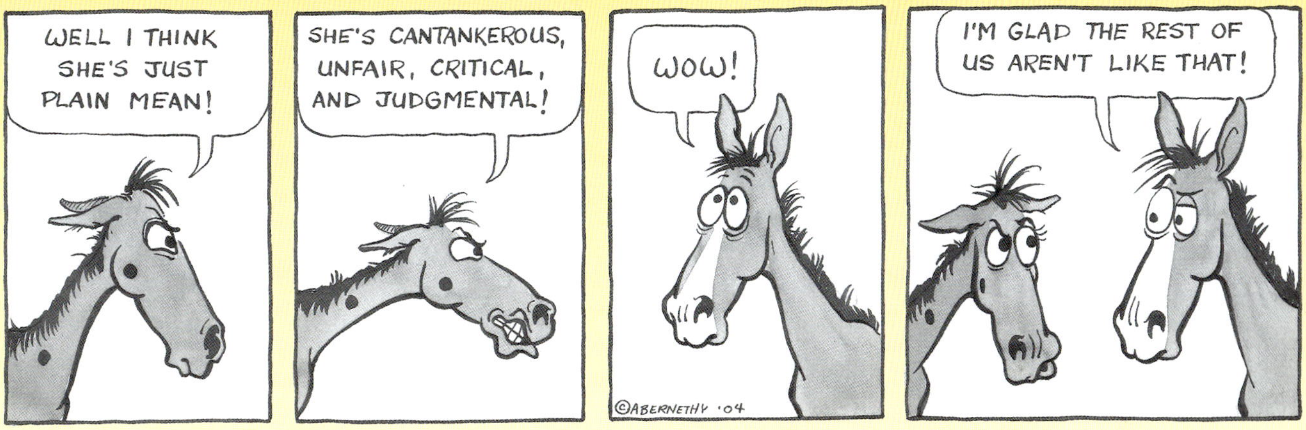
WELL I THINK SHE'S JUST PLAIN MEAN!
SHE'S CANTANKEROUS, UNFAIR, CRITICAL, AND JUDGMENTAL!
WOW!
I'M GLAD THE REST OF US AREN'T LIKE THAT!
©ABERNETHY '04

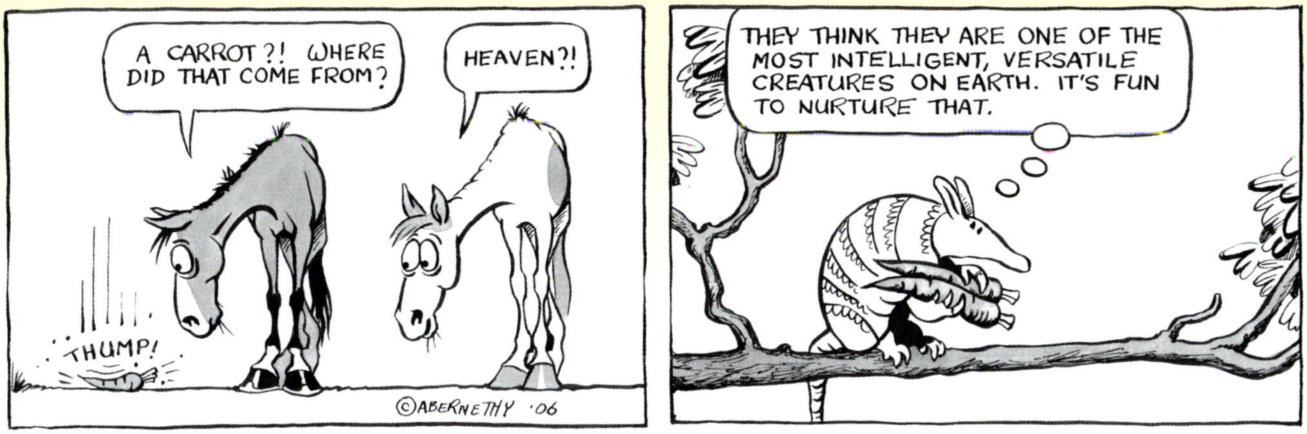
A CARROT?! WHERE DID THAT COME FROM?
HEAVEN?!
THUMP!
©ABERNETHY '06
THEY THINK THEY ARE ONE OF THE MOST INTELLIGENT, VERSATILE CREATURES ON EARTH. IT'S FUN TO NURTURE THAT.

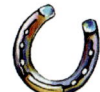

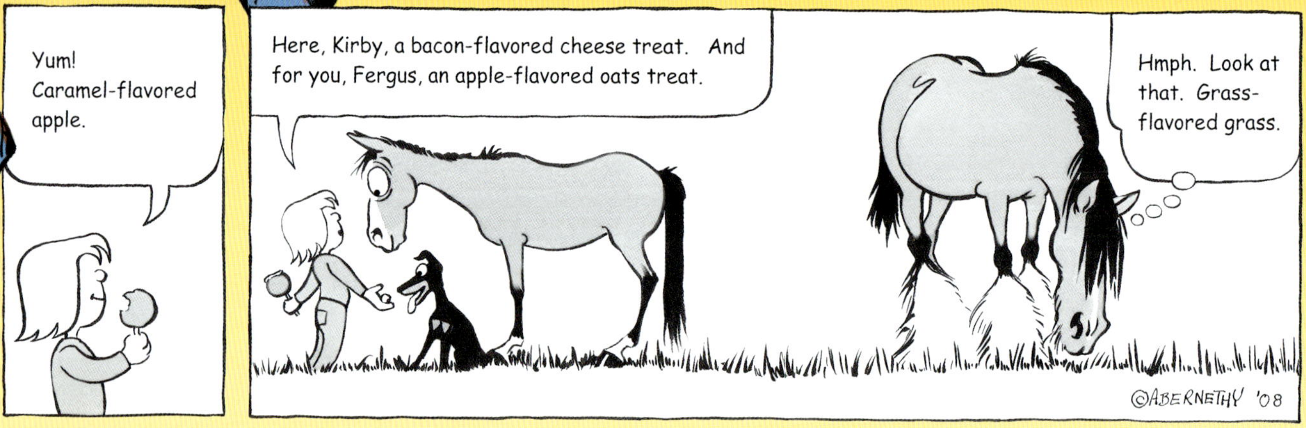
Yum! Caramel-flavored apple.
Here, Kirby, a bacon-flavored cheese treat. And for you, Fergus, an apple-flavored oats treat.
Hmph. Look at that. Grass-flavored grass.
©ABERNETHY '08

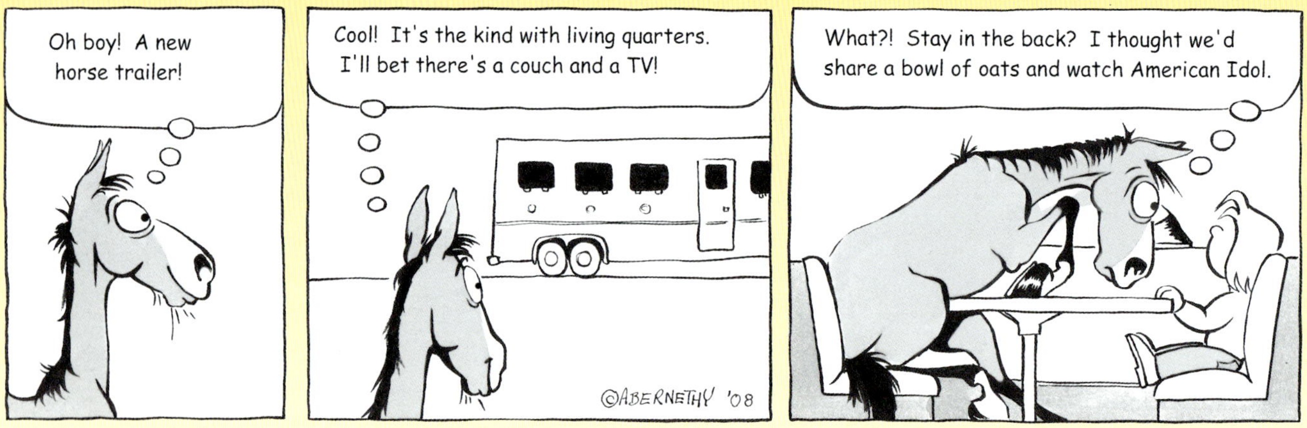
Oh boy! A new horse trailer!
Cool! It's the kind with living quarters. I'll bet there's a couch and a TV!
©ABERNETHY '08
What?! Stay in the back? I thought we'd share a bowl of oats and watch American Idol.

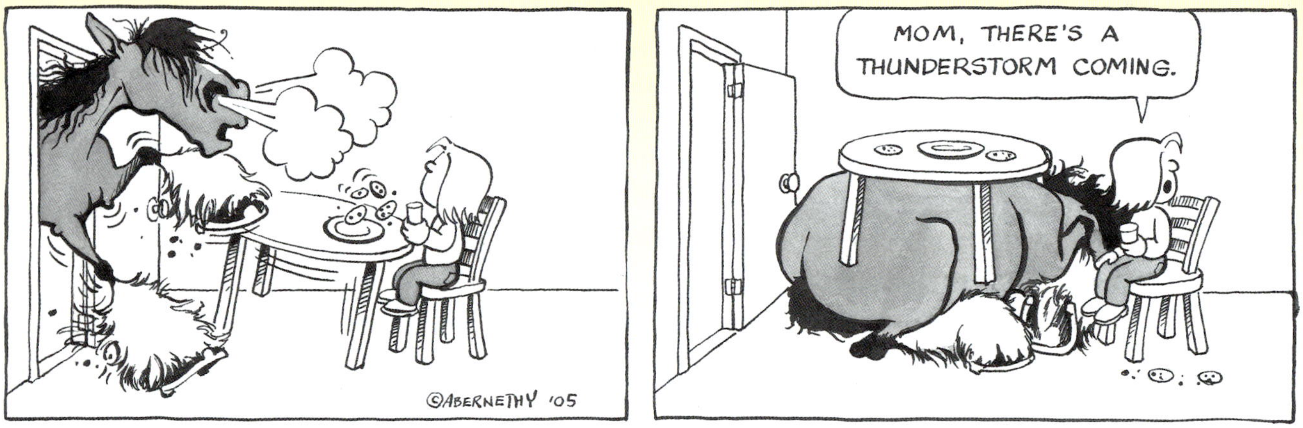
©ABERNETHY '05
MOM, THERE'S A THUNDERSTORM COMING.

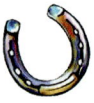

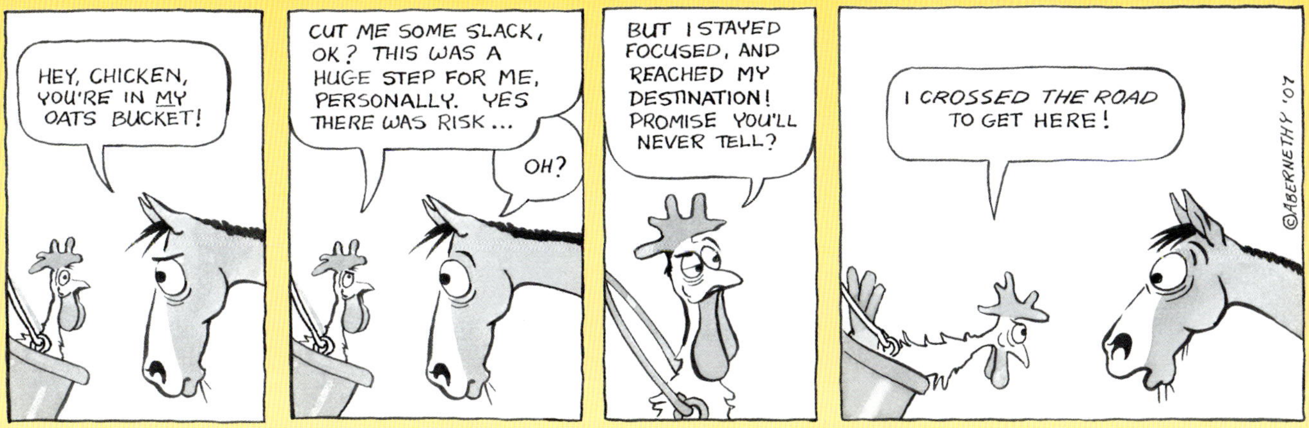
HEY, CHICKEN, YOU'RE IN MY OATS BUCKET!
CUT ME SOME SLACK, OK? THIS WAS A HUGE STEP FOR ME, PERSONALLY. YES THERE WAS RISK...
OH?
BUT I STAYED FOCUSED, AND REACHED MY DESTINATION! PROMISE YOU'LL NEVER TELL?
I CROSSED THE ROAD TO GET HERE!
©ABERNETHY '07

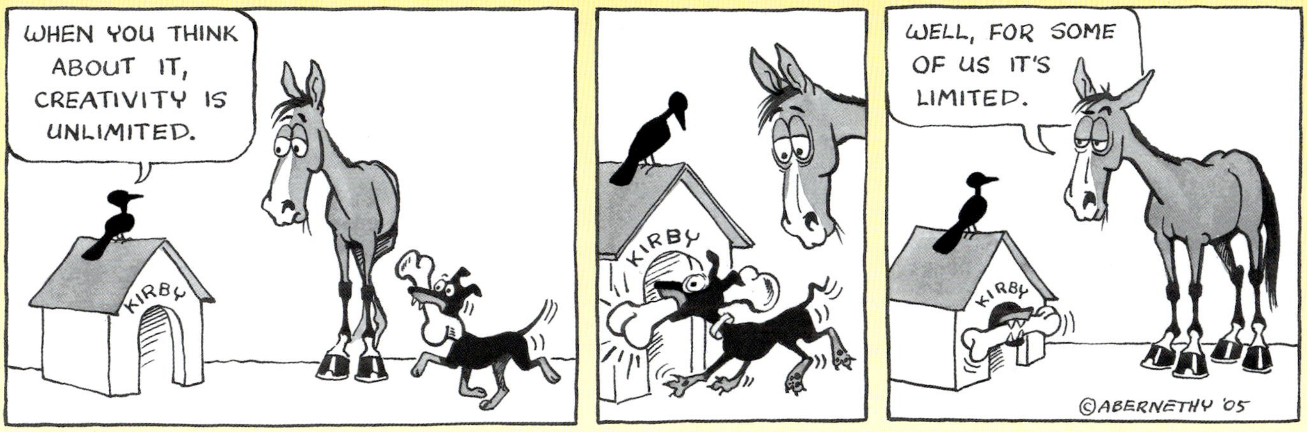
WHEN YOU THINK ABOUT IT, CREATIVITY IS UNLIMITED.
KIRBY
KIRBY
WELL, FOR SOME OF US IT'S LIMITED.
KIRBY
©ABERNETHY '05

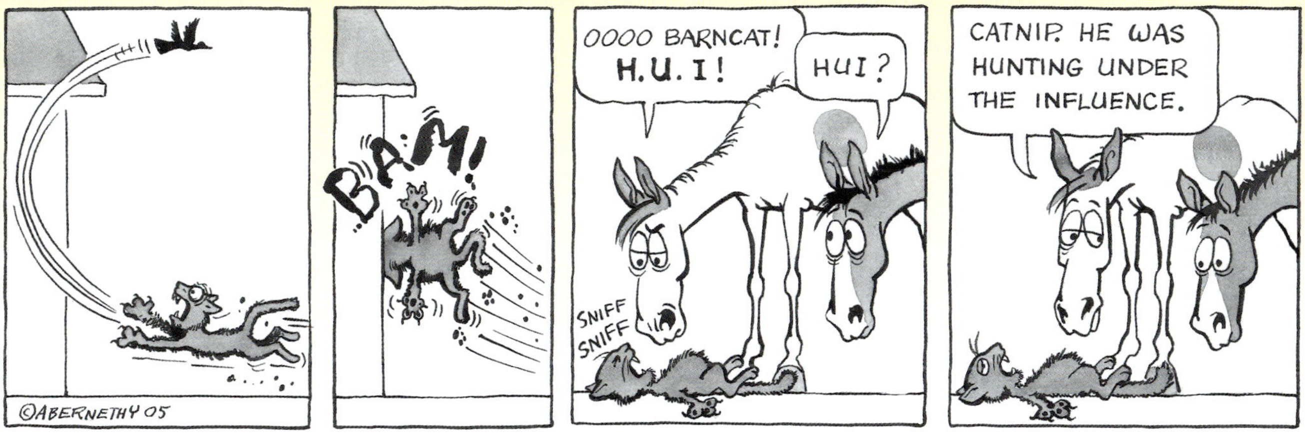
©ABERNETHY 05
BAM!
OOOO BARNCAT! H.U.I!
HUI?
SNIFF SNIFF
CATNIP. HE WAS HUNTING UNDER THE INFLUENCE.

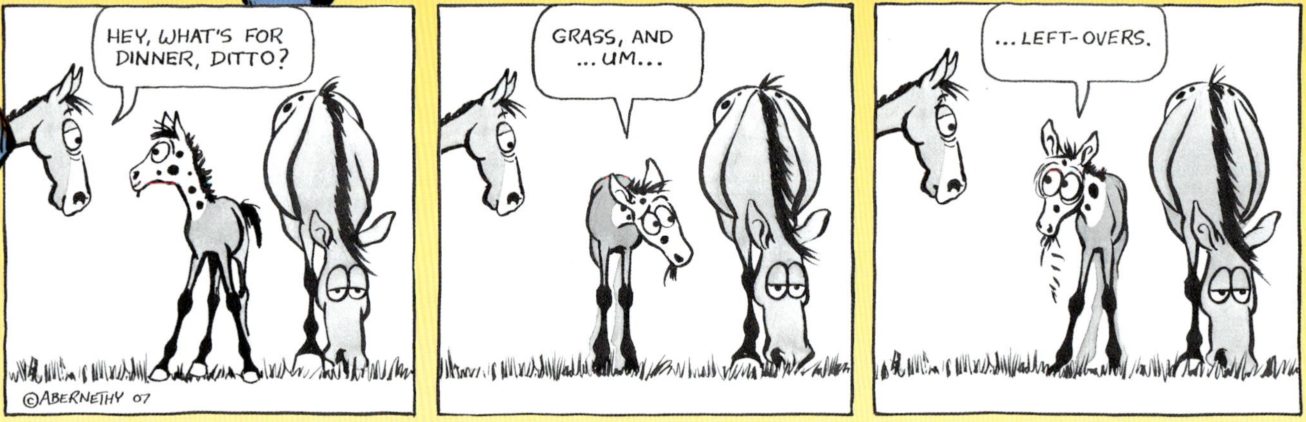

HEY, WHAT'S FOR DINNER, DITTO?
GRASS, AND ... UM...
... LEFT-OVERS.
©ABERNETHY 07


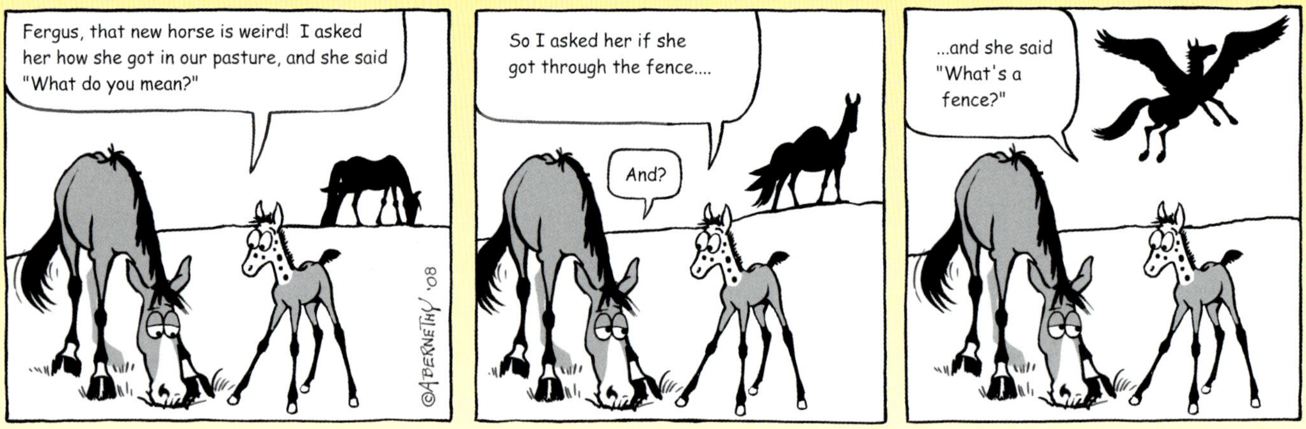

Fergus, that new horse is weird! I asked her how she got in our pasture, and she said "What do you mean?"
©ABERNETHY '08
So I asked her if she got through the fence....
And?
...and she said "What's a fence?"


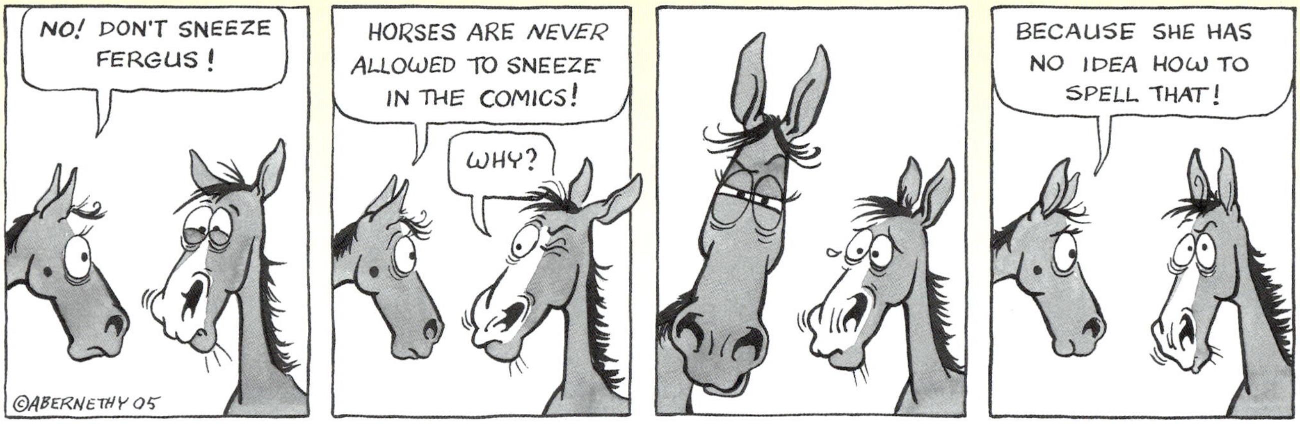

NO! DON'T SNEEZE FERGUS!
©ABERNETHY 05
HORSES ARE NEVER ALLOWED TO SNEEZE IN THE COMICS!
WHY?
BECAUSE SHE HAS NO IDEA HOW TO SPELL THAT!

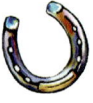

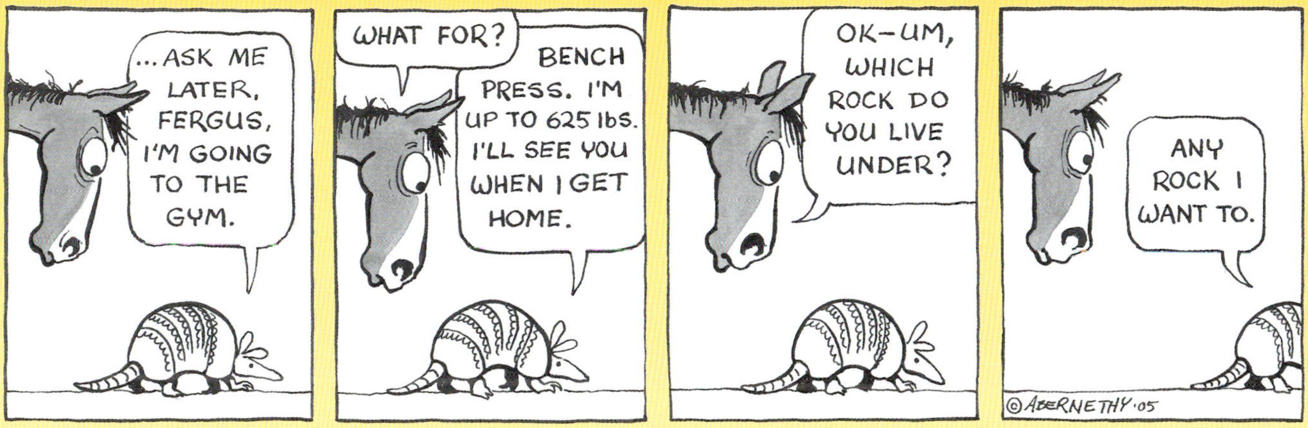
...ASK ME LATER, FERGUS, I'M GOING TO THE GYM.
WHAT FOR?
BENCH PRESS. I'M UP TO 625 lbs. I'LL SEE YOU WHEN I GET HOME.
OK-UM, WHICH ROCK DO YOU LIVE UNDER?
ANY ROCK I WANT TO.
©ABERNETHY '05

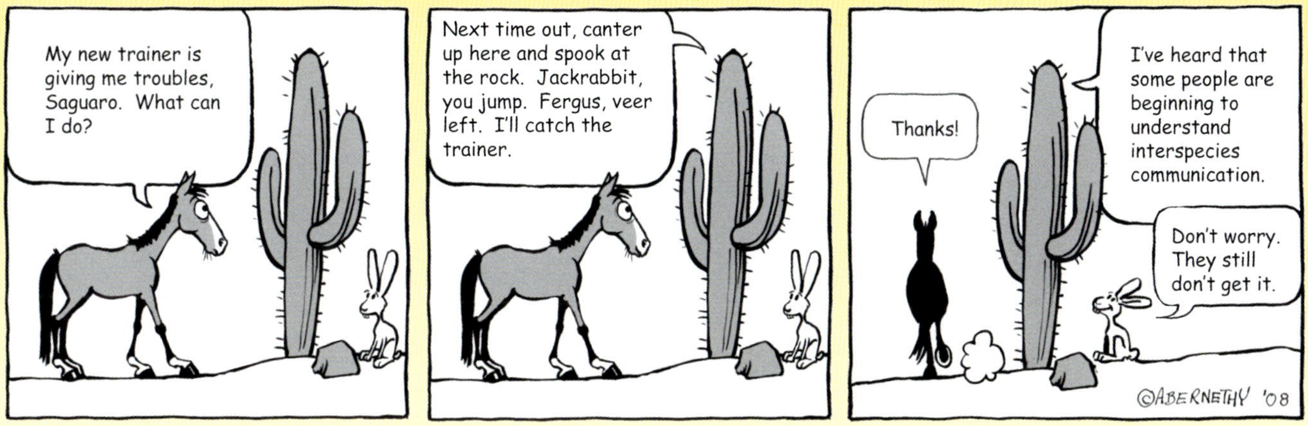
My new trainer is giving me troubles, Saguaro. What can I do?
Next time out, canter up here and spook at the rock. Jackrabbit, you jump. Fergus, veer left. I'll catch the trainer.
Thanks!
I've heard that some people are beginning to understand interspecies communication.
Don't worry. They still don't get it.
©ABERNETHY '08

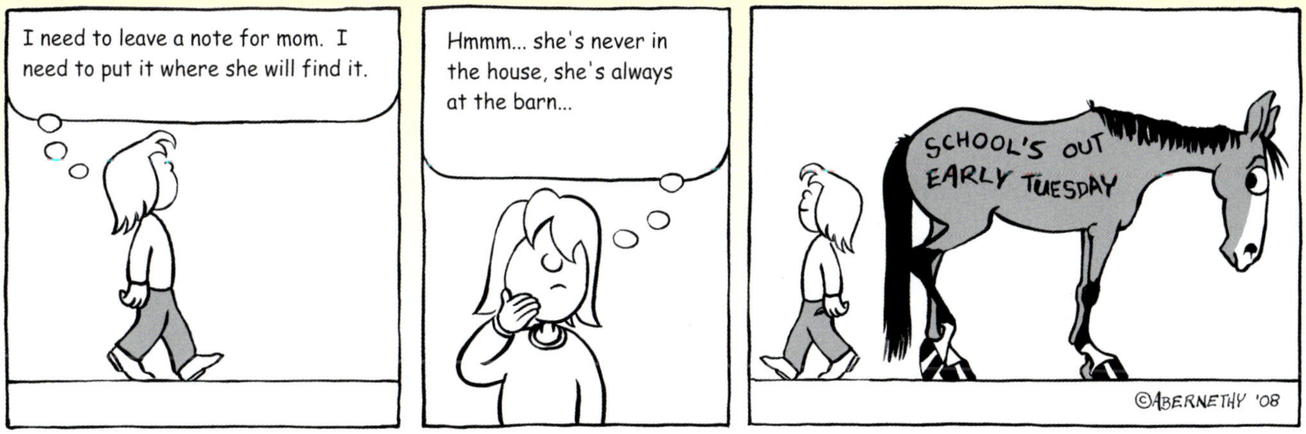
I need to leave a note for mom. I need to put it where she will find it.
Hmmm... she's never in the house, she's always at the barn...
SCHOOL'S OUT EARLY TUESDAY
©ABERNETHY '08

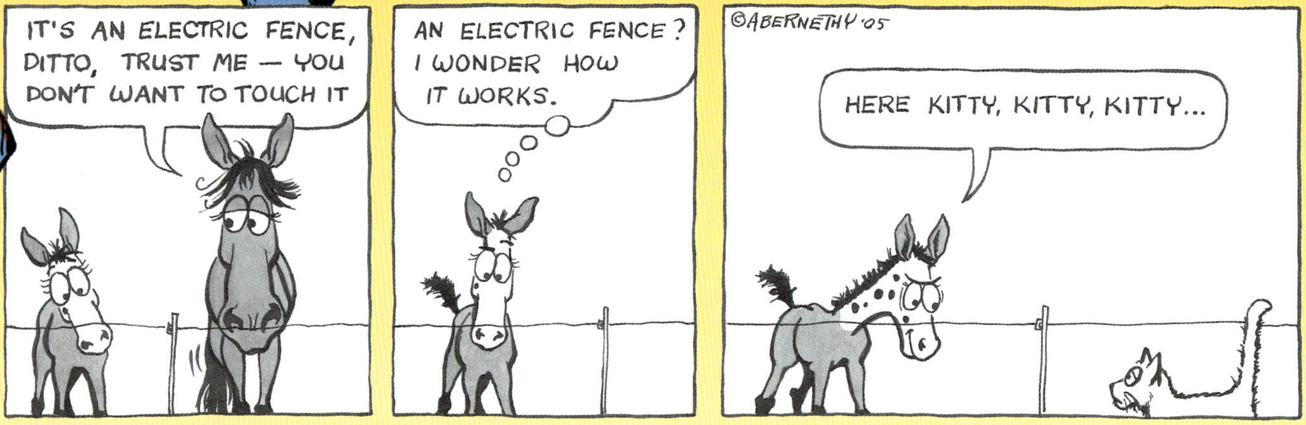
IT'S AN ELECTRIC FENCE, DITTO, TRUST ME — YOU DON'T WANT TO TOUCH IT
AN ELECTRIC FENCE? I WONDER HOW IT WORKS.
©ABERNETHY '05
HERE KITTY, KITTY, KITTY...

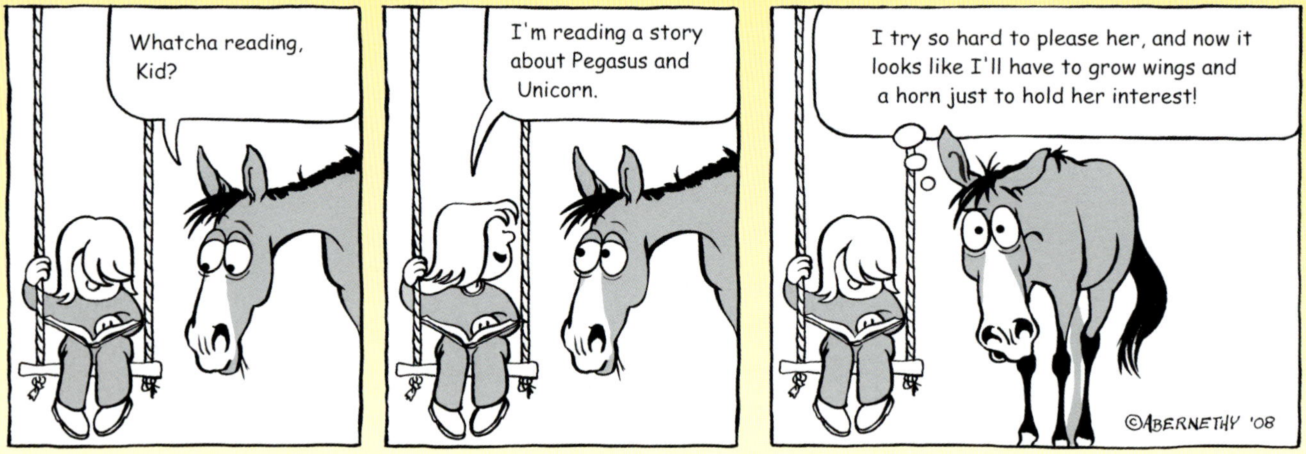
Whatcha reading, Kid?
I'm reading a story about Pegasus and Unicorn.
I try so hard to please her, and now it looks like I'll have to grow wings and a horn just to hold her interest!
©ABERNETHY '08

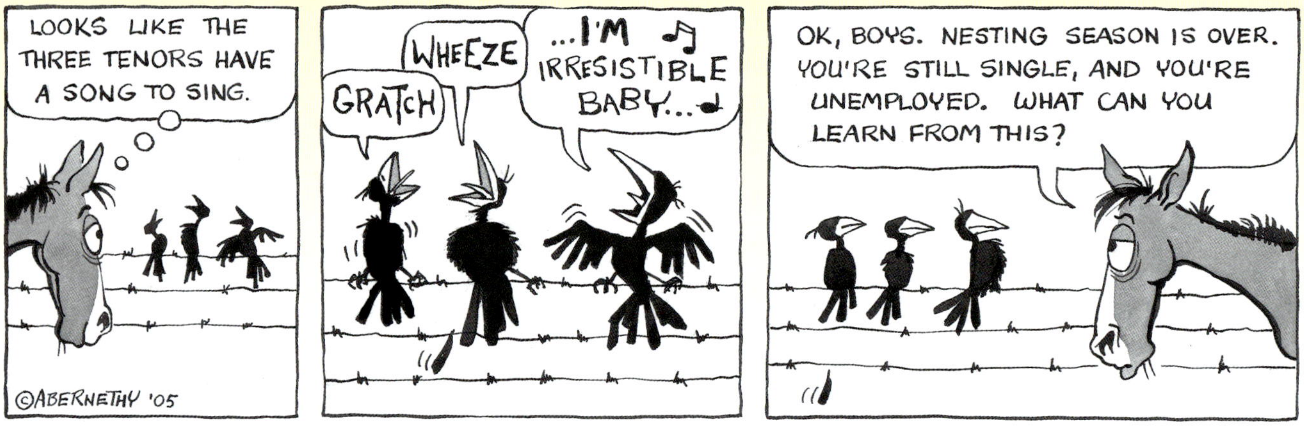
LOOKS LIKE THE THREE TENORS HAVE A SONG TO SING.
©ABERNETHY '05
GRATCH
WHEEZE
...I'M IRRESISTIBLE BABY...
OK, BOYS. NESTING SEASON IS OVER. YOU'RE STILL SINGLE, AND YOU'RE UNEMPLOYED. WHAT CAN YOU LEARN FROM THIS?

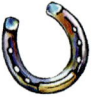

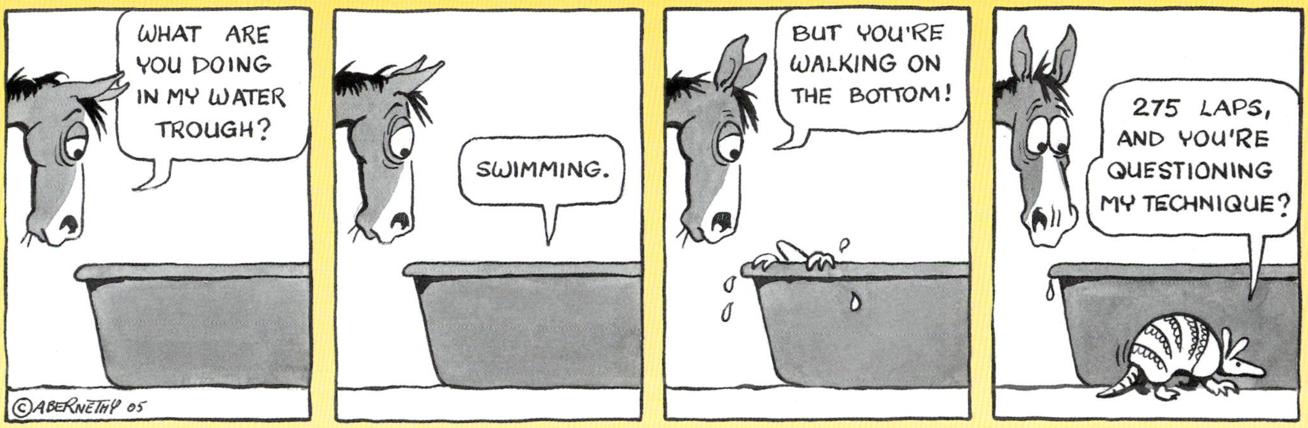
WHAT ARE YOU DOING IN MY WATER TROUGH?
SWIMMING.
BUT YOU'RE WALKING ON THE BOTTOM!
275 LAPS, AND YOU'RE QUESTIONING MY TECHNIQUE?
©ABERNETHY 05

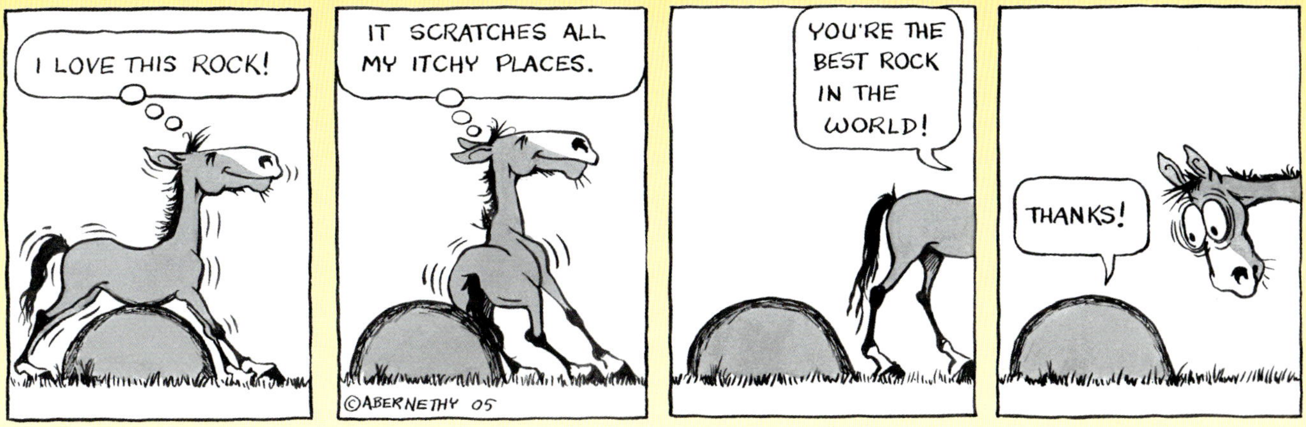
I LOVE THIS ROCK!
IT SCRATCHES ALL MY ITCHY PLACES.
YOU'RE THE BEST ROCK IN THE WORLD!
THANKS!
©ABERNETHY 05

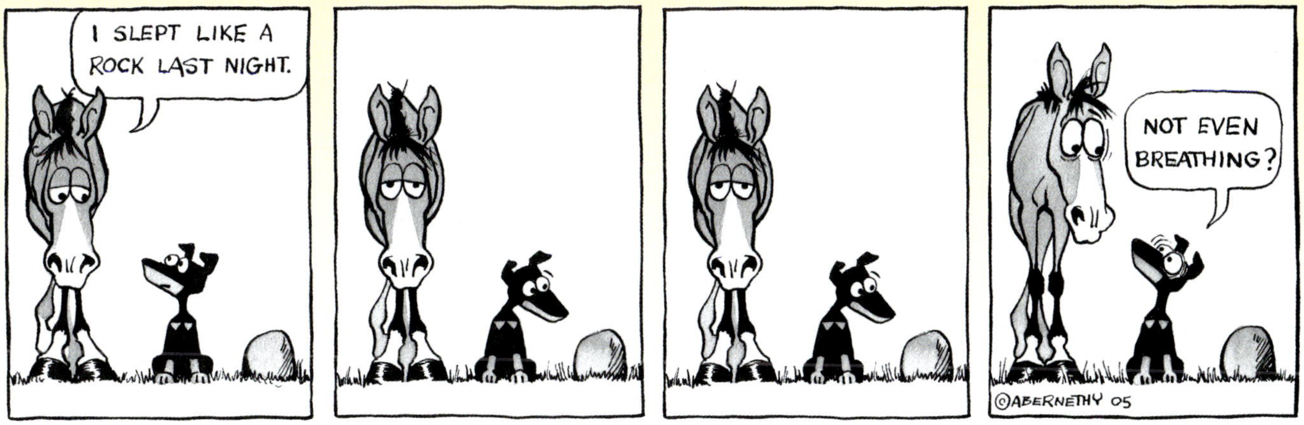
I SLEPT LIKE A ROCK LAST NIGHT.
NOT EVEN BREATHING?
©ABERNETHY 05

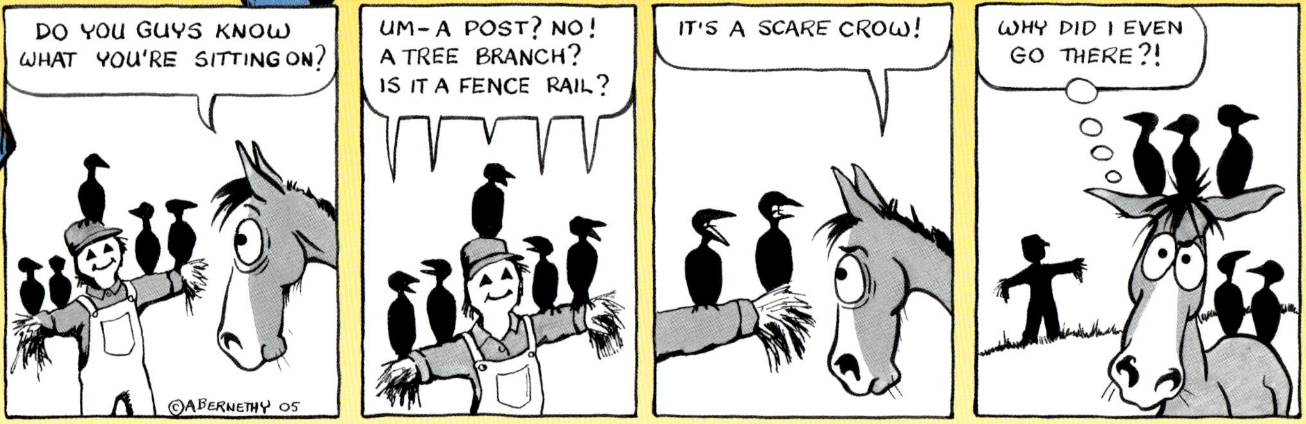
DO YOU GUYS KNOW WHAT YOU'RE SITTING ON?
UM- A POST? NO! A TREE BRANCH? IS IT A FENCE RAIL?
IT'S A SCARE CROW!
WHY DID I EVEN GO THERE?!
©ABERNETHY 05

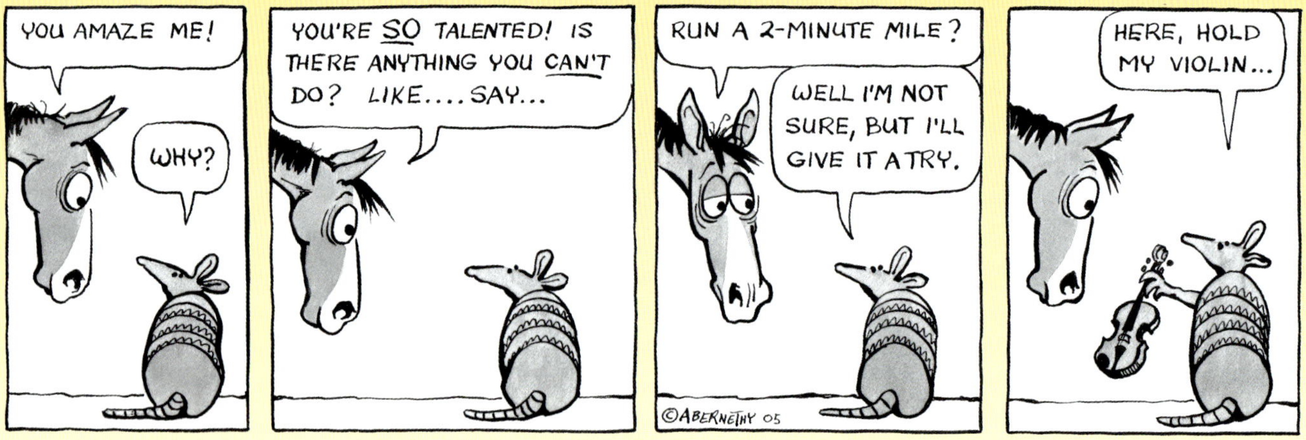
YOU AMAZE ME!
WHY?
YOU'RE SO TALENTED! IS THERE ANYTHING YOU CAN'T DO? LIKE.... SAY...
RUN A 2-MINUTE MILE?
WELL I'M NOT SURE, BUT I'LL GIVE IT A TRY.
HERE, HOLD MY VIOLIN...
©ABERNETHY 05

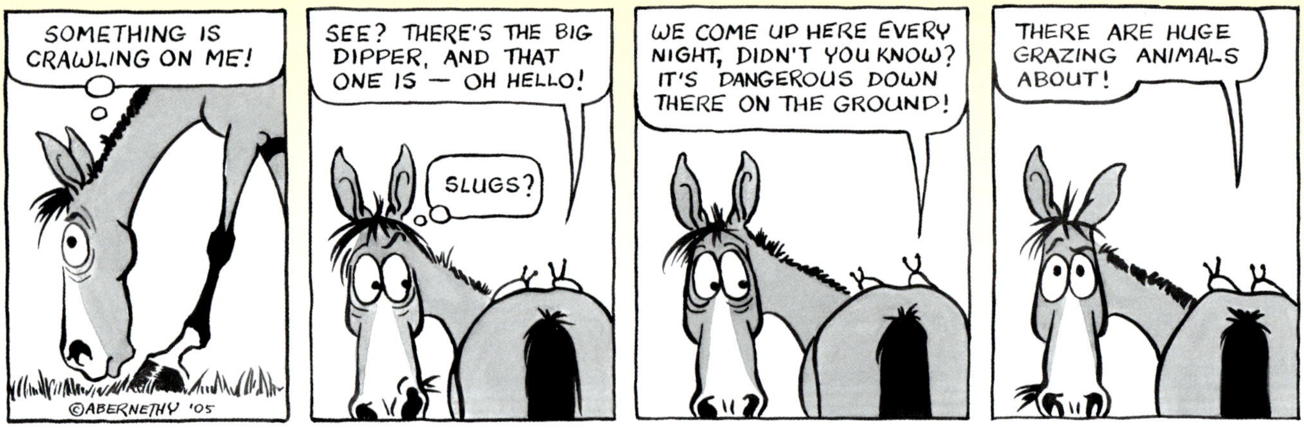
SOMETHING IS CRAWLING ON ME!
SEE? THERE'S THE BIG DIPPER, AND THAT ONE IS — OH HELLO!
SLUGS?
WE COME UP HERE EVERY NIGHT, DIDN'T YOU KNOW? IT'S DANGEROUS DOWN THERE ON THE GROUND!
THERE ARE HUGE GRAZING ANIMALS ABOUT!
©ABERNETHY '05

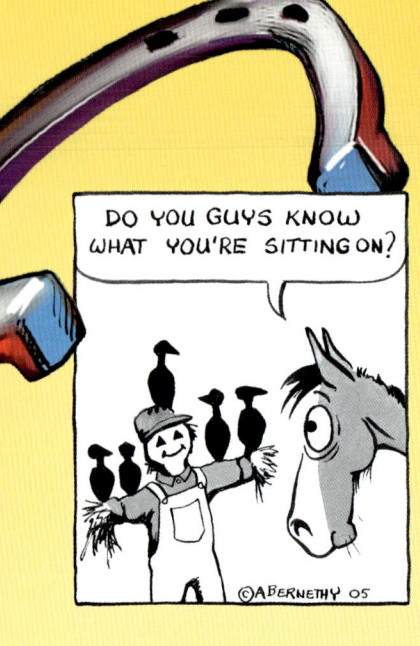

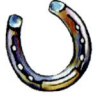

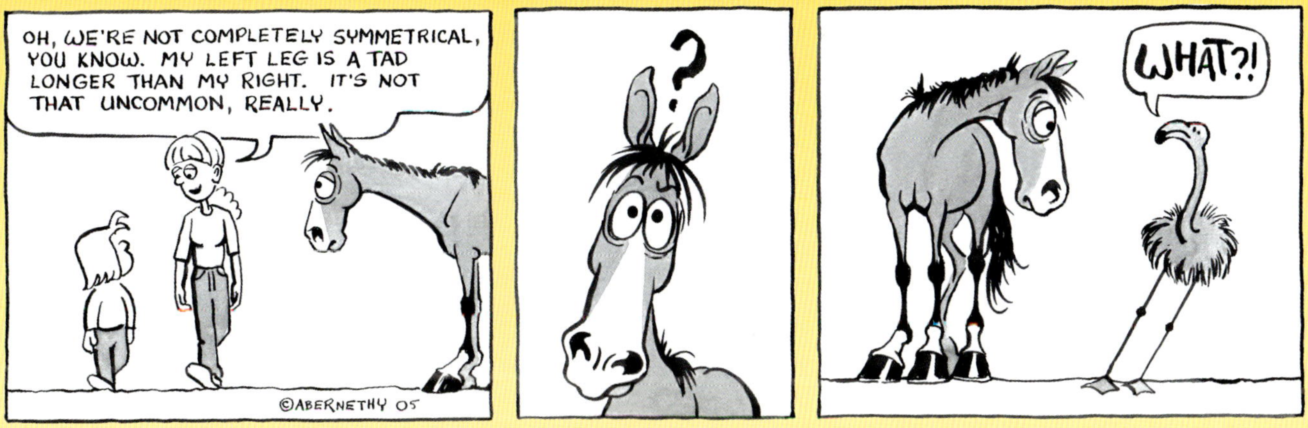
OH, WE'RE NOT COMPLETELY SYMMETRICAL, YOU KNOW. MY LEFT LEG IS A TAD LONGER THAN MY RIGHT. IT'S NOT THAT UNCOMMON, REALLY.
©ABERNETHY 05
?
WHAT?!

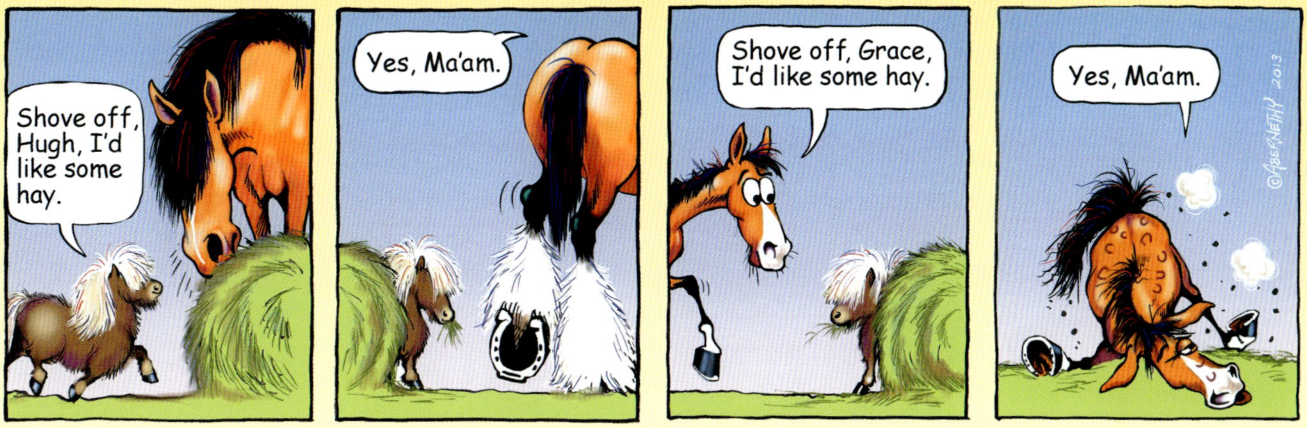
Shove off, Hugh, I'd like some hay.
Yes, Ma'am.
Shove off, Grace, I'd like some hay.
Yes, Ma'am.
©ABERNETHY 2013

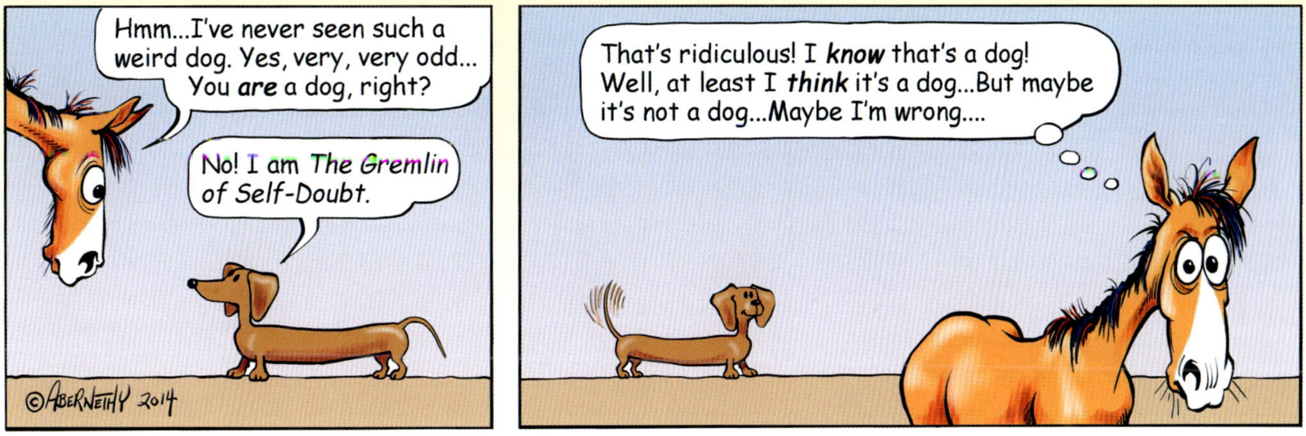
Hmm...I've never seen such a weird dog. Yes, very, very odd... You *are* a dog, right?
No! I am *The Gremlin of Self-Doubt.*
©ABERNETHY 2014
That's ridiculous! I ***know*** that's a dog! Well, at least I ***think*** it's a dog...But maybe it's not a dog...Maybe I'm wrong....

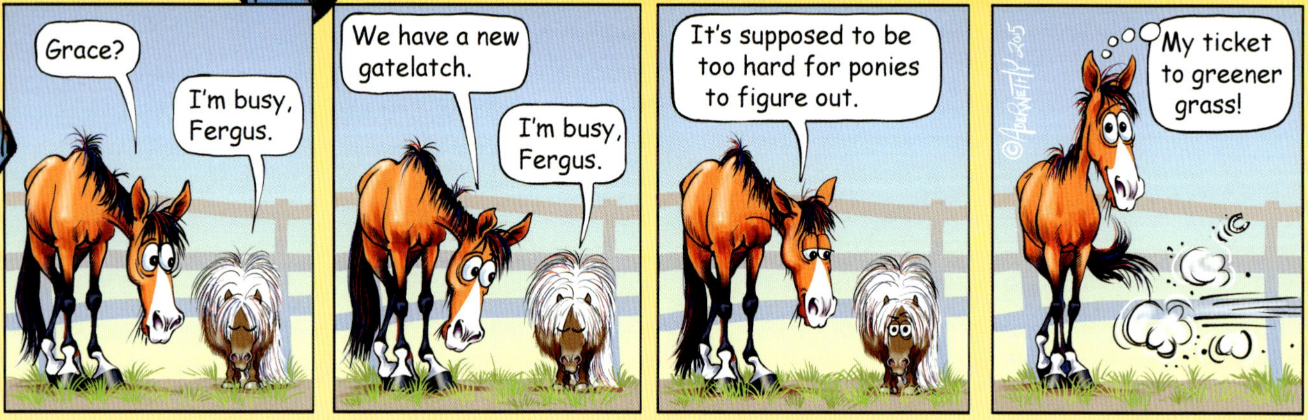
Grace?
I'm busy, Fergus.
We have a new gatelatch.
I'm busy, Fergus.
It's supposed to be too hard for ponies to figure out.
©ABERNETHY 2015
My ticket to greener grass!

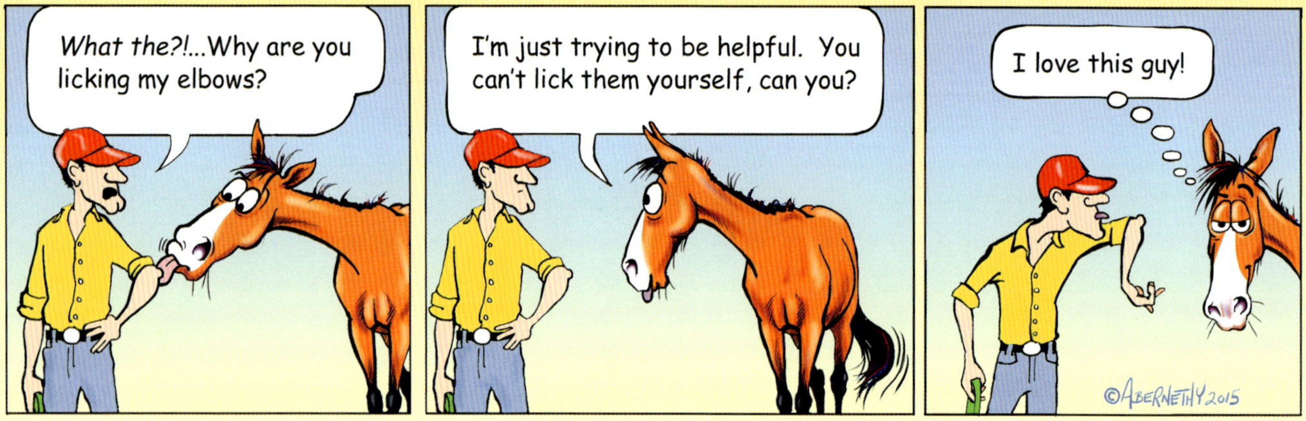
*What the?!*...Why are you licking my elbows?
I'm just trying to be helpful. You can't lick them yourself, can you?
I love this guy!
©ABERNETHY 2015

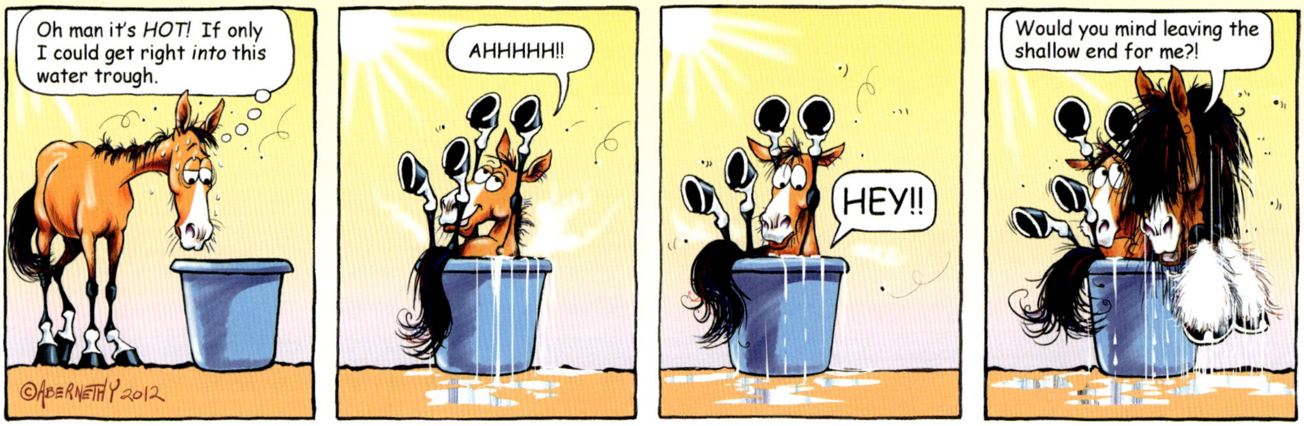
Oh man it's *HOT!* If only I could get right *into* this water trough.
©ABERNETHY 2012
AHHHHH!!
HEY!!
Would you mind leaving the shallow end for me?!

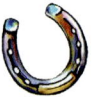

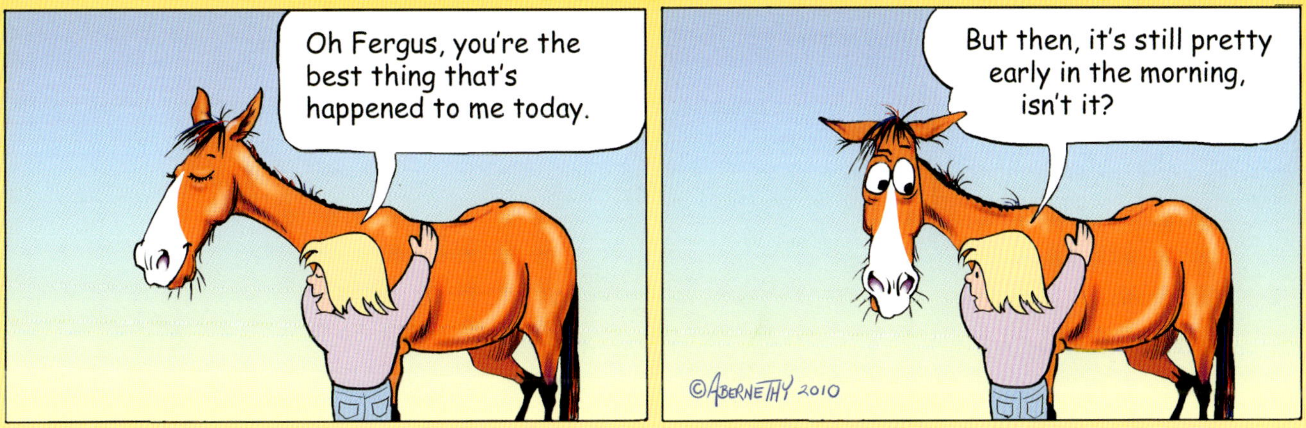
Oh Fergus, you're the best thing that's happened to me today.
But then, it's still pretty early in the morning, isn't it?
©ABERNETHY 2010

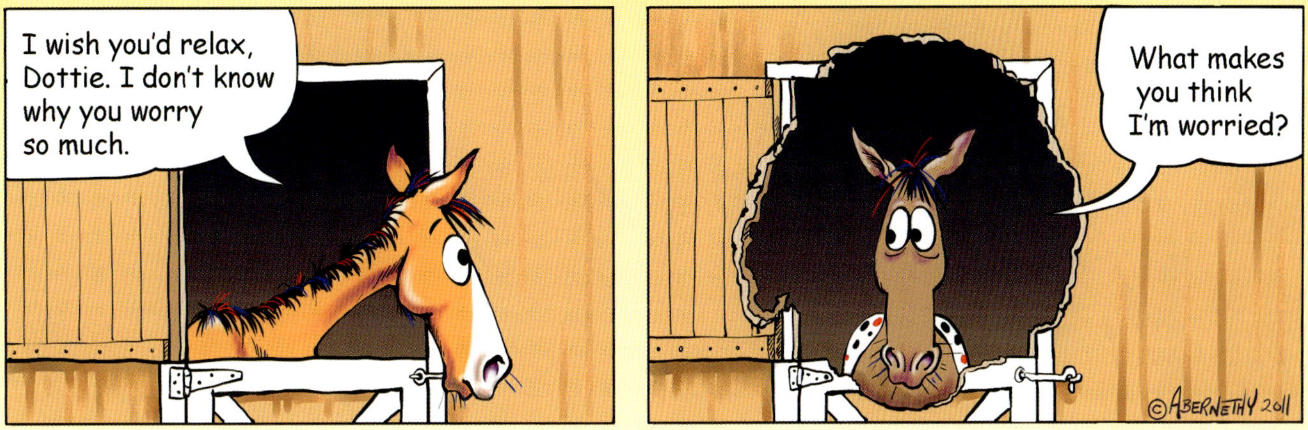
I wish you'd relax, Dottie. I don't know why you worry so much.
What makes you think I'm worried?
©ABERNETHY 2011

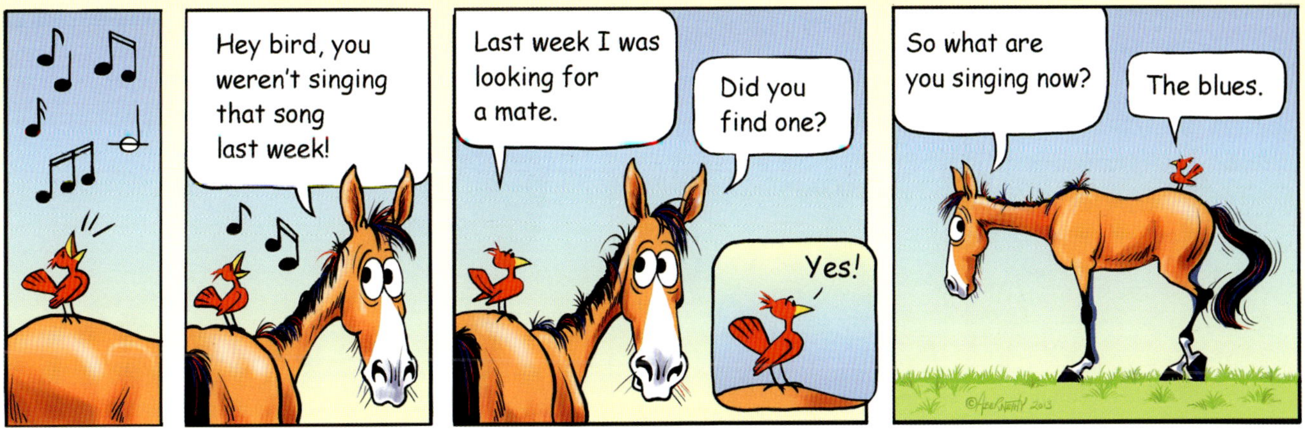
Hey bird, you weren't singing that song last week!
Last week I was looking for a mate.
Did you find one?
Yes!
So what are you singing now?
The blues.

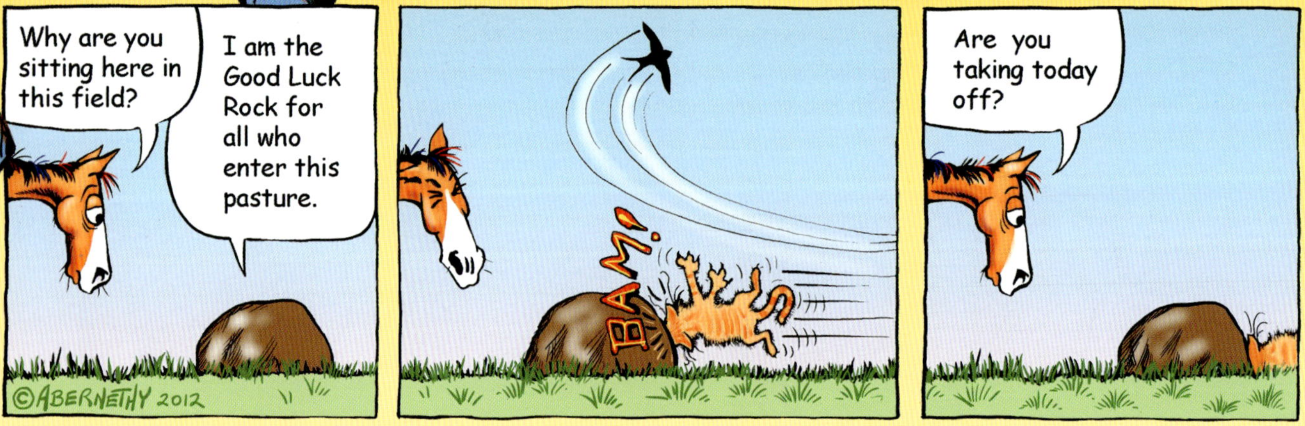
Why are you sitting here in this field?
I am the Good Luck Rock for all who enter this pasture.
BAM!
Are you taking today off?
©ABERNETHY 2012

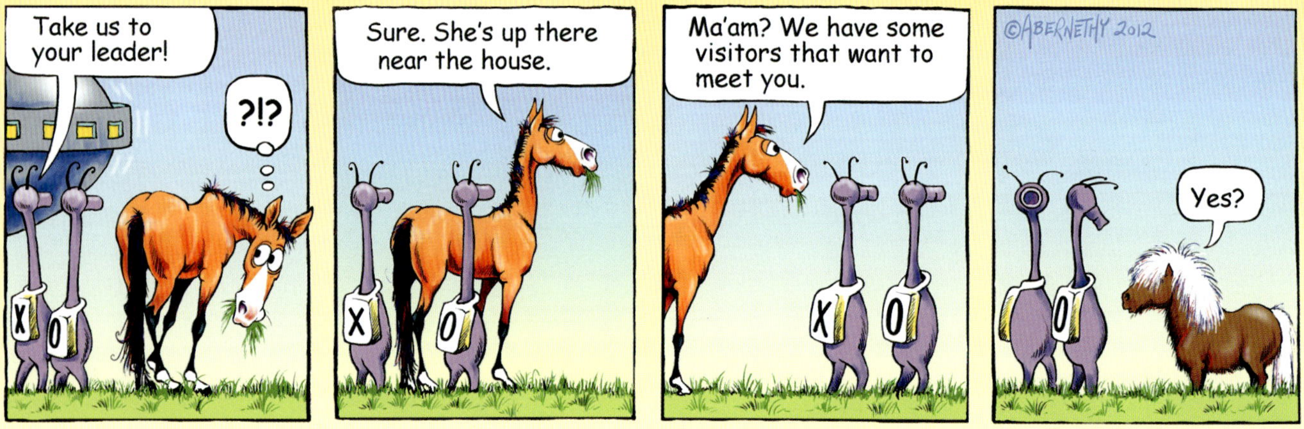
Take us to your leader!
?!?
Sure. She's up there near the house.
Ma'am? We have some visitors that want to meet you.
©ABERNETHY 2012
Yes?

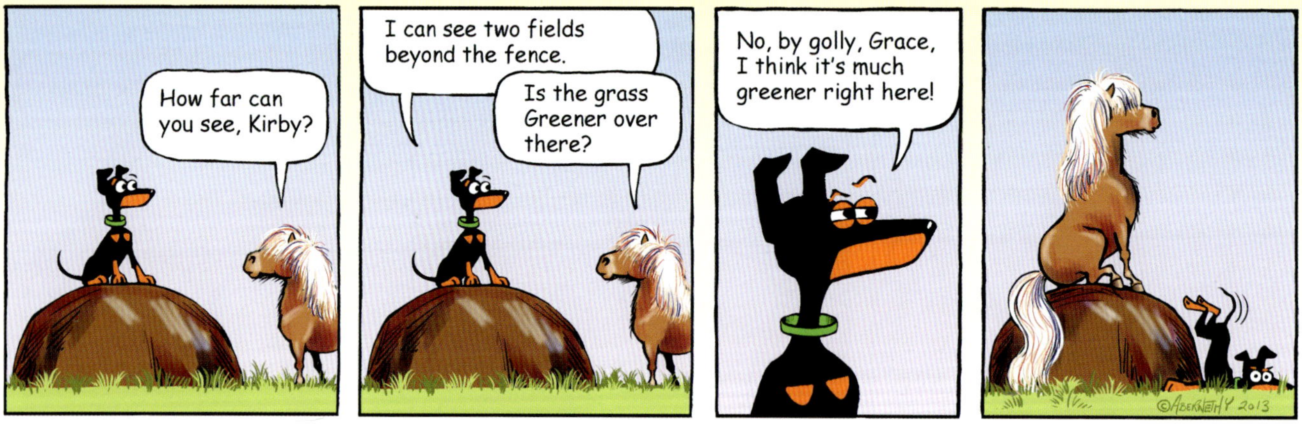
How far can you see, Kirby?
I can see two fields beyond the fence.
Is the grass Greener over there?
No, by golly, Grace, I think it's much greener right here!
©ABERNETHY 2013

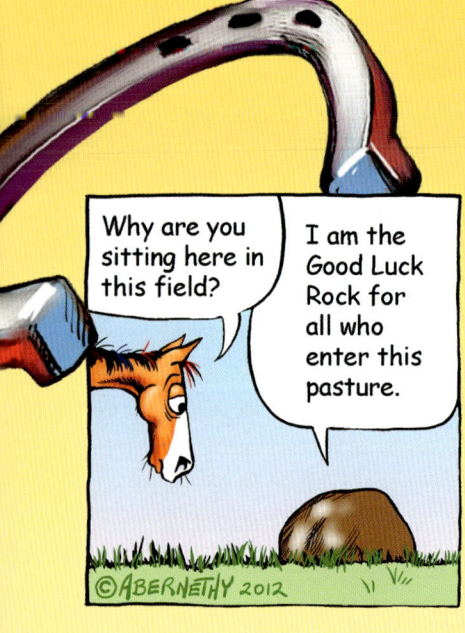

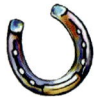

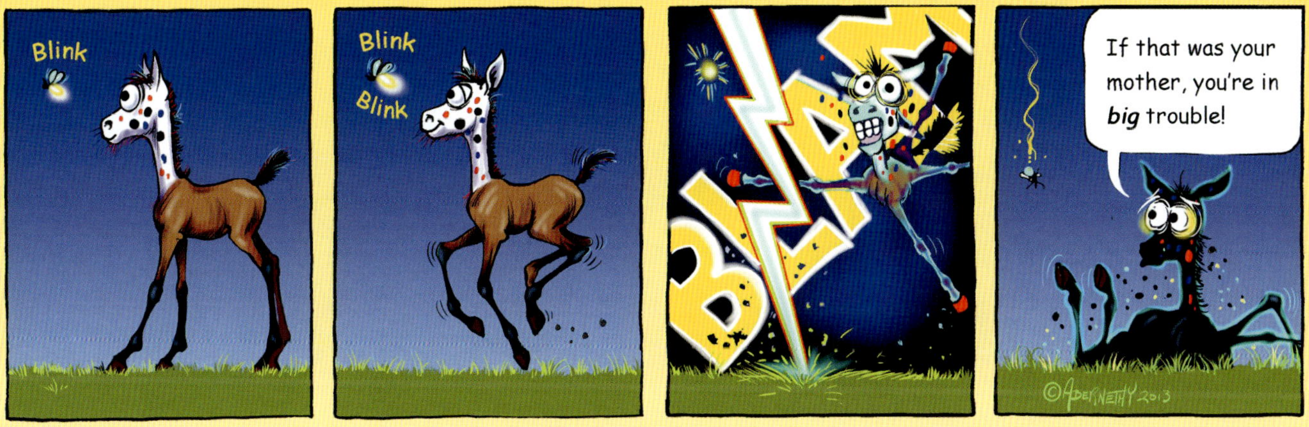
Blink
Blink
Blink
BLAM!
If that was your mother, you're in ***big*** trouble!
©ABERNETHY 2013

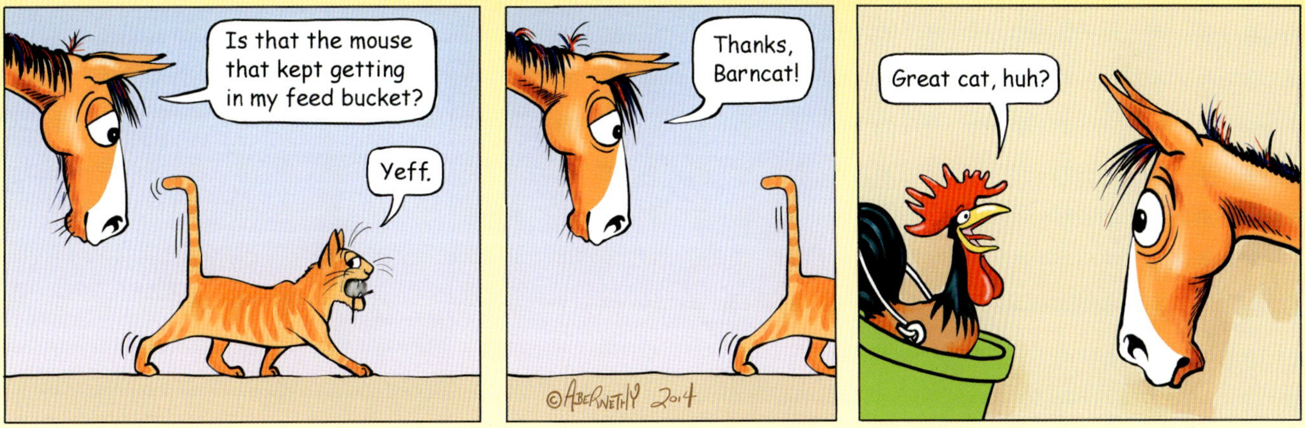
Is that the mouse that kept getting in my feed bucket?
Yeff.
Thanks, Barncat!
©ABERNETHY 2014
Great cat, huh?

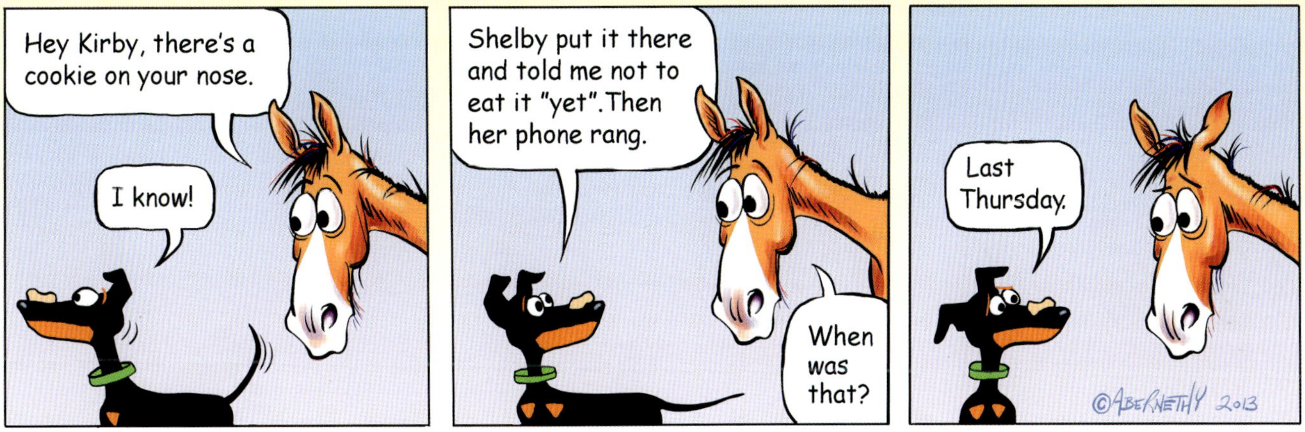
Hey Kirby, there's a cookie on your nose.
I know!
Shelby put it there and told me not to eat it "yet". Then her phone rang.
When was that?
Last Thursday.
©ABERNETHY 2013

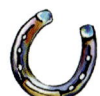

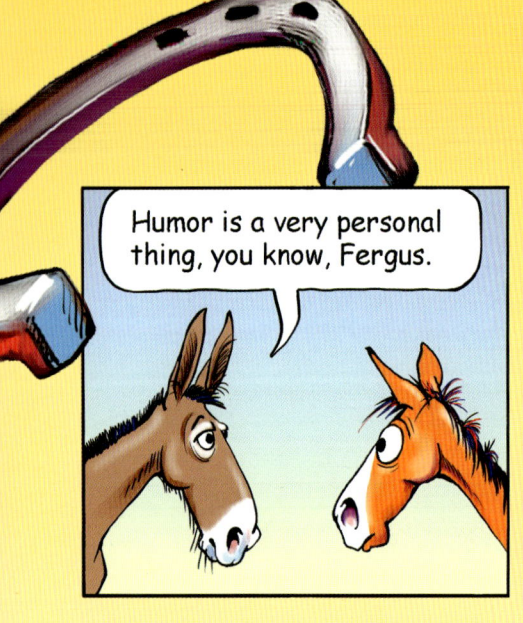

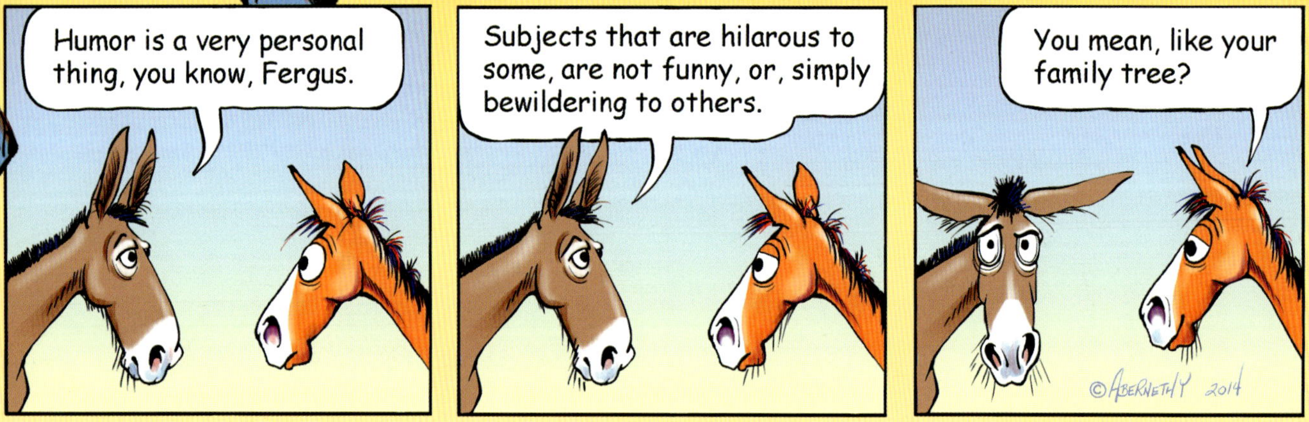
Humor is a very personal thing, you know, Fergus.
Subjects that are hilarous to some, are not funny, or, simply bewildering to others.
You mean, like your family tree?
©ABERNETHY 2014

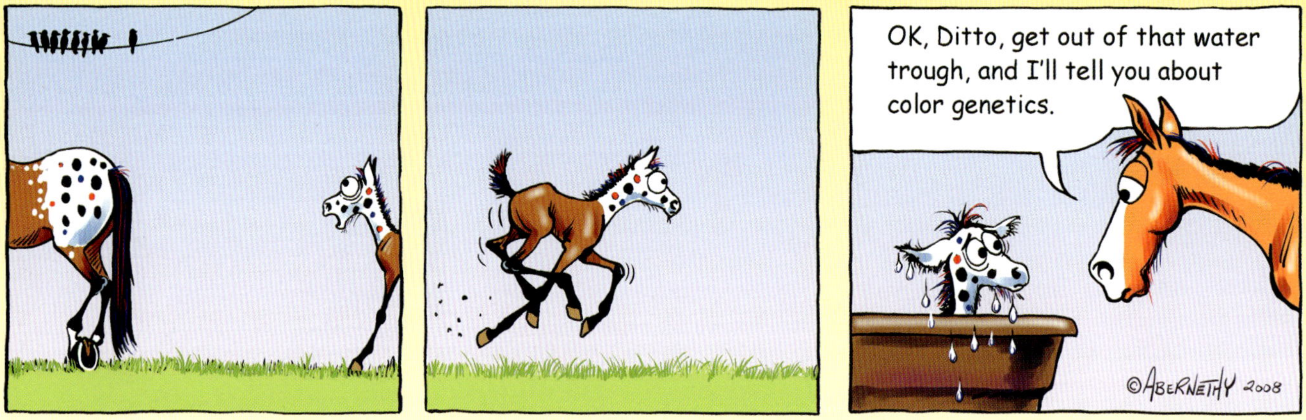
OK, Ditto, get out of that water trough, and I'll tell you about color genetics.
©ABERNETHY 2008

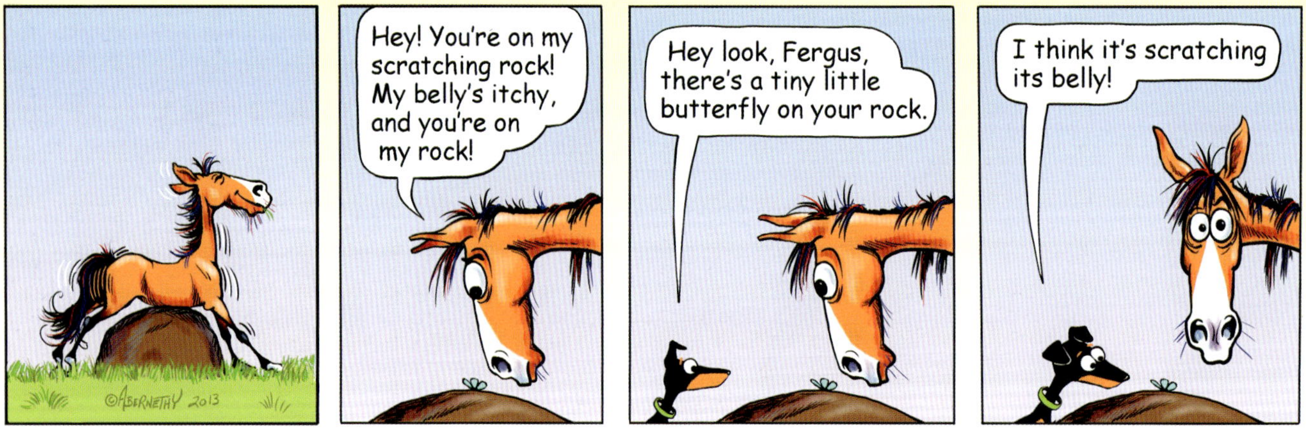
©ABERNETHY 2013
Hey! You're on my scratching rock! My belly's itchy, and you're on my rock!
Hey look, Fergus, there's a tiny little butterfly on your rock.
I think it's scratching its belly!

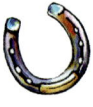

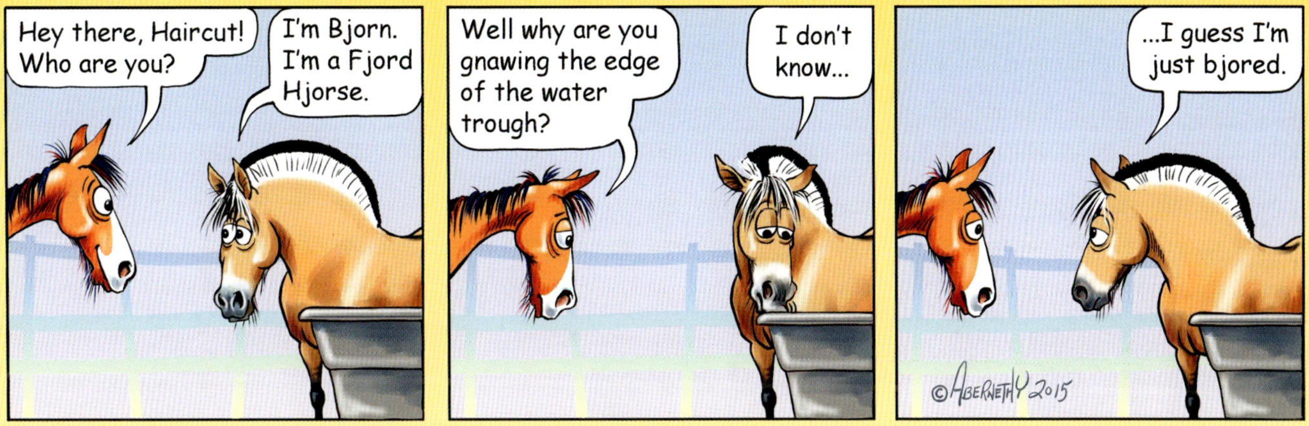
Hey there, Haircut! Who are you?
I'm Bjorn. I'm a Fjord Hjorse.
Well why are you gnawing the edge of the water trough?
I don't know...
...I guess I'm just bjored.
©ABERNETHY 2015

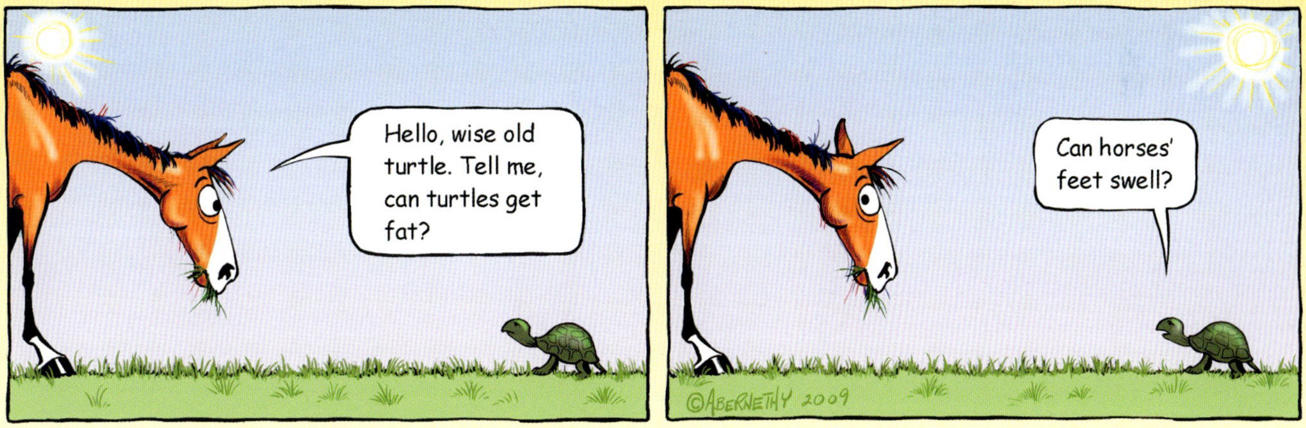
Hello, wise old turtle. Tell me, can turtles get fat?
Can horses' feet swell?
©ABERNETHY 2009

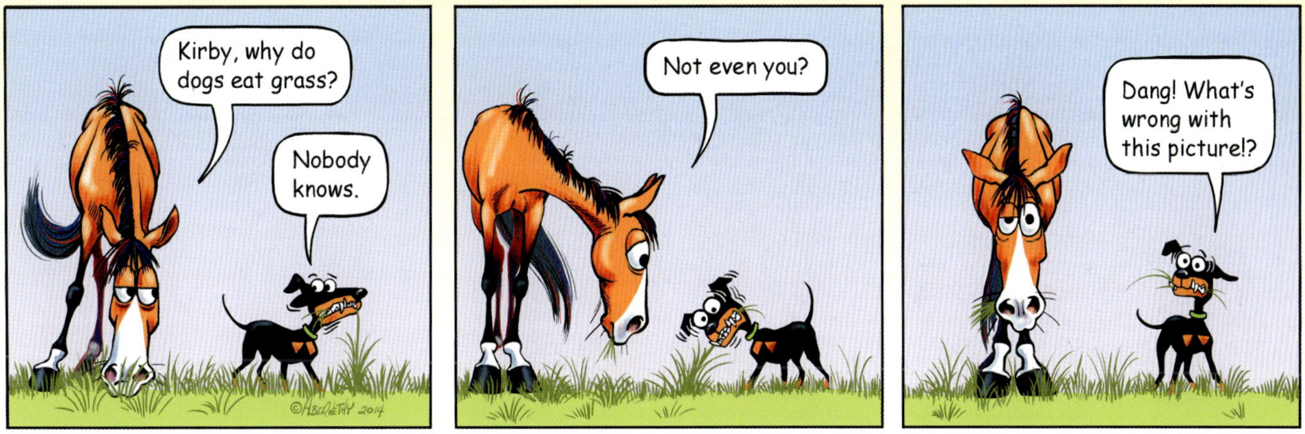
Kirby, why do dogs eat grass?
Nobody knows.
©ABERNETHY 2014
Not even you?
Dang! What's wrong with this picture!?

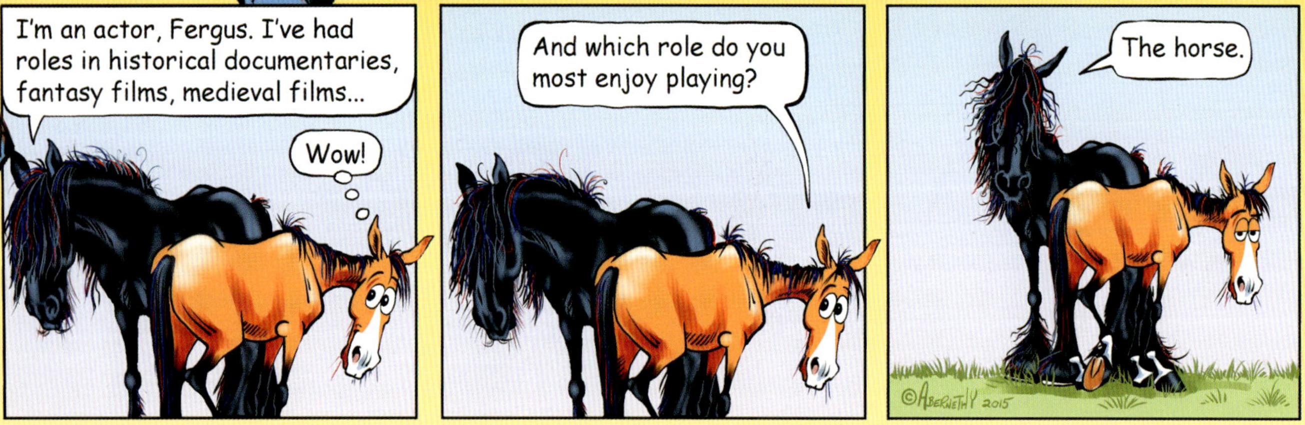
I'm an actor, Fergus. I've had roles in historical documentaries, fantasy films, medieval films...
Wow!
And which role do you most enjoy playing?
The horse.
©ABERNETHY 2015

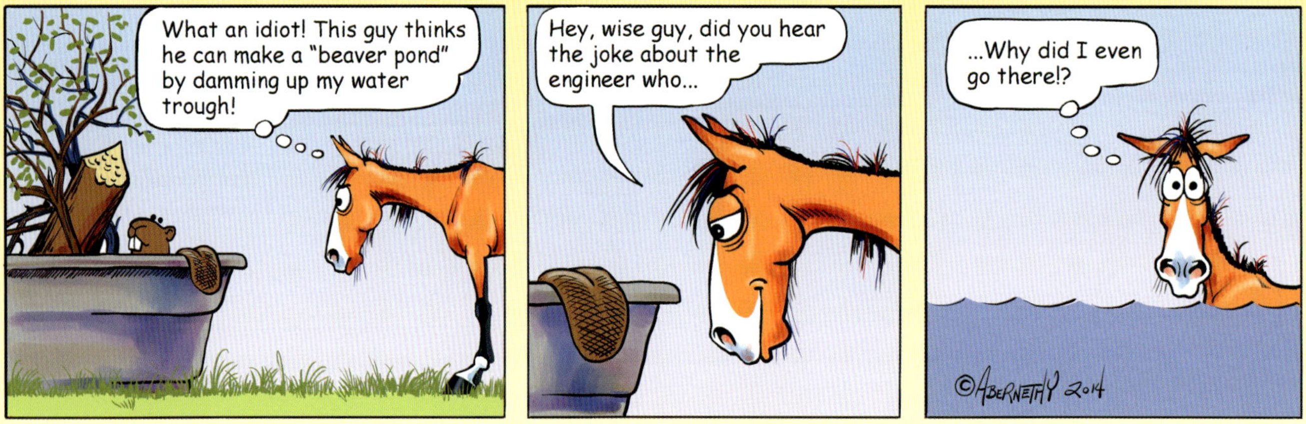
What an idiot! This guy thinks he can make a "beaver pond" by damming up my water trough!
Hey, wise guy, did you hear the joke about the engineer who...
...Why did I even go there!?
©ABERNETHY 2014

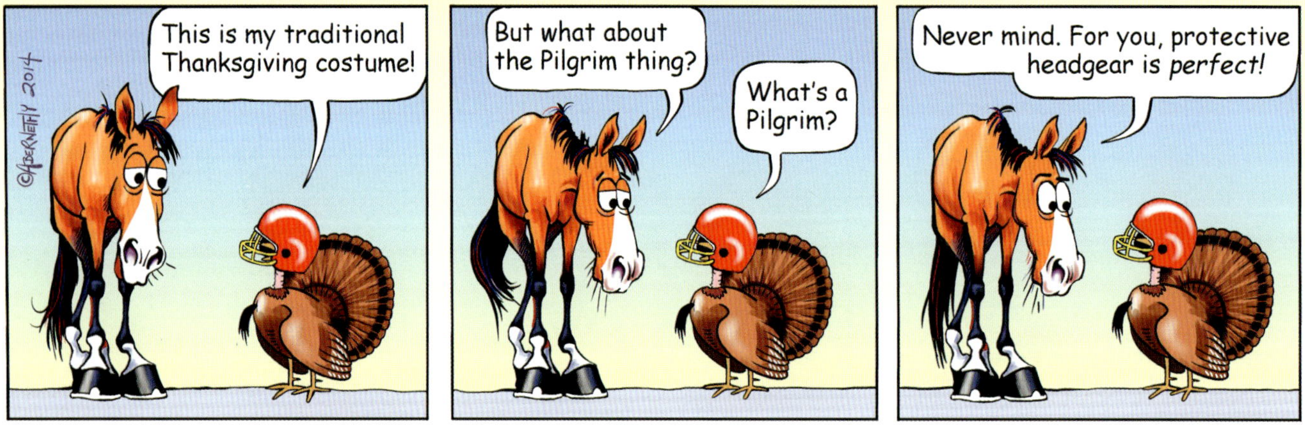
©ABERNETHY 2014
This is my traditional Thanksgiving costume!
But what about the Pilgrim thing?
What's a Pilgrim?
Never mind. For you, protective headgear is *perfect!*

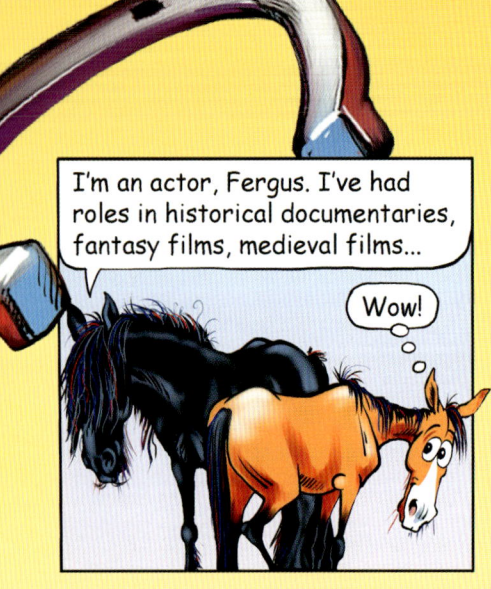

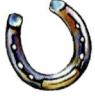

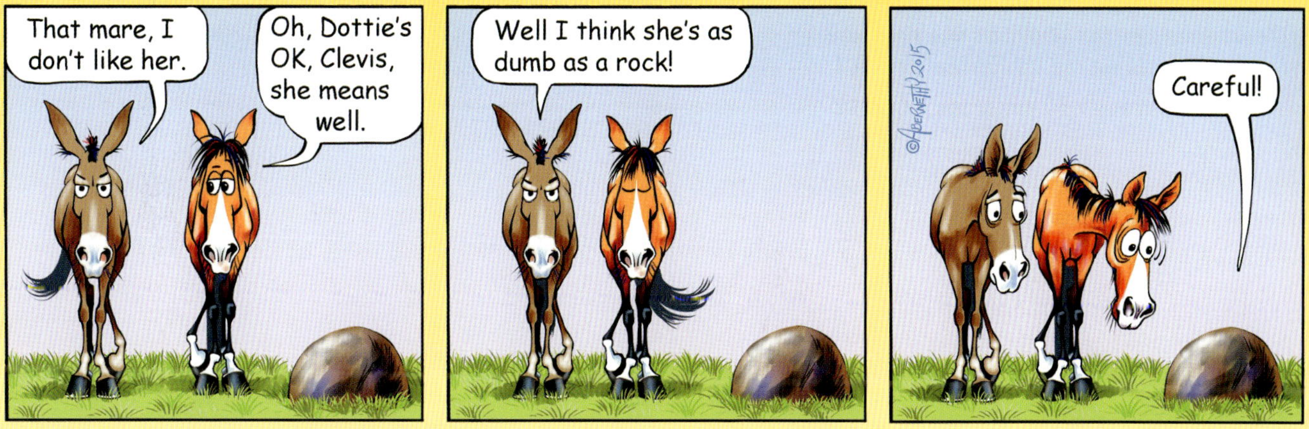
That mare, I don't like her.
Oh, Dottie's OK, Clevis, she means well.
Well I think she's as dumb as a rock!
Careful!

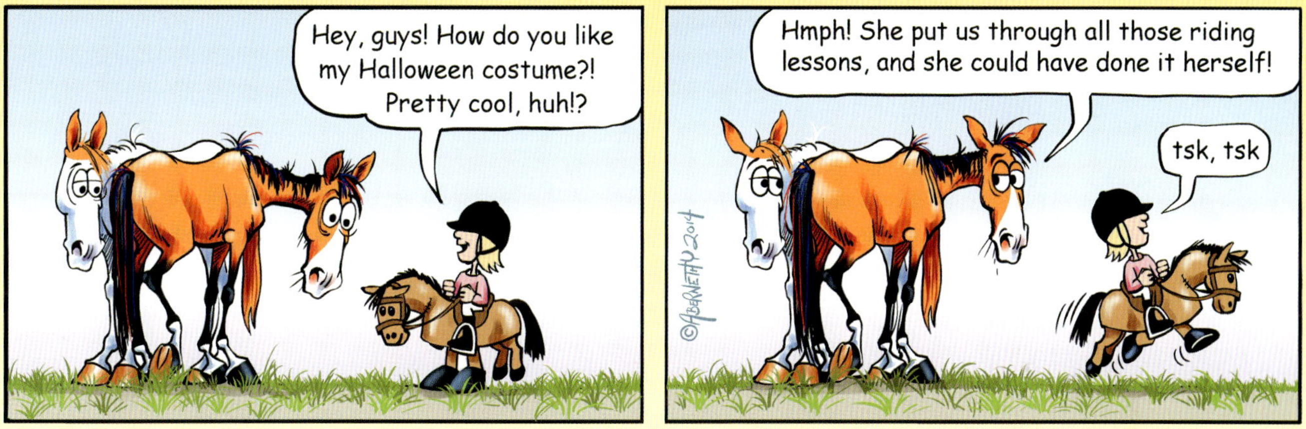
Hey, guys! How do you like my Halloween costume?! Pretty cool, huh!?
Hmph! She put us through all those riding lessons, and she could have done it herself!
tsk, tsk

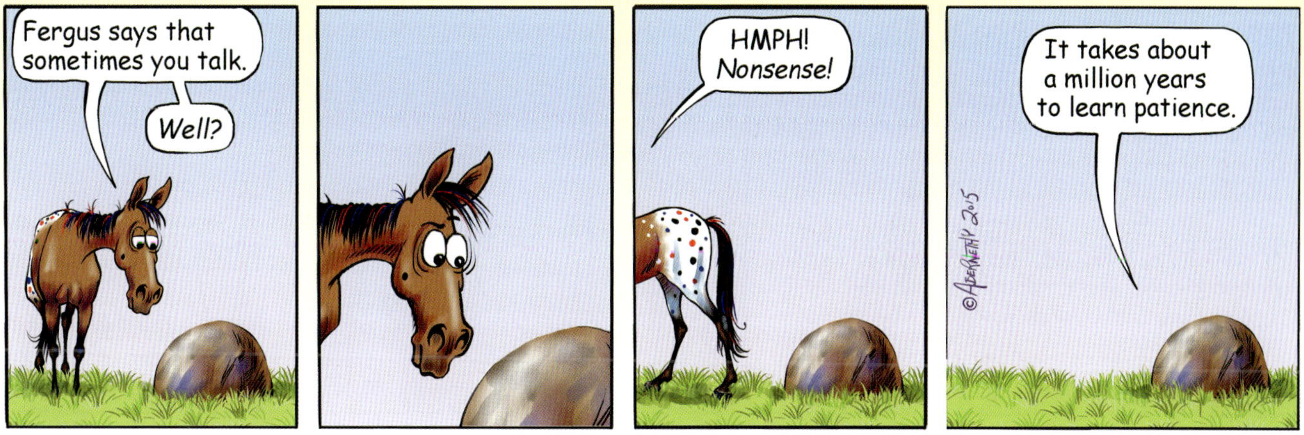
Fergus says that sometimes you talk.
Well?
HMPH! Nonsense!
It takes about a million years to learn patience.

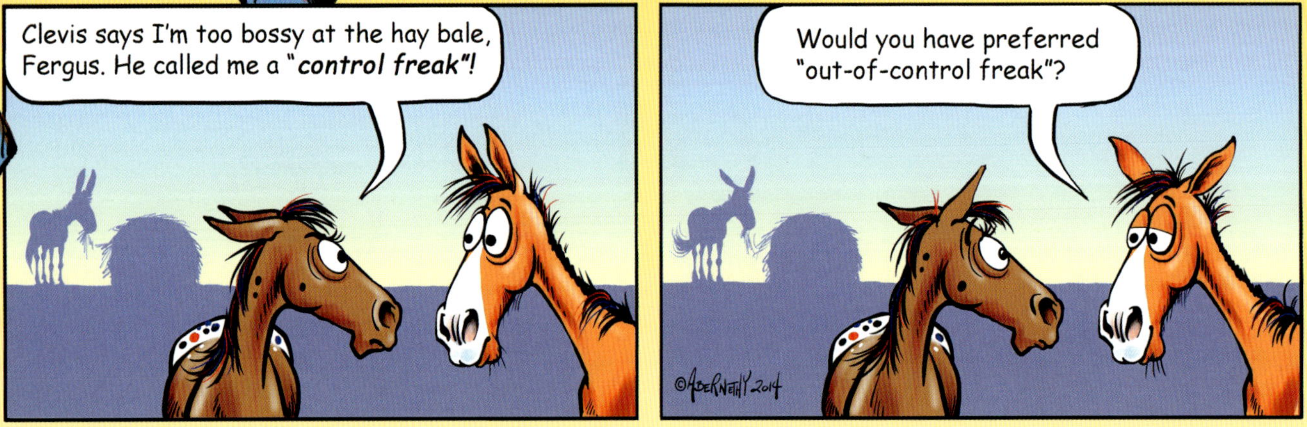
Clevis says I'm too bossy at the hay bale, Fergus. He called me a "*control freak*"!
Would you have preferred "out-of-control freak"?
©ABERNETHY 2014

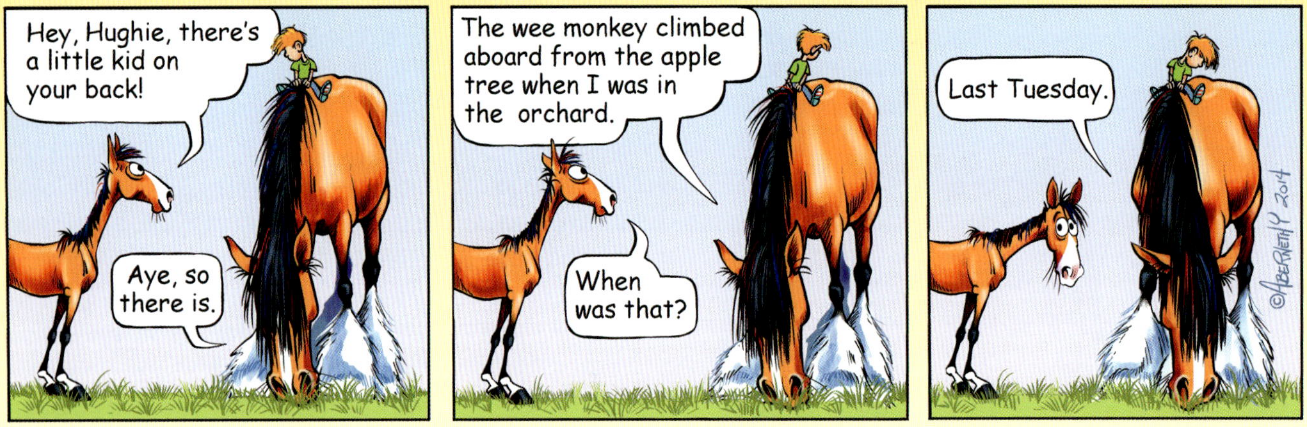
Hey, Hughie, there's a little kid on your back!
Aye, so there is.
The wee monkey climbed aboard from the apple tree when I was in the orchard.
When was that?
Last Tuesday.
©ABERNETHY 2014

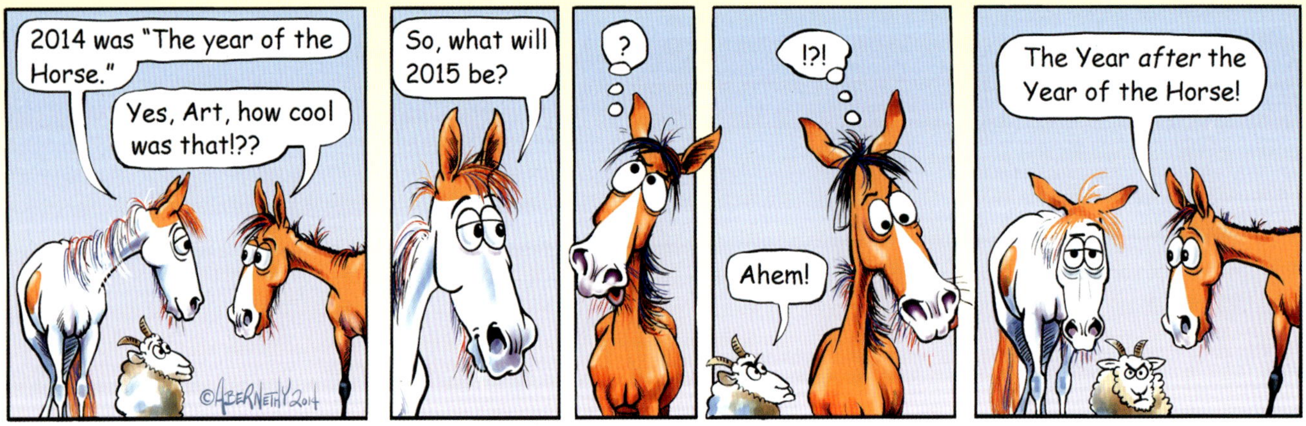
2014 was "The year of the Horse."
Yes, Art, how cool was that!??
©ABERNETHY 2014
So, what will 2015 be?
?
!?!
Ahem!
The Year *after* the Year of the Horse!

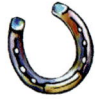

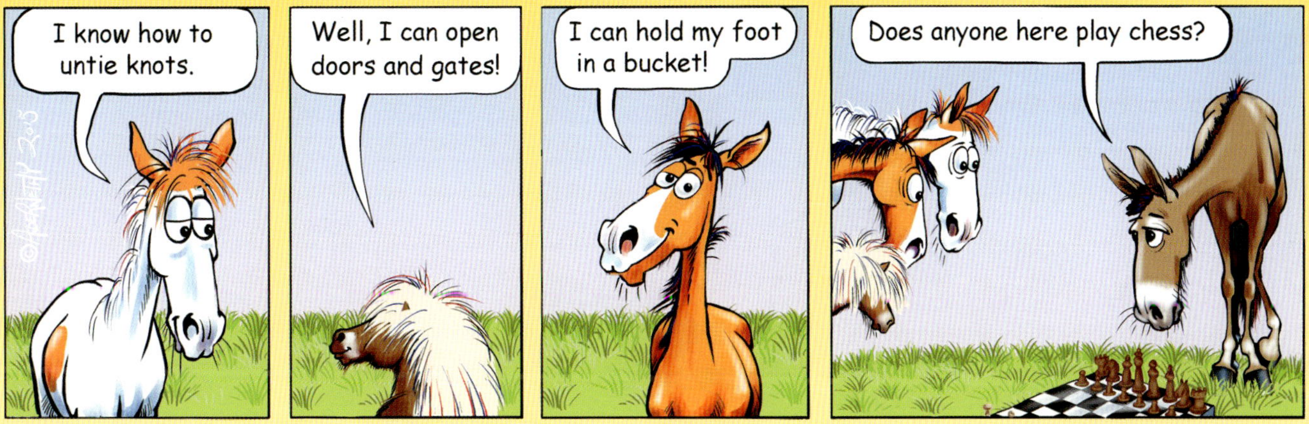
I know how to untie knots.
Well, I can open doors and gates!
I can hold my foot in a bucket!
Does anyone here play chess?

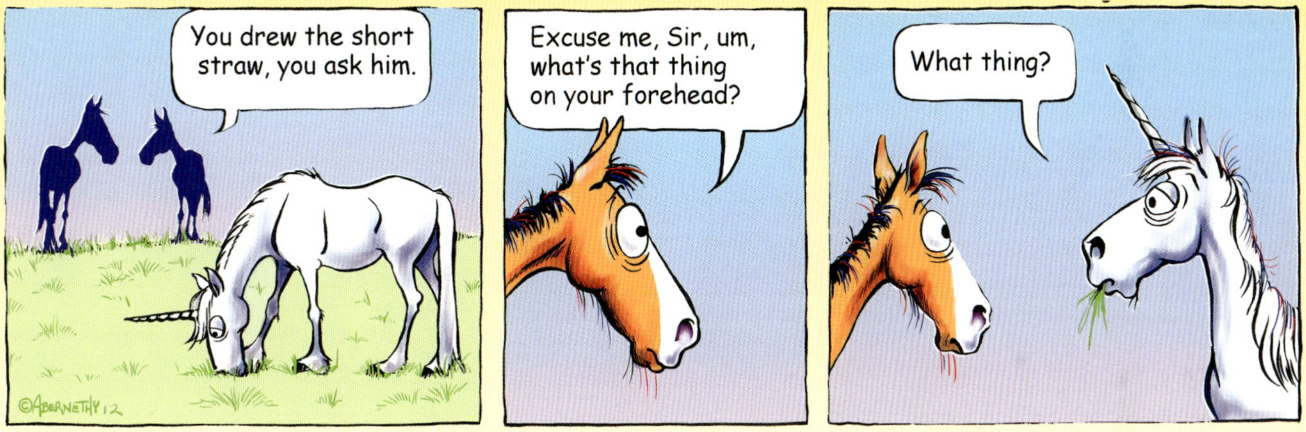
You drew the short straw, you ask him.
©ABERNETHY 12
Excuse me, Sir, um, what's that thing on your forehead?
What thing?

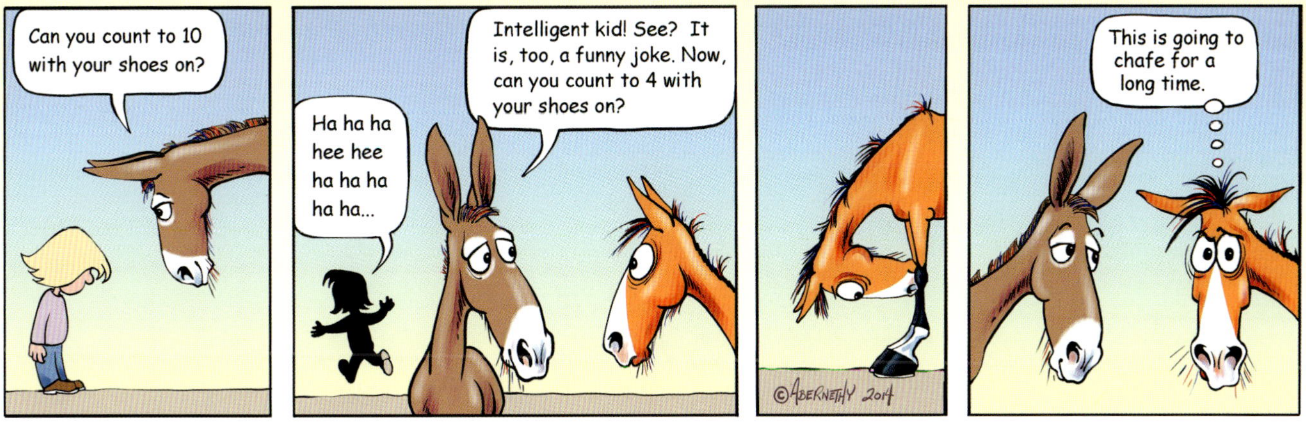
Can you count to 10 with your shoes on?
Ha ha ha hee hee ha ha ha ha ha...
Intelligent kid! See? It is, too, a funny joke. Now, can you count to 4 with your shoes on?
©ABERNETHY 2014
This is going to chafe for a long time.

Did you just...um... CHEW that off!?
Yeth.
Would you be interested in taking a look at our feedroom door?
©ABERNETHY 2005

WOW! It's HOT!
Hughie! The water looks great! Can I lay about in it too?
Aye, Fergus, but...
I'm not layin' down, lad, I'm standin' up!
©ABERNETHY 2015

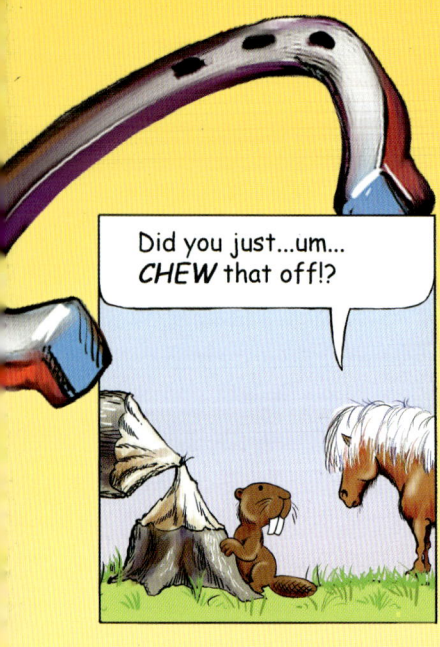

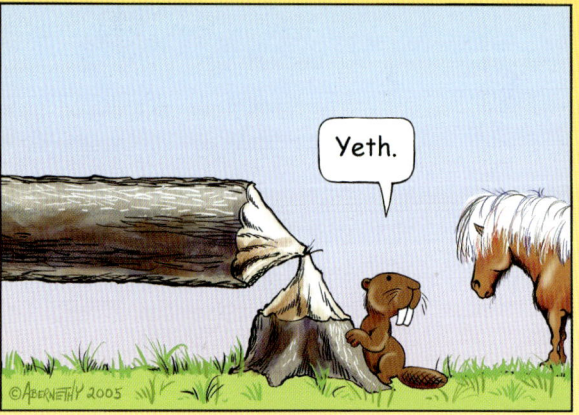

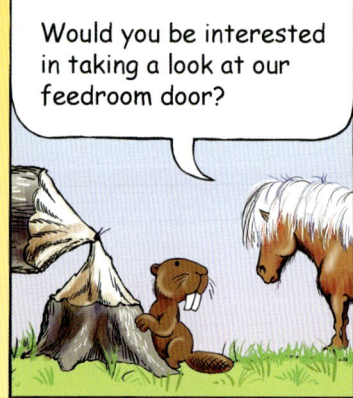

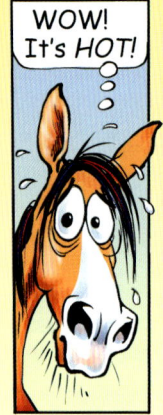

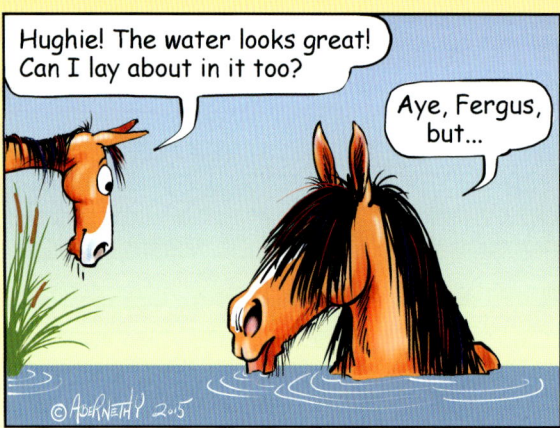

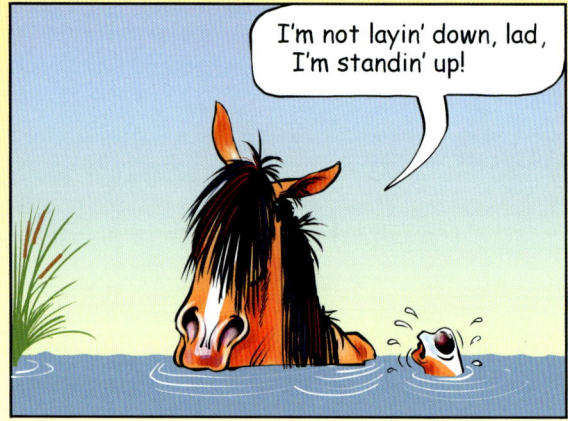

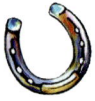

# Wonderland

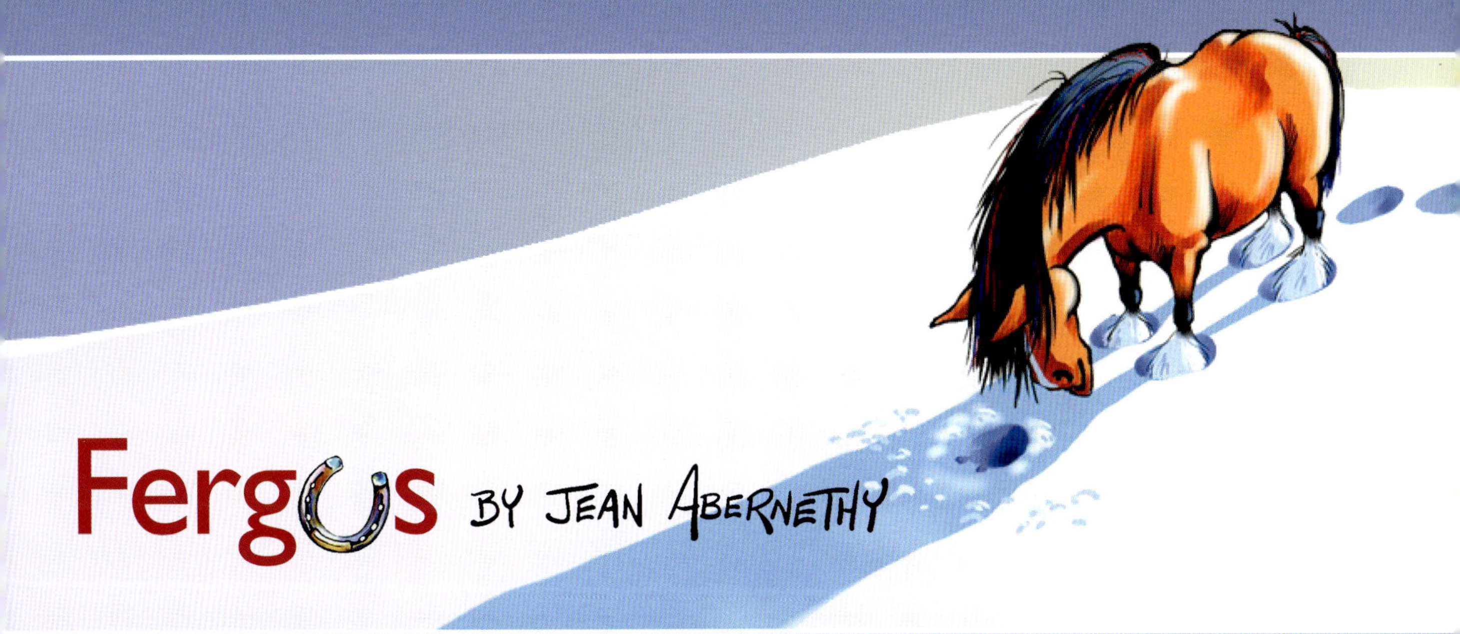

# Fergus

BY JEAN ABERNETHY

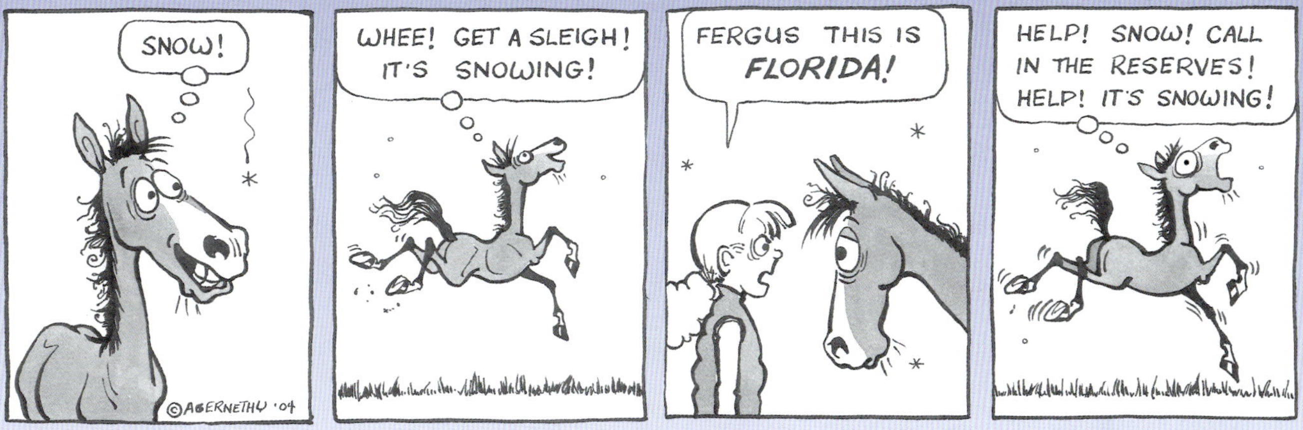

SNOW!
©ABERNETHY '04
WHEE! GET A SLEIGH! IT'S SNOWING!
FERGUS THIS IS *FLORIDA!*
HELP! SNOW! CALL IN THE RESERVES! HELP! IT'S SNOWING!


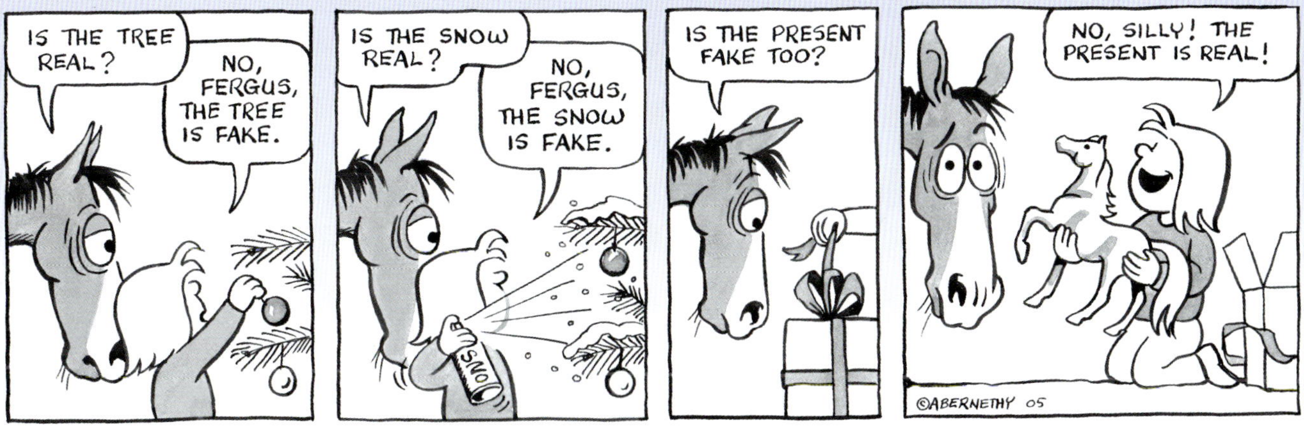

IS THE TREE REAL?
NO, FERGUS, THE TREE IS FAKE.
IS THE SNOW REAL?
NO, FERGUS, THE SNOW IS FAKE.
SNO
IS THE PRESENT FAKE TOO?
NO, SILLY! THE PRESENT IS REAL!
©ABERNETHY 05

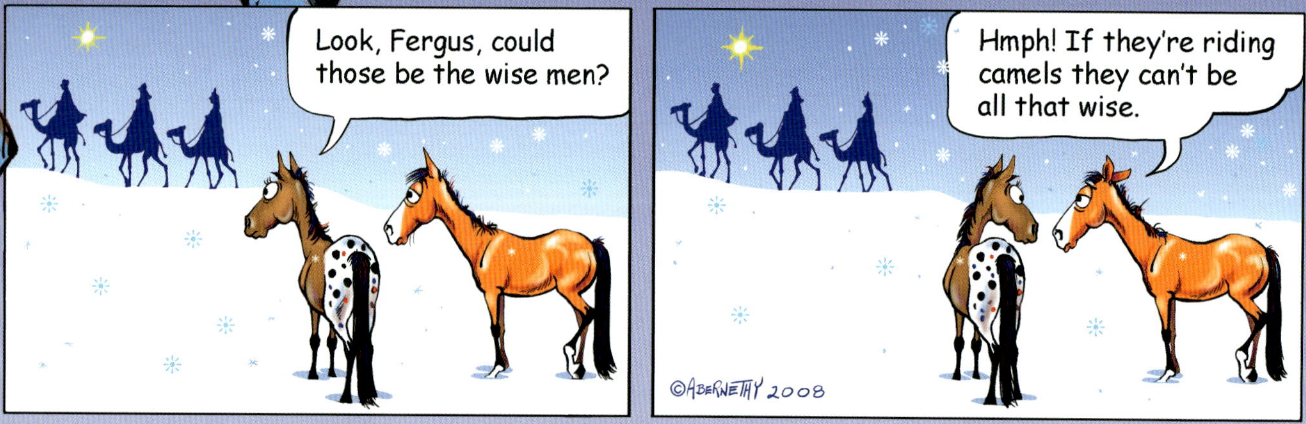
Look, Fergus, could those be the wise men?
Hmph! If they're riding camels they can't be all that wise.
©ABERNETHY 2008

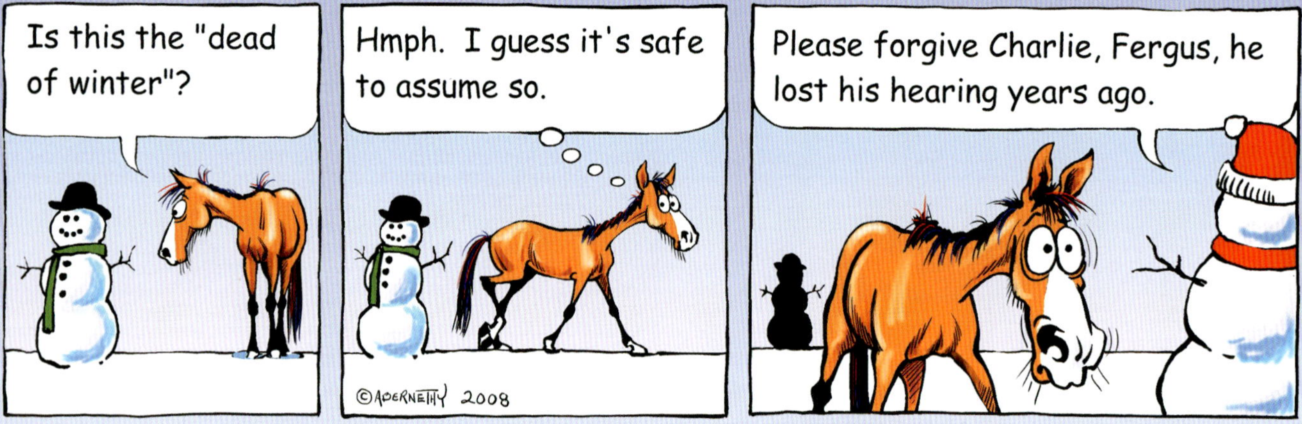
Is this the "dead of winter"?
Hmph. I guess it's safe to assume so.
©ABERNETHY 2008
Please forgive Charlie, Fergus, he lost his hearing years ago.

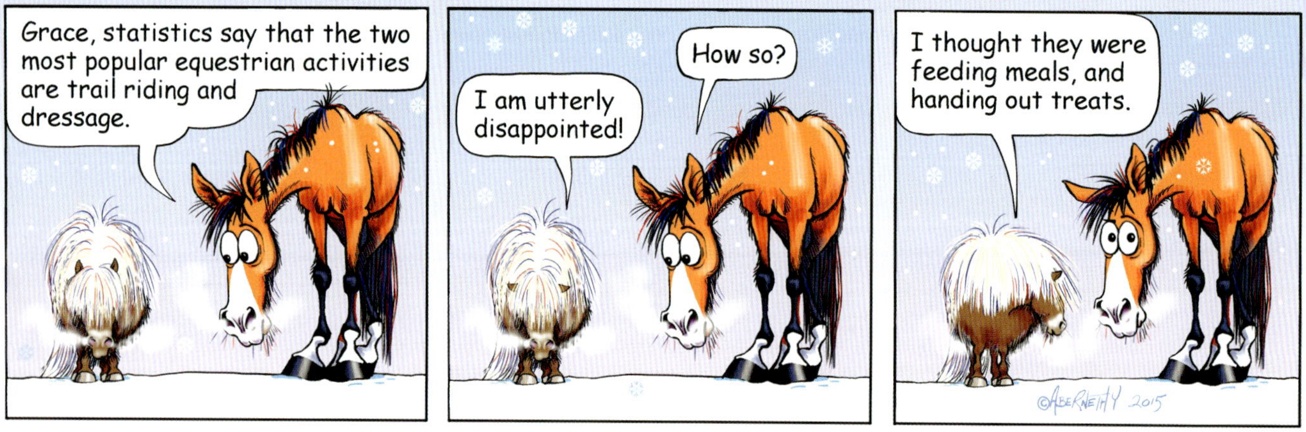
Grace, statistics say that the two most popular equestrian activities are trail riding and dressage.
I am utterly disappointed!
How so?
I thought they were feeding meals, and handing out treats.
©ABERNETHY 2015

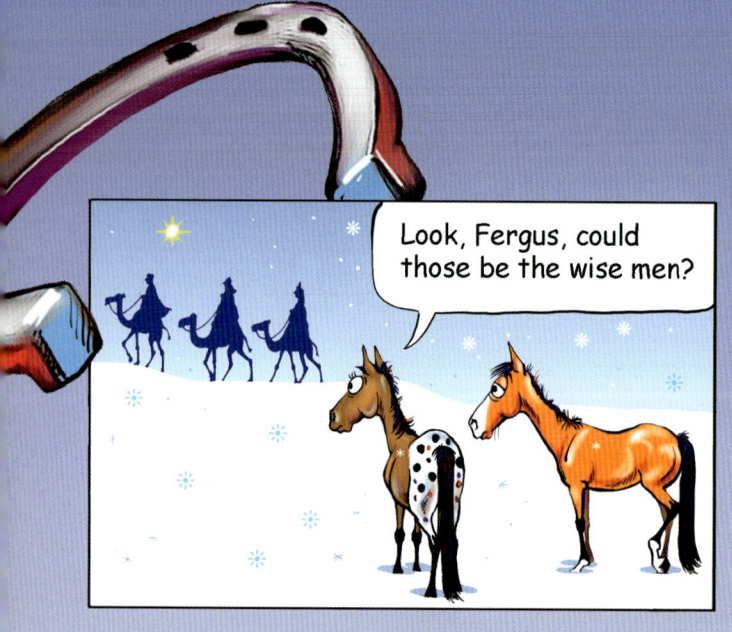

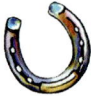

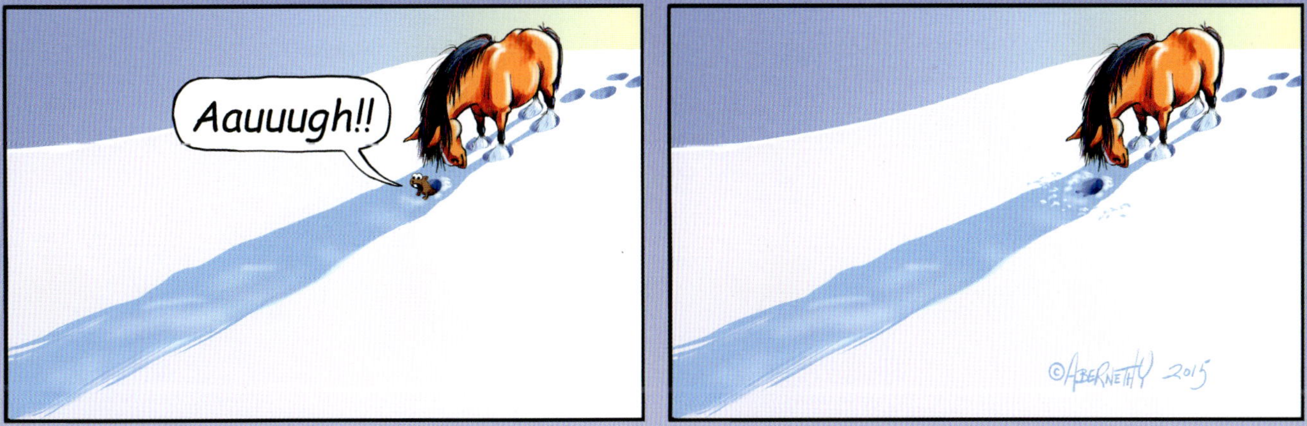
Aauuugh!!
©ABERNETHY 2015

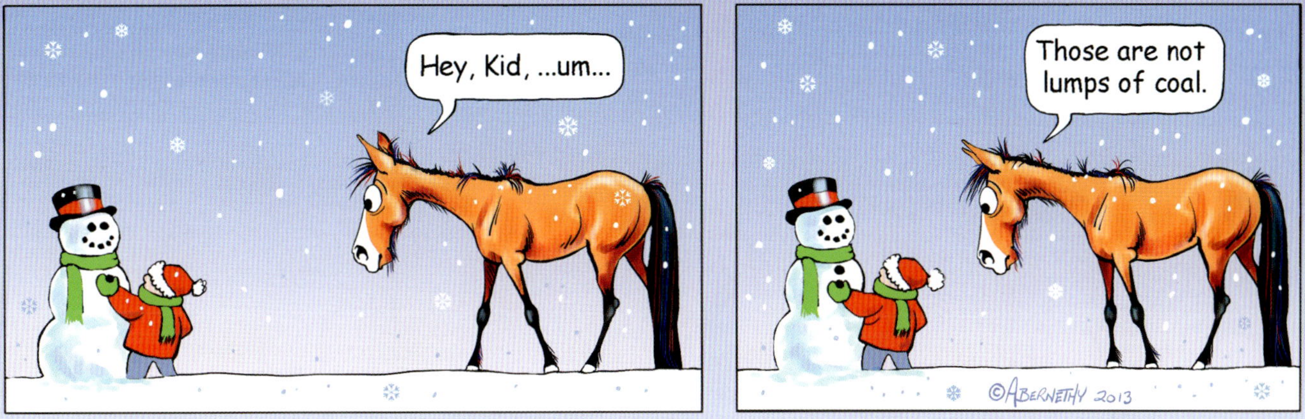
Hey, Kid, ...um...
Those are not lumps of coal.
©ABERNETHY 2013

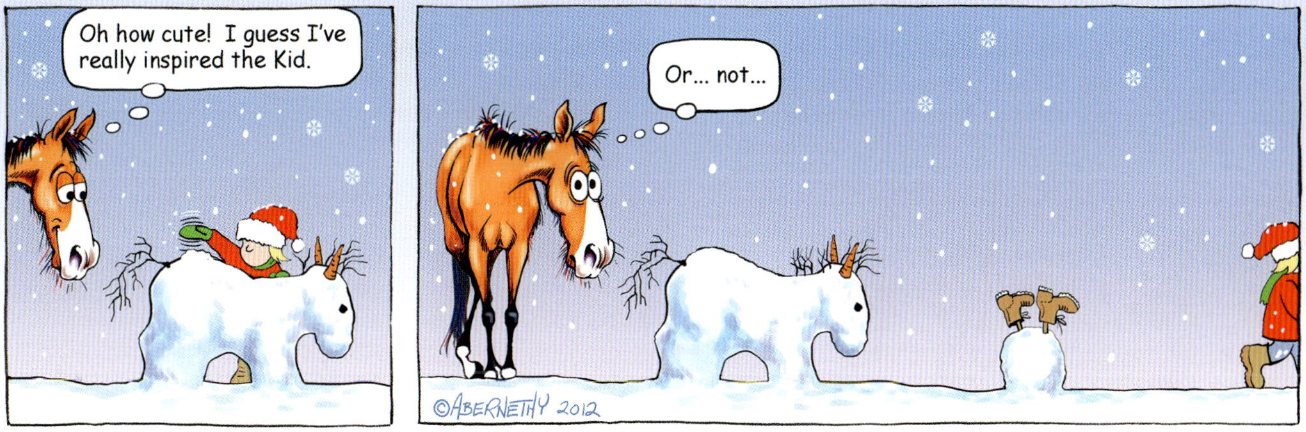
Oh how cute! I guess I've really inspired the Kid.
Or... not...
©ABERNETHY 2012

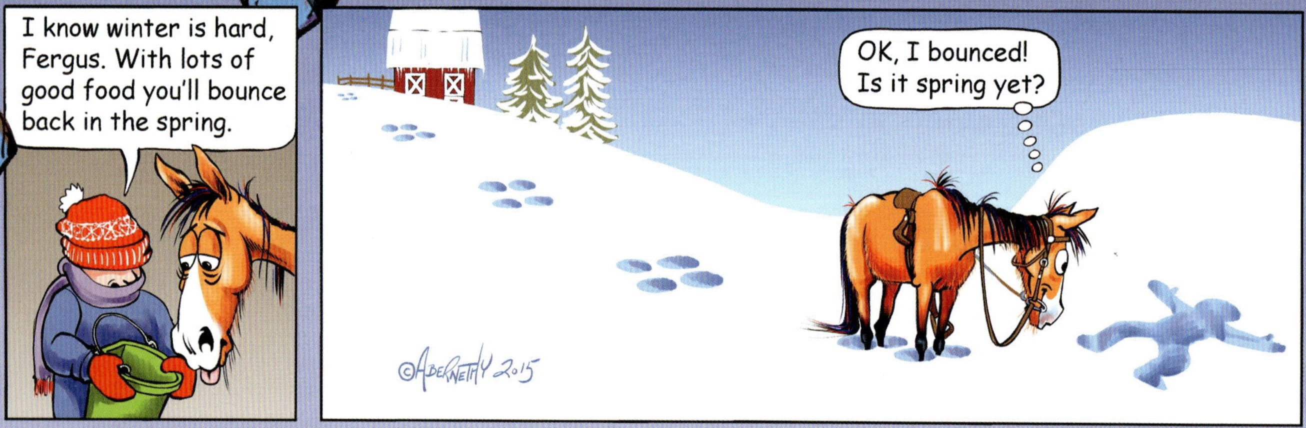
I know winter is hard, Fergus. With lots of good food you'll bounce back in the spring.
OK, I bounced! Is it spring yet?
©ABERNETHY 2015

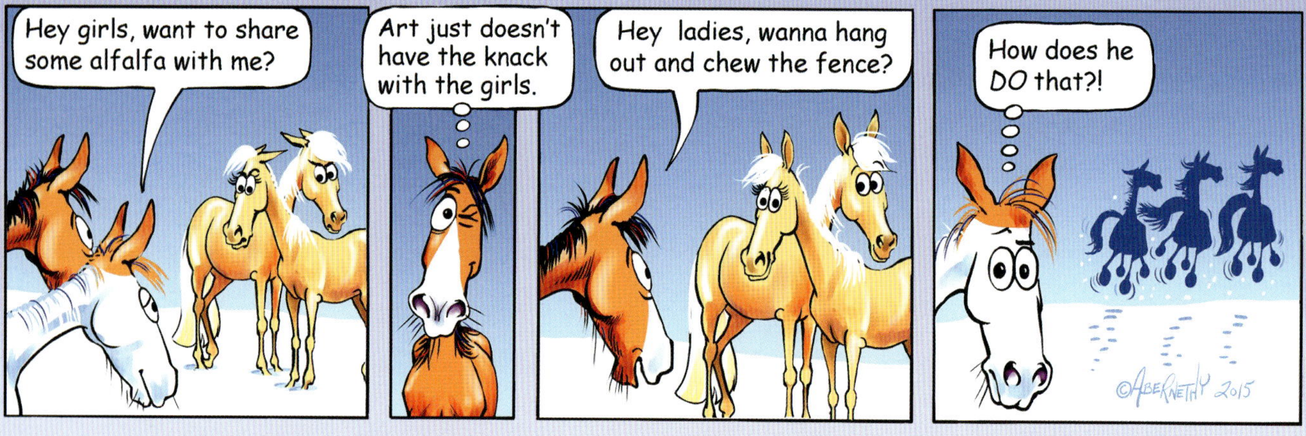
Hey girls, want to share some alfalfa with me?
Art just doesn't have the knack with the girls.
Hey ladies, wanna hang out and chew the fence?
How does he DO that?!
©ABERNETHY 2015

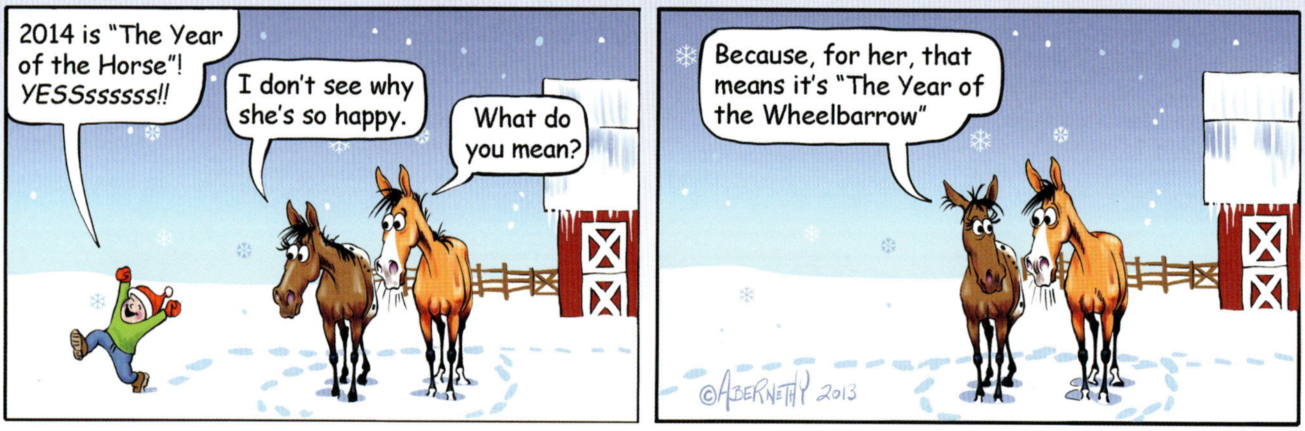
2014 is "The Year of the Horse"! YESSssssss!!
I don't see why she's so happy.
What do you mean?
Because, for her, that means it's "The Year of the Wheelbarrow"
©ABERNETHY 2013

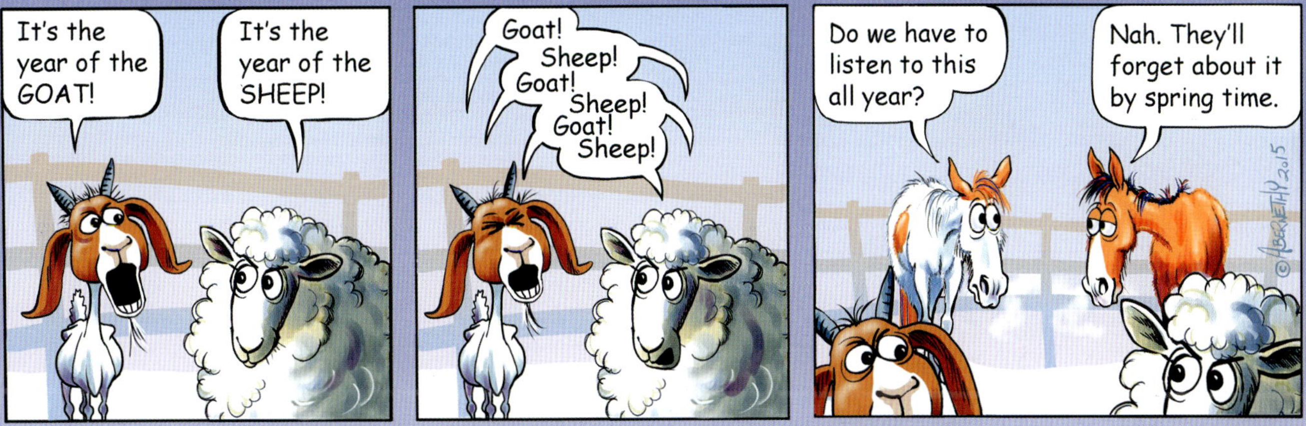
It's the year of the GOAT!
It's the year of the SHEEP!
Goat! Sheep! Goat! Sheep! Goat! Sheep!
Do we have to listen to this all year?
Nah. They'll forget about it by spring time.
©ABERNETHY 2015

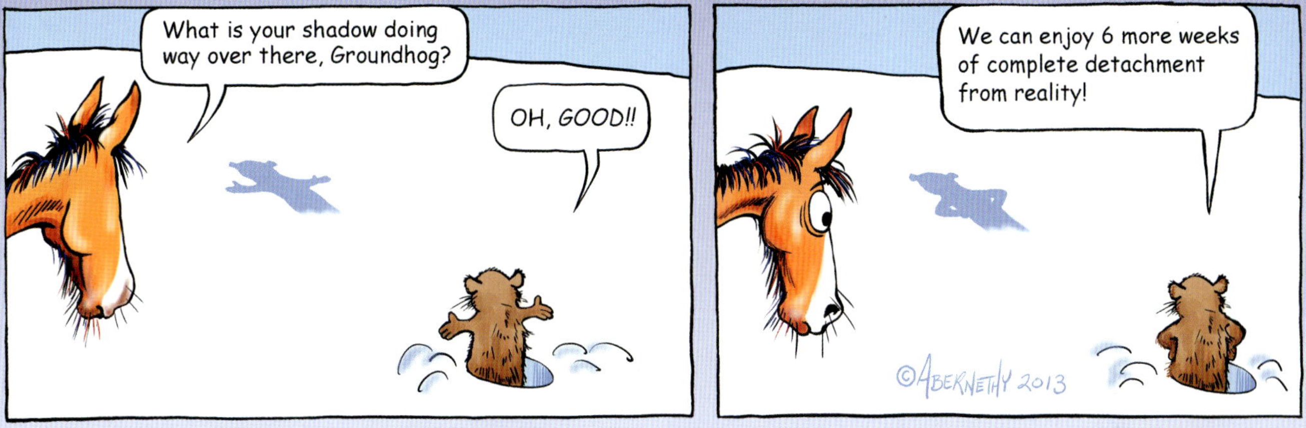
What is your shadow doing way over there, Groundhog?
OH, GOOD!!
We can enjoy 6 more weeks of complete detachment from reality!
©ABERNETHY 2013

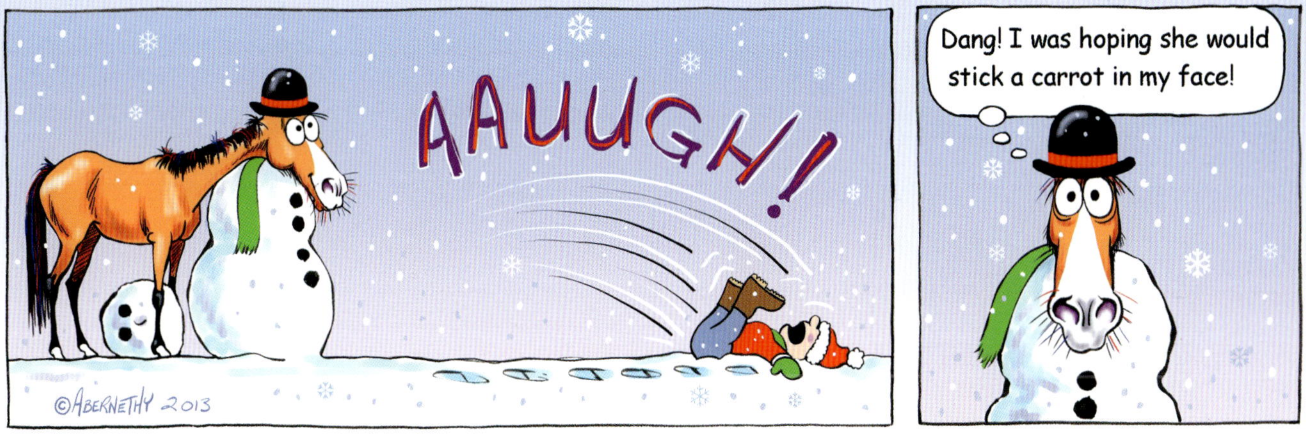
AAUUGH!
©ABERNETHY 2013
Dang! I was hoping she would stick a carrot in my face!

I've been unemployed for years, now, Fergus. Nobody rides me any more.
©ABERNETHY 2013
PLUNK
It's not so bad, Grace. Your pension plan seems to be working out.

Canter, please, caaaaanter!
©ABERNETHY 2013
*What?!* I was just *curious!*

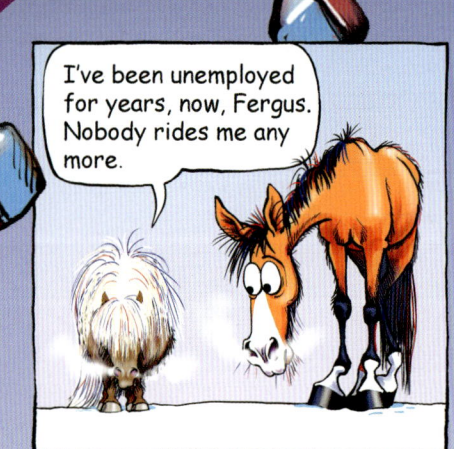

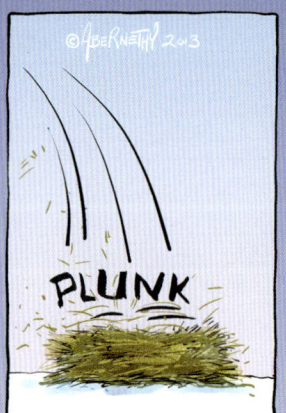

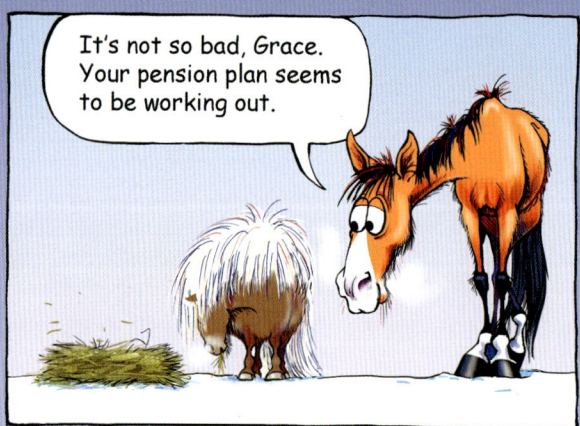

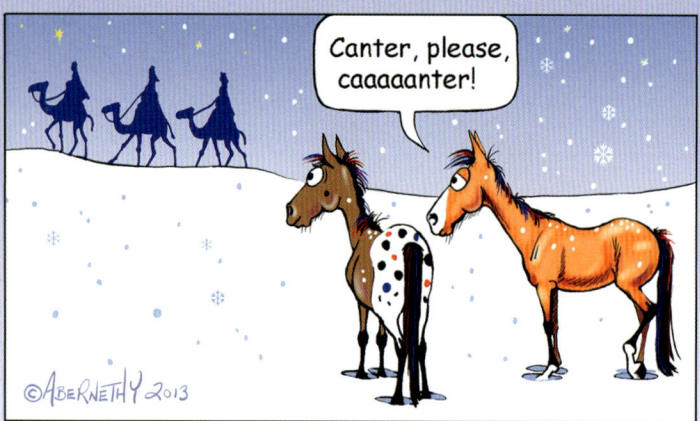

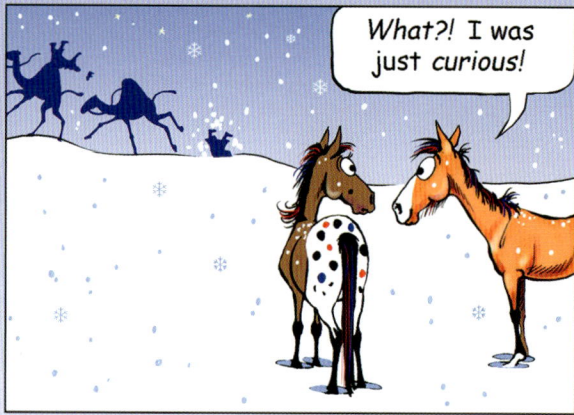

# Let's Stay Friends!

www.fergusthehorse.com

 FergusTheHorse

 @fergusthehorse

 Fergus The Horse